SHOW TIME

SHOW TIME

The Logic and Power of Violent Display

Lee Ann Fujii

Edited by Martha Finnemore
Epilogue by Elisabeth Jean Wood

CORNELL UNIVERSITY PRESS   ITHACA AND LONDON

First published 2021 by Cornell University Press

Library of Congress Cataloging-in-Publication Data

Names: Fujii, Lee Ann, author. | Finnemore, Martha, editor. | Wood, Elisabeth Jean, 1957– writer of supplementary textual content.
Title: Show time : the logic and power of violent display / Lee Ann Fujii ; edited by Martha Finnemore ; epilogue by Elisabeth Jean Wood.
Description: Ithaca [New York] : Cornell University Press, 2021. | Includes bibliographical references and index.
Identifiers: LCCN 2020051078 (print) | LCCN 2020051079 (ebook) | ISBN 9781501758546 (hardcover) | ISBN 9781501758553 (epub) | ISBN 9781501758560 (pdf)
Subjects: LCSH: Violence—Social aspects—History—20th century. | Violence—Psychological aspects—History—20th century. | Political violence—Social aspects—Rwanda—History—20th century. | Genocide—Social aspects—Rwanda—History—20th century. | Massacres—Social aspects—Bosnia and Herzegovina—History—20th century. | Political violence—Social aspects—Bosnia and Herzegovina—History—20th century. | Lynching—Social aspects—Maryland—History—20th century.
Classification: LCC HM1121 .F855 2021 (print) | LCC HM1121 (ebook) | DDC 303.60967571—dc23
LC record available at https://lccn.loc.gov/2020051078
LC ebook record available at https://lccn.loc.gov/2020051079

Contents

Preface

Filling another scholar's shoes is hard, particularly when those shoes are leopard print boots, which is what Lee Ann was wearing the last time I saw her. At the time of her death, Fujii was polishing this manuscript for submission to Cornell University Press. I had seen her give a talk on the book the week before she died (available on YouTube) and knew how good it would be. Like all of Fujii's work, the project was intellectually eye-opening and urgent. It dove deep into acts of public racialized violence done by and to ordinary people. It asked not just why and how these public displays of violence happen but how processes of enacting public violence transform everyone concerned. Particularly compelling was Fujii's treatment of racial violence in the United States, specifically lynching, as being of a piece with violence in Rwanda and Bosnia, episodes Americans often treat with detachment, as bizarre events happening "over there," to other people. The book needed to be published, but I had no copy of the full manuscript; neither did Roger Haydon at Cornell.

Devorah Manekin, of the Hebrew University of Jerusalem, supplied the most complete draft we were able to locate, sent to her by Fujii four weeks before her death in March 2018. That version was polished but lacked a conclusion. Elisabeth Jean Wood graciously agreed to fill this void with an epilogue that not only draws together important themes of the book but situates the project in larger conversations and in the arc of Fujii's work.

Research for the book depends heavily on interviews conducted on the Eastern Shore of Maryland, in Bosnia, and in Rwanda. Fujii thought deeply about interview techniques and the ethics thereof, and the book reflects both concerns. Her detailed comments about the importance and reliability of interviews for qualitative research can be found in the chapter "Intermission" in this book and in her *Interviewing in Social Science Research* (Fujii 2017). She conducted her interviews with the aid of research assistants. We know the identity of one of them—Linda Duyer, who is mentioned in the text and who graciously helped answer questions about Eastern Shore materials and made some of these available to us. Other primary sources are briefly described in the section "The Data and Sources" in the introduction to *Show Time*.

Fujii followed an informed consent procedure with all informants, detailed in an agreement on confidentiality (technically an Ethics Review Protocol Submission to the Office of Research Ethics at the University of Toronto) that has been made available to us by Antoinette Handley, chair of the political science department, and her colleagues at that university's Research Ethics Office. As Fujii noted in the original Protocol Submission,

> The main risks [to participants] are psychological and social. With survivors and witnesses of violence, there is always the danger of retraumatization. . . . The social risks have to do with making neighbors or acquaintances suspicious or jealous of their participation in a research project and/or their perceived relationship with an outsider (and generally an "elite" outsider by local standards). I try to minimize these risks by promising anonymity in any published work to all participants. I also promise confidentiality and tell people that I will not share anything they have said to me with anyone besides my research assistant, including government officials.

Confidentiality for interview participants is assured in this instance not only by these binding agreements with the Office of Research Ethics but also because Fujii's laptop is password protected (as she had agreed to do in the Submission). No one has yet located the password.

Citations to interviews are thus cryptic. Fujii told Haydon by email in May 2014, about an early chapter draft, "The cites and the other nomenclature (e.g., 'Fil' and 'Col') which are 'code' for my interview sources, I will clean up toward the end to make the prose readable. . . . I will also include a footnote to explain however I end up citing my interviews." She was unable to complete that work, we do not know to whom the citations refer, and they were not standardized in the version of the manuscript we have. Fujii also used several primary documents. We have left all citations as Fujii presented them in the manuscript with which we have worked. The mixture of sources, and citation challenges they created, vary across the three research sites.

Bosnia: Quotations from Fujii interviews are sourced in text in square brackets, for instance, [Bra #1/2]. Quotations from testimony given at the International Criminal Tribunal for the former Yugoslavia (ICTY) are noted in the same form; for example, quotations from the Brdjanin indictment appear as [Brdj XXXX] and are taken from https://www.icty.org/en/case/brdanin. English-language transcripts for all ICTY cases are at icty.org.

Maryland: Quotations from Fujii interviews are sourced in text in square brackets. Some interviews are dated, some are not. In this, the oldest of the case studies, most information comes from local newspapers as well as the recollections of elderly residents of the area and court and inquest testimony. *Testimony Given before Coroner Edgar A. Jones, at the Inquest of George Armwood on October 24, 1933* is quoted from Johnny Robins IV private papers, a PDF given to Fujii and Linda Duyer. Access information for this PDF appears in the references section of this book.

Rwanda: Quotations from Fujii's interviews are sourced in text variously, in square brackets as [Chau #7/8 22] and in parentheses as (Fieldnotes, Dec. 2011), sometimes dated and sometimes not.

We could not have undertaken this task without the gracious permission and assistance of Carey Fujii and the Fujii family. They, and a great many friends of Fujii's, helped with the search for a polished manuscript. In the end, it was Dvora Yanow who put us in touch with Devorah Manekin and alerted us to the existence of this version. Grants and material assistance from an array of sources supported Fujii's research and writing. Those we know of are the Institute for Advanced Study at Princeton University, the Ford Foundation's Diversity Fellowship program, the Russell Sage Foundation, the Social Science and Humanities Research Council of Canada, the National Council for Eurasian and East European Research, the University of Toronto's Connaught Fund, the United States Institute of Peace, and George Washington University's Dilthey Fellowship program.

Lee Ann herself would have had a very long list of people to thank for the many, many forms of assistance and kindness that go into any research project of this size. She was always generous about giving credit. We can only hope that you know who you are and regret we are unable to acknowledge so many of the people who made important contributions to the creation of this book.

Martha Finnemore

Acronyms

BCS   Bosnian-Croatian-Serbian (language)

Brdj.   Brdjanin indictment at the International Criminal Tribunal for the former Yugoslavia. The indictment appears at http://www.icty.org/x/cases/brdanin/trans/en/990712IA.htm.

CDR   Coalition pour la défense de la république. Radical wing of the MRND party in Rwanda.

ICTR   International Criminal Tribunal for Rwanda

ICTY   International Criminal Tribunal for the former Yugoslavia

JNA   Jugoslovenska narodna armija. Yugoslav national army.

MDR   Mouvement Démocratique Républicain. Rwandan political party founded in 1991.

MRND   Mouvement Révolutionnaire National pour le Développement. Ruling party in Rwanda, 1974–94, led by Juvenal Habyarimana.

NDH   Nezavisna Država Hrvatska. The independent state of Croatia, created in 1941.

PSD   Parti social démocrate. Opposition party based in the south of Rwanda.

RPA   Rwandan Patriotic Army. Military wing of the RPF.

RPF   Rwandan Patriotic Front. Ruling party in Rwanda since 1994, led by Paul Kagame.

RS   Republika Srpska. Proclaimed a sovereign state 1992–95. Since 1995 one of two political entities comprising Bosnia and Herzegovina.

SDA   Stranka demokratske akcij. Muslim party in Bosnia, headed by Alija Izetbegović.

SDS   Srpska demokratska stranka. Serb nationalist party in Bosnia.

SHOW TIME

Introduction

A man is dead. Everyone knows who did it. Just as everyone knows who added a few extras as they killed him: a gratuitous kick, some well-chosen words, a finger cut off as a prized souvenir. Many cheered as the scene unfolded; others gawked in amazement, while a few looked away, not wanting to see more.

The people responsible for the killing are the man's neighbors, many of whom exchanged hellos with him each morning. Daily greetings are like ritual in small communities. They mark time and space, drawing boundaries between those who belong and those who do not. Here, as elsewhere, people live like families do—with gestures of kindness and generosity, but also with long-standing resentments, jealousies, and prejudices. Most resentments and jealousies are personal while prejudice, by its nature, is impersonal. Rarely, however, had any of these sentiments erupted in violence, let alone in murder.

The day after the killing, people talk amongst themselves, some to brag, others to hear what they missed. Many stay quiet, shocked or cowed into silence. Time passes. Years, decades. The talking ends, yet details persist. They remain stuck in people's minds, like flies trapped in amber. No one who was there can ever really forget, for memory has a life of its own. Some remember what they saw, others what they heard. Many try not to remember at all, because doing so may implicate their families in ways they would rather not face.

In Bosnia, this scene occurred against the backdrop of nationalist wars that vivisected the country then known as Yugoslavia. In Rwanda, the context was genocide, a campaign of mass murder aimed at exterminating an entire category of persons. In the United States, the setting was the Jim Crow South, where white supremacy ruled through law, custom, and violence. Taken singularly, each episode evokes a particular history and setting. Taken together, they raise similar questions. Why execute a man in such a drawn-out way? Why go to all the trouble? Why include extralethal acts, such as mutilation and degradation? Why not just shoot the man and go home? And why do all this with so many neighbors in attendance, laughing and cheering with delight? The answers lie in how we view these incidents. I argue that each is an instance of "violent display." Violent displays are collective efforts at staging violence for people to see, notice, and take in. This book investigates specific episodes across diverse contexts with the aim of explaining and theorizing how and why collectives of all sorts—neighbors, nationalists, and nobodies—express themselves by putting violence on display. The main contribution is to shine a light on an underappreciated dimension of collective violence: the critical importance of embodied action in transforming how people see and experience themselves and others. But for bodies moving and acting in particular ways, these displays would never come to be; nor would they have the power to draw in new audiences over time and place.

The Concept

What does it mean to put something on display? Rendering something visible is not about revealing that which is hidden, but bringing to life that which exists in the imaginary (Goldstein 2004; Handelman 1997; Taylor 1997, 2016). Display makes the imagined "real" by giving it materiality, visibility, and three-dimensional form. In doing so, it draws attention to certain "realities" while keeping others hidden or tucked away in the background. By structuring what people see, displays simultaneously structure what people do not see (Ferme 2001).

When actors put violence on display, they are bringing to life ideas about how the world should be and more specifically, how it should be ordered—who should have power and who should be included and on what basis people should claim belonging. Defined as a collective effort to stage violence for people to see, notice, and take in, violent display is both a social and aesthetic affair. The term *collective* points to the highly social nature of this act. When putting violence on display, people work together, not at cross purposes. The notion of "staging" means that participants share a general concern for creating a certain "look and feel" through the display process. "For people to see, notice, and take in" means that actors have a sense of playing to an audience or to multiple audiences at the same time. These audiences might include those present at the scene physically (spectators) as well as more distant publics throughout the world.

The key element that constitutes an episode as a violent display is staging, a theatrical term that refers to how the director physically arranges bodies, objects, lights, sound, and set pieces to create a particular stage picture. Just as in theater where the possibilities for staging a play are nearly limitless, violent displays, too, can take many different forms. Staging might involve forcing bodies to enact crude, pornographic scenes, as American soldiers did at Abu Ghraib when they made prisoners create naked human pyramids (Danner 2004; Fisher 2004; Norton 2011). It can also involve precise positioning of bodies, as when ISIS videotaped the beheadings of American hostages James Foley and Steven Sotloff and British aid workers David Haines and Alan Henning. To record these murders, ISIS members scouted the location, set up multiple cameras, adjusted the lighting, shot the scene from different angles, then edited the various takes before uploading the videos to the internet (Callimachi 2014)

Staging might also involve choreographed movement and forcing people to don costumes and props. In Nazi-occupied Belarus, for example, German soldiers forced six thousand Jews to enact a mock parade commemorating the Bolshevik Revolution. The soldiers had the prisoners wave Soviet flags, sing revolutionary songs, and smile for the camera as they paraded in two columns. At the end of the parade, the soldiers killed the captives en masse (Snyder 2010, 225–26). Perpetrators, too, might don costumes and props and put themselves in the scene. One of the most infamous photos from Abu Ghraib shows Lynndie England gesturing with her hands toward a line of naked prisoners forced to masturbate in front of her. A cigarette dangles from her mouth, adding to the mocking tone of her stance.

Another form of staging is showcasing souvenirs taken from a violent encounter (which may or may not have been a violent display) (Bourke 1999; Sledge 1981; Wood 2009). These "mementoes" might include body parts, such as the skull of a dead Vietnamese that General George S. Patton III, son of the famed World War II general, kept on his desk during the Vietnam War (Turse 2013, 264); or photographs of the violence, such as the thousands of pictures that soldiers at Abu Ghraib snapped of the prisoners at their most degraded. Actors might also showcase entire dead bodies. During the Dirty War in Argentina, one of the favorite practices of the junta was to "disappear" alleged "subversives" by snatching them off city streets in broad daylight. After torturing and executing their victims in undisclosed locations, the junta would "reappear" their dead bodies by leaving them in places where people would be sure to see them, such as "on sidewalks" or "in trash cans" (Taylor 1997, 98).

Despite varying in all manner of ways, violent displays share a common logic—one that is focused on aesthetics. When actors put violence on display, they are creating a certain "look and feel" that engages the body and all its senses: sight, sound, taste, touch, and smell. From American soldiers at Abu Ghraib to ISIS in Syria, Nazis in Belarus, and the junta in Argentina, actors do what they do in the way they do to create an immediate, bodily experience for all who participate as well as those who look on from afar or after the fact.

The Puzzle

The puzzle of violent displays is why they occur at all, given the risks and costs. One of the biggest risks is undermining larger political goals or interests. The sexual tortures that American soldiers inflicted on Iraqi prisoners at Abu Ghraib, for example, were not simply detrimental to the reputation of the US military; they also harmed US-Iraqi relations at the very moment when the Bush administration was trying to rebuild the country after toppling Saddam Hussein (Hersh 2004).

Violent displays might be counterproductive in other ways as well. They may draw the wrong kind of attention to the region or town where the displays took place. Lynchings in the United States, for example, tended to provoke virulent criticism and condemnation of the communities where they occurred (Carr 2006; Phillips 2016; Smead 1986; Tyson 2017). This negative attention had far-ranging economic and social ramifications. As Arthur Raper (1933, 41–42) concluded in his study of all mob executions that occurred in the United States in 1930: "The lynchings focused attention on these communities, not as places where labor conditions are settled and life and property are safe, but rather as places where human relations are unstable and life and property are subject to the whims of a mob. Every lynching gives unfavorable publicity not onto the immediate community involved, but to the whole section." More recent studies support Raper's claim. Cynthia Carr (2006) argues that the double lynching of Tommy Shipp and Abe Smith in her hometown of Marion, Indiana, on August 7, 1930, is the principal reason why Marion never developed economically over the ensuing decades. Patrick Phillips (2016) tells a similar story about Forsyth County, Georgia. He argues that a 1912 campaign of relentless antiblack terror stymied local efforts at developing the county economically and transforming the county seat into a regional hub.

Putting violence on display is also costly at the organizational, institutional, or group level. It takes time, energy, and resources to pose dead bodies, stage a mock parade, or cut off body parts as souvenirs. Resources are always in limited supply, particularly during wartime when engaging in violent display means diverting energy and attention from other tasks and priorities. Such "diversions" can be counterproductive to campaigns that put a premium on speed or efficiency, such as mass killing or ethnic cleansing.

Putting violence on display is also costly on an individual level. Participating can exact an emotional and psychological toll that can last a lifetime (Fair 2016; Stone 2004, 57; Vietnam Veterans Against the War 1972). Numerous memoirs and testimonies from former soldiers who served in Vietnam and Iraq, for example, attest to the psychological, emotional, and physical costs of committing atrocities, many of which fit my definition of violent display. Varnado Simpson, for example, was a soldier in Charlie Company, the unit that committed all manner of atrocity against unarmed civilians at the villages Americans called My Lai. Before taking his own life at the age of forty-eight, Simpson lived as a total recluse, having literally locked himself inside his home, taking numerous medications as a result of his wartime activities (Sim 1989).

Putting violence on display also entails individual risks. Participants can face censure, demotion, reprimand, prosecution, and even prison time. One of the first to stand trial at the International Criminal Tribunal for the former Yugoslavia (ICTY), for example, was Duško Tadić, accused of committing atrocities at the Omarska prison camp. Similarly, the American soldiers responsible for committing sexual tortures at Abu Ghraib also learned firsthand the risks of putting violence on display. The US Army eventually tried and sentenced eleven of the soldiers and reprimanded, demoted, and dishonorably discharged others. Several officers also received reprimands and demotions (though only one was tried but was later acquitted of all charges) (CNN Library 2016).

Given these risks and costs, the puzzle of violent display is why they occur at all, especially when the option to engage in less "show-y" forms of violence remains. In fact, in many situations, un-displayed violence may be just as or more effective at helping actors to achieve their goals than violence put on display.

The Argument and Theory

I argue that despite these risks and costs, actors put violence on display because such displays can do "things" that undisplayed violence cannot. By putting violence on display, actors are telling others who they are. In this way, violent displays reinscribe what it means to belong to a specific category, group, or "side" and make going along with the violence the basis for belonging. They also enable actors to bring to life a new political order and to broadcast power, authority, sovereignty, and other political claims *in the most graphic terms possible* (Richards 1996).

This argument draws from an eclectic literature on violence, performance, and race and ethnicity. Its singular contribution is to expand the analytic lens to view violence as a *process* of group making rather than a product of groups; to examine how all those on the scene make a moment special, rather than focus solely on those committing physical violence; to take seriously the effects beyond actors' intentions, such as inscribing meaning and transforming how actors see and experience themselves.

In this effort, the book draws insights from scholarship that points to the strategic value of putting violence on display. Actors in a civil or interstate war might use violent displays to issue warnings or to punish defectors to a rival side (Grossman 1995; Kalyvas 1999, 2006). Armed groups might also use violent displays to give the impression of greater military strength than actually exists, as the RUF rebel group did when it began cutting off the arms and hands of villagers during the war in Sierra Leone (Coll 2000; Richards 1996).[1] Putting violence on display might also enable actors to demonstrate their compliance, devotion or enthusiasm to those in power (Hinton 2002; McCord 2001; Su 2011); and/or to induct new recruits into the norms and expectations of their group or organization (Checkel 2017; Cohen 2016; Rodgers 2017; Theidon 2007).

In addition to its strategic value, violent display might also be important for its expressive capacity. Actors might put violence on display to "talk back" to those in power, for example. During the Vietnam war, when the men of Charlie Company tortured, burned, and raped their way through My Lai with abandon, they were sending a powerful rebuke to the military command and its obsession with body counts as the only measure of success in the war (Fujii 2013). At the same time, the men were also talking back to the elusive Vietnamese enemy, which fought the war not through open battles but hidden booby traps, minefields, and ambushes (Greiner 2009).

Scholars have also offered possible answers to the related question of why actors would participate in a violent display, especially one that features "overkill" or more force than is necessary in a given moment. For Randall Collins (2006, 2008), the answer lies in a specific situational dynamic that he calls "forward panic." Forward panic occurs when pent-up tension and fear in a conflict situation (such as war) can finally be released. In these moments of release, soldiers do not retreat quietly but instead surge forward in an "emotional rush," which generally involves a frenzy of aggression and using more force than is necessary. Collins uses forward panic to explain such incidents as the US attack on Hamburger Hill during the Vietnam war (Caputo 1977) and the Rape of Nanking during World War II. Stefan Klusemann (2010) builds on Collins's theory to explain Ratko Mladić's order to have all the male refugees at Potočari (near Srebrenica) killed after the UN peacekeepers surrendered to him.

This body of work provides an important starting point for the study. Violent displays may well have both strategic *and* expressive value. Microsituational dynamics might also be key to explaining certain *outcomes* of violence, such as displays that feature more force than is necessary. Many questions remain, however. What explains violent displays that seem to undermine rather than serve larger goals or displays that occur outside forward panic? The guards at Abu Ghraib, for example, were under orders to "soften up" the prisoners for interrogation; no one ordered them to subject the detainees to endless sexual tortures, which resulted in little to no actionable "intel." In addition, the men were not releasing pent-up tension or fear when they forced prisoners to degrade themselves while they snapped endless pictures to amplify the humiliation.

Similarly, when actors use violence to "talk back" or when they do find themselves in a situation of forward panic, why do actors respond to the same situational dynamics in such different ways? The men of Charlie Company, for example, responded to the situation at My Lai in varied ways. Some soldiers shot at people, animals, and structures while hooting and hollering while some wandered through the carnage without firing a shot. Some raped women and burned hooches but refused a direct order to fire into a group of villagers (Fujii 2013; Hammer 1970; Hersh 1970).

The framework I adopt focuses on the performative dimensions of violence—or the importance of "doing" things in a particular way in a particular context because such actions constitute a particular identity (gender, national, local) and order, rather than just referencing those ideas (Butler 1999; Taylor 1997). In much the same way, certain speech acts—"I do" or "I bet"—uttered the right way in the right moment constitute actions in their own right, rather than simply describing or referencing those actions, as John Austin (1962) points out. Viewing violence and violent displays performatively means paying attention to what participants do with and through their own and others' bodies. By "participants" I do not only mean those shooting a gun or wielding a machete. I mean anyone and everyone who takes part in whatever way they take part, such as those who bring a rope or gasoline to the scene, gawk or jeer at victims, cheer on others, snap and circulate photos of the scene, or grab a souvenir and show it off later. In addition, participants might include the unwitting passer-by or neighbor who, by dint of their proximity to the scene, cannot help but see and hear what is happening. I analyze the sum total of these actions, rather than parsing them singularly, to understand how collectively doing things in a particular way helps to generate a special occasion or mark off the moment as special (Burke 2005). Gauntlets and manhunts, for example, are not just opportunities to beat or chase others; they are also occasions for taking part in a special type of collective act.

By focusing on the meaning-making power of embodied action, I seek to add to a large literature that explores how actors "perform" social identities such as "fascist," "citizen," "nation," or "gender" (Berezin 1997; Butler 1999; Goldstein 2004; Guss 2000; Hinton 2005; Jarman 1997; Taylor 1997). I also draw on theories of the body that point to the ways the human body can signify larger, more abstract, social "bodies" and the relationship between these two different kinds of "bodies" (Foucault 1995). As Mary Douglas (1966, 1996) points out, the human body does not just represent anatomical concepts; it also signifies the social values, distinctions, taboos, and boundaries that order daily life. "The physical body," she observes, "is a microcosm of society, facing the centre of power, contracting and expanding its claims in direct accordance with the increase and relaxation of social pressures" (Douglas 1996, 80). Douglas's insights could not be more applicable when talking about violent displays. Through violence enacted through and with the individual bodies of victims, violent displays can simultaneously speak to larger, societal concerns about order and ordering, such as who should have power and who should not, which segments of society merit which rights and privileges over which others, and which parts of the social body should be amputated or excised completely.

The body's communicative power stems from its capacity to stand in for entire categories of persons. This capacity is not limitless. As Douglas (1996, 69) points out, "The social body constrains the way the physical body is perceived." It is social bodies that invest physical bodies with various kinds of meaning. These meanings are not random or fixed. On the surface, they may appear static or taken for granted; but underneath often lie contradictory layers. These layers are evidence of the emergent nature of meanings and the meaning-making process more generally. Meanings are always in the process of becoming; they are never endpoints. They do not adhere or affix to bodies in unproblematic or automatic ways, for no body comes premade or prepackaged in a particular category. Rather, social bodies construct and deconstruct notions of rich or poor, foreigner or native, real or unreal Serb, and other distinctions through everyday interactions as well as extraordinary moments of collective violence, such as violent displays. Violent displays are not necessarily about affirming extant understandings about what it means to be white or black, Tutsi or Hutu; often, they are radically *rewriting* what it means to belong to a given category. What it means to be white before a lynching is different than what it means after taking part in one.

Violent displays create new meanings by harnessing the fungibility of the human body—its capacity to stand in for larger social bodies and entire social categories. Putting violence on display turns the body of the victim into a stand-in for an entire imagined category of persons. The body becomes a canvas for the whole, such that what perpetrators carve on one (individual body) is automatically inscribed on the other (collective body). In this way, the body serves as both content and carrier, billboard and slogan. It is both the object of display as well as the medium for inscribing meanings.

In addition to constructing or rewriting what it means to belong, violent displays also transform and reconstitute actors in new and novel ways. The process of putting violence on display can certify participants as members of a group, such as a mob, fraternity, street gang, or army. Indeed, this is precisely the reason that many organizations use violence to induct new members and to socialize them to group norms and expectations (Checkel 2017; Cohen 2016; Garot 2007, 2010; Winslow 1999). In addition to constituting participants as full-fledged members of the group, putting violence on display can also deepen or expand members' sense of "groupness" within an existing collective, strengthening norms of solidarity (Brubaker 2004a; Fujii 2017; Goldstein 2004; Guss 2000; McCall 1995).

Through the process of display, actors can also become transformed. By assembling, running, milling, clapping, laughing, jeering, tying, driving, among other actions, actors not only enact the moment, they experience it firsthand—through their body and bodily senses. As Amy Louise Wood (2009, 11) writes about the experience of watching a lynching:

> Spectators heard the speeches of the mob, the shouts of the crowd, the confessions of the victim, and most of all, his dying shrieks and cries. In cases where the victim was burned, to witness a lynching was also to smell it. And, in all instances, the feel and push of the crowd created the sense of belonging and commonality that sustained the violence. In this respect, spectators did not watch or consume a lynching as much as they witnessed it—that is, they beheld or experienced it with active engagement.

The same "active engagement" occurs in other types of violent display as well. The soldiers at Abu Ghraib, for example, were also consuming the displays they themselves were putting on. They heard the cries or protests of the victims, they felt the pull of dogs on a leash (which they used to terrorize the detainees), they smelled the victims' sweat, urine, and defecation, and felt their friends' celebratory slaps on the back, high fives, or other gestures of "belonging and communality that sustained the violence" (Wood 2009, 11).

In addition to experiencing displays through their bodies and senses, participants also experience new forms of power, belonging, and hierarchy. These forms of power might be novel, new, and titillating. The large crowd at the lynchings of Sam Hose, Claude Neal, or Jesse Washington may well have experienced the power over life and death for the first (and possibly only) time in their lives (Dray 2003; SoRelle 1983).

Understanding the communicative, constitutive, and performative power of violent displays helps to explain why a variety of actors would participate in them. It also provides insight into the larger political effects of putting violence on display in terms of inscribing meanings, making claims, and broadcasting power—effects that might lie outside actors' intentions, interests, or preferences. In this investigation, I follow Glenn Bowman (2001, 28) who asks: "What else does violence do?'" a question to which I would add another: What else does violence have the power *to do*?

Violent displays, I argue, have the power to pull in participants—both willing and unwilling, witting and unwitting. To explain how different people come to take part in these shows, I propose a theory of casting. Casting is the process by which actors take on roles and roles take on actors. These roles include not only those featured in the center of the violent action in starring, costarring, or supporting parts, but also those on the sidelines engaging in smaller, bit parts or playing the vital role of "spectator." Taken together, these roles give the display its form, content, and meaning. They bring the display to "life." The process is dynamic and interactive. As people take on roles, the display begins to emerge. As the display begins to take shape, new roles become available as others fade. At each step of the process, roles make possible new ways of acting and taken together, make the show what it is. They transform a murder into a lynching, for example, or prison detention into pornographic fun and games (Norton 2011). Casting is a process of continual inclusion. It not only enables the most eager and willing to become part of the show; it also pulls in the unwitting and unwilling.

The Approach

To investigate how the process of putting violence on display unfolds at the local level, I examine episodes that occurred in divergent contexts. I define an episode as an instance of violence within a larger campaign of organized violence. An episode is generally temporally bounded, taking place within a single day or afternoon. But in some cases, certain forms of violent display might become so routine that temporal boundaries start to blur, as occurred with the extralethal shows at the Bosnian Serb–run camp of Omarska. I make no claims these episodes are representative of the larger organized violence that was taking place at the same time. Neither do I claim that comparing episodes is the equivalent of comparing a lynching to a genocide or a genocide to ethnic cleansing—to the contrary. I focus not on the national-level terrain but on small, face-to-face communities, where differences and distinctions are not always what they seem, but under the right circumstances, can become a matter of life and death.

The episodes I examine in detail allow us to see how different displays "look" and "feel" depending on the extent and type of stagecraft they feature. I examine episodes that I dub "main attractions" (chapter 3) as well as those I call "sideshows" (chapter 5). These displays vary along multiple dimensions. Some involve large crowds; others, a select few. Some feature adults and children as spectators; others are restricted to a select few. Some last a brief moment; others days, weeks, and months. Some feature elaborate choreography and props; others very little. Some take place in public settings, while others occur in closed-off locations, such as prison camps. Finally, they vary in their levels of extralethal violence. Extralethal violence is any act of bodily harm that transgresses shared norms and understandings about the proper treatment of persons or bodies (Fujii 2013). Some are comprised almost entirely of extralethal violence, while others are largely devoid of such acts.

Of the three "main attractions" the least showy is the killing of a prominent family during the Rwandan genocide. The genocide was the project of threatened extremists in the capital, but was carried out, with different degrees of initiative and enthusiasm, by local elites who organized residents to carry out the killings. The designated targets were Tutsi and anyone opposed to the extremists in power. In the community of Ngali, one Tutsi family stood out as the most prominent. Various groups of attackers hunted down members of the family. A large group even hunted down three children from the family. Though the violence was clearly for show, it had the fewest elements of staging among all the episodes. It also featured no extralethal acts, such as mutilation or desecration of the bodies.

The second showed more evidence of staging. In the spring of 1992, Bosnian Serbs began forcibly taking over northern and eastern parts of the country and declaring them "autonomous regions." On July 10, 1992, in one of the villages located in Bosnian Serb-controlled territory, soldiers rounded up all Muslim men of "fighting age," paraded them through the neighborhood, held them captive in a primary school, then killed them that afternoon. The actual killings were not on display. Neither was the disposal of the bodies. This episode shows how actors might put certain portions of the violence on display, while keeping others parts out of view.

The third is the lynching of a twenty-two-year-old black farmhand named George Armwood that occurred in the Eastern Shore of Maryland. On the evening of Wednesday, October 18, 1933, a mob estimated to be in the thousands descended on the jail in Princess Anne. After milling for hours, the crowd broke into the jail, seized Armwood from his cell, hanged him in two different locations, then lit his body on fire. This episode is the most elaborately staged of the three and features the highest levels of extralethal acts.

While the contexts for these episodes differ in significant ways—temporally, politically, culturally—each emerged during a period of economic and political crises that affected all strata of society. In Bosnia, the demise of the Communist Party following Tito's death in 1980 gave rise to a bevy of nationalist leaders, each more radical than the next, and a sagging economy that featured runaway inflation. In Rwanda, growing pressures for democratic opening radicalized a group of elites who were determined to maintain their monopoly on power. A drop in global coffee prices simultaneously plunged the country into dire economic straits, while the invasion by the RPF rebel group created a grave security crisis. In the United States, the Great Depression wiped out entire family fortunes and made the poor even poorer. Maryland governor Albert Ritchie made matters worse by refusing federal aid. In response to these crises, political elites and entrepreneurs in all three settings deployed a language of imminent and existential threat and identified the enemy as coming from within. The solution many called for was lethal violence against the embedded foe.

Crises, however, present opportunities, not destinies. They do not lead people in one direction, but in multiple ways (Bergholz 2016). We cannot explain local-level violence by simply referring to the "master narrative" (Kalyvas 2003), because there are too many ways for actors to interpret, deviate, and appropriate master scripts. In addition, political elites can and do move from radical to more moderate positions and back again, depending on electoral incentives and other political exigencies (Gagnon 2004; Wilkinson 2004). Moreover, what political elites say does not always align with what they do. In Rwanda genocide leaders at all levels went to great lengths to protect their Tutsi wives, mistresses, and family members even as they worked hard to ensure the extermination of all Tutsi. In other words, stark differences at the macro level begin to fade at the neighbor level where local relations and power hierarchies shape how people act on and act out directives from the top (Fujii 2009).

The method for uncovering and theorizing the process of violent display is comparison. Comparing cases across divergent settings is common in studies of comparative genocide (Melson 1996), contentious politics (McAdam, Tarrow, and Tilly 2001; Tilly 2008), democratization (Wood 2000), riots (Horowitz 2001), and other political phenomena. What makes this book different from others studies, however, is that its core concept—violent display—cuts across different forms of organized violence. And because the concept does not neatly coincide with any one type, it invites new avenues for analysis and explanation, while pushing against the tendency among specialists to work largely in isolation from scholars working on other forms of violence (Jackman 2002; Krupa 2009). As Randall Collins (2008, 1) argues: "We need to break down the usual categories—homicides in one research specialty, war in another, child abuse in another, police violence yet elsewhere—and look for the situations that occur within them." For Collins, outward differences should not preclude analysts from looking for patterns that arise across divergent forms of violence. William Beik (2007, 78) makes a similar argument in his study of riots over time and place. As Beik argues, the "point is to highlight elements they had in common, not to deny or ignore the many ways that riots differ in purpose and form." Following Collins and Beik, I seek to locate similarities in the processes that produced violent displays at the local level while also trying to theorize how those processes unfold across diverse settings.

The comparison I undertake is not the usual. I place diverse episodes in conversation with one another not to control for difference, but rather to bend and alter the looking glass. Examining one episode through the lens of another can highlight new bases for comparing and theorizing that more traditionally designed studies might miss. Rather than working from a deductively derived, normative theory of how violent displays *should* unfold, I use each episode as a model for one possible pathway that actors might take to put violence on display. The lens each episode provides is one of context—historical, political, social, and cultural—as well as process. Points of similarity and difference are a function of which episode(s) is/are providing the light for viewing other(s). Particular elements may appear more or less similar depending on which direction the analytic light is bending. For example, the wartime contexts of Rwanda and Bosnia might seem to contrast with the peacetime setting of the United States in the 1930s. Yet, surface differences occlude meaningful similarities. For most black people, daily life under Jim Crow was not that much different than life under Bosnian Serb control for non-Serbs or life under the genocidal regime in Rwanda for those who opposed the mass killing. In all three contexts, those who did not support the power structure in place were forced to navigate—with extreme care—the do's and don'ts mandated by each regime. "Acting" the right away was key to survival (Taylor 1997, 104–5).

The Data and Sources

In the following chapters, I weave together narratives from an array of sources. Many of the data came from interviews I conducted in three different research sites, one in each country. The sites were all small, rural communities that experienced violence. In each place, I spoke with approximately forty to fifty people who were living in the community when the violence occurred. Their perspectives varied but all had direct and personal experiences of the violence.

In addition to talking to local residents, I also met with other interlocutors in each site. In Bosnia, they included local journalists, researchers, and people who worked for or led local organizations. In the Eastern Shore, I talked with community leaders, professors from local universities, and local (nonacademic) historians, many of whom did not come from the Eastern Shore, but had lived there for many years. In Rwanda, I had countless conversations with Rwandan friends and colleagues, American and European scholars who have conducted field research in Rwanda, and a handful of currently imprisoned detainees who were not from my research site but were willing to talk with me during my regular visits to the central prison nearest my research site of Ngali. I spoke to everyone at least once and multiple times with several individuals. I asked participants what they recalled about the violence and what daily life was like before the violence began to sketch a social history of the local community in the period before violence. To conduct these interviews and meetings, I worked closely with a research assistant who came from the community or region where the research site is located. All were fluent in the local language and familiar with local people, place names, landmarks, and cultural norms. In Rwanda and Bosnia, my assistants also helped to interpret between the local language and my own working languages.[2] In Maryland, my interpreter also spoke the local vernacular of people and place names, a language with which I was wholly unfamiliar when I began research and acquired only slowly after repeated trips to the field.

In each locale, I tried to find people of different social backgrounds and experiences. In Rwanda, I spoke with people who had been targeted for killing as well as those tasked with carrying them out. I also talked with people who fit neither category. In Bosnia, I tried to interview people on all sides of the nationalist divide and talked with many who did not identify with any side at all. Post-Dayton realities meant that few Serbs from my site, which I call "Selo," returned to live there full time.[3] This made it difficult to find local Serbs to interview, though I did find a few. In the Eastern Shore, I interviewed people from both the black and white communities. I focused my efforts on finding people who were alive at the time of the lynching. This meant that most interviewees were in their eighties and nineties when I met with them; two were a hundred years old and still living on their own.

Everyone I spoke with was of sound enough body and mind to consent to an interview and to understand what consenting to an interview meant. I told all participants that I would not use any real names or other identifiers in order to protect everyone's identities. Not every person agreed to be interviewed. A few in each site turned down my request, an indication that not everyone felt pressured to say yes to a foreign researcher. (In the Eastern Shore, I was also considered a "foreigner" since I hailed from the "Western Shore.") Subsequent attempts to reinterview a few individuals in Maryland were unsuccessful because the person had grown too infirm. It was usually adult children who would tell me if it was or was not possible to come back. In Selo, my research site in Bosnia, some follow-up attempts (by family members) to persuade relatives or friends to talk with me were also unsuccessful. I respected everyone who declined my request and did not press further.

In addition to interviews, I managed to collect a rich trove of primary sources. These were particularly helpful in the Armwood case. Much of the case study literature on lynching relies heavily on newspaper accounts, but local papers, especially those aimed at a white readership, tend to provide highly partisan and partial accounts of white-perpetrated violence against black victims (Perloff 2000; Tyson 2017, chap. 4, fn 2; Vinikas 1999).[4] One source that helped to offset this bias was the *Afro-American*, a black newspaper based in Baltimore, which sent reporters to the lynchings of Matthew Williams and George Armwood (Clark 1933) as well as the execution of Euel Lee in Baltimore.

Another set of sources invaluable to my understanding of the Armwood lynching came from the private papers of John B. Robins IV. These documents included sworn testimony by state police who were on the scene before and during the Armwood lynching; a transcript of the coroner's inquest, which took place one week after the lynching; and attorney work product by the state's attorney at the time. The police affidavits provide eyewitness accounts of violence, while the transcript of the coroner's inquest gives a glimpse inside the jail at the precise moment when the mob seized Armwood from his cell.

The key set of written sources I use for the Bosnia case is written transcripts and audio recordings of the trial of Marko Samardžija, the commander of the unit that rounded up a group of civilian men who were executed the same day. Samardžija was tried in the State Court of Bosnia-Herzegovina, an institution established by the international community at the war's end to prosecute war and economic crimes. These trials were conducted in the local language and simultaneously translated into English for the panel of international judges, all of whom came from outside the former Yugoslavia. Most of the transcripts and tapes I draw from are the English-language version, but in a few instances, I use the Bosnian-Croatian-Serbian version which I translated myself. My translations were double-checked by a native speaker language teacher.

In addition to these sources, I also availed myself of personal memoirs, journalists' accounts, and reports by human rights organizations and the US State Department. I also consulted the vast secondary literature for each region so that my view of the local context never became untethered from the larger political machinations that were occurring in the rest of country at the time of violence.

To analyze these data, I read the sources in the context in which they were produced, whether at a deposition taken shortly after events or at an interview taking place decades later. I remained mindful about why an actor would tell his or her story one way and not another. My goal was not to adjudicate between facts and falsehoods, but rather to identify whatever truths—moral, emotional, psychological, official—that a given source might contain (Cole 2010; Fujii 2010, 2018; Portelli 1991). Some accounts might be lacking in a certain factual accuracy, but may nevertheless reveal the person's aspirations, disappointments, fears, or hopes. The recollections of Sidney Hayman, for example, a prominent white man who lived in downtown Princess Anne, decades after the lynching might minimize his knowledge of plans to lynch Armwood, but they may still provide emotional truths about how it felt when he heard and saw the large lynch mob move past his home.

The narratives I present in the following chapters are pieced together from these various sources and fragments. They do not represent a singular truth, as if only one truth existed, but rather an argument about how these displays took form and shape, how and why people joined in, and what the consequences were in terms of people's understandings about the world and their place in it.

The Chapters

The book traces both the local- and supralocal process of violent display making. The weighting of episodes varies by chapter. One region or episode might feature more prominently than others, depending on what needs to be accentuated, highlighted, theorized, or explained (Gourevitch 1986, 68).

The first part of the book lays theoretical and historical groundwork. Chapter 1 examines how the state and ordinary people deployed social categories before the period of violence. It argues that lines of difference were more changeable and context dependent than nationalist claims would imply. Chapter 2 begins developing the theory of violent display by examining the process of political takeover at the national, regional, and local levels. This chapter argues that establishing a new political order is, in large part, an embodied process. It requires people to abandon their old habits of relating to one another and to adopt new habits that signify the rupture of former friendships and other social ties.

Chapter 3 focuses on the main show in each episode. Here the lynching case from Maryland takes center stage, mainly because the rich detail that the source materials provide enables us to see people moving in and out of different roles in a given moment and over time. To put this display in comparative perspective, I also discuss violent displays in Rwanda and Bosnia. Both pale in comparison to the lynching in terms of their brutality and extralethality. And yet, these less spectacular displays, I argue, still express notions of power and belonging.

Chapter 4, titled "Intermission," marks a break from the narrative that constitutes the book's argument. In this chapter, I examine silencing narratives or those versions of "what happened" that have endured over time despite evidence to the contrary and that work to foreclose other possible ways of constructing past incidents of violence. In discussing these narratives, I highlight key moments during the research process that informed my understanding of the local context. Because all empirical data are only as trustworthy as the researcher's own methods, integrity, and reflexivity (Schwartz-Shea 2014), these moments merit more than a quick footnote. I view these encounters as instances of "accidental ethnography" that helped me to understand what was possible to see and not to see, to ask and not to ask, and to delve into more deeply or to overlook altogether (Fujii 2014).

Chapter 5 extends the analysis by looking at extralethal displays that occurred in Bosnia and Rwanda. In Bosnia, I examine the violence that occurred in the Omarska prison camp, arguably the most notorious of all the Bosnian Serb-run camps during the war. I look at various forms of extralethal acts, from the mundane (forcing prisoners to sing Serb nationalist songs) to the more spectacular (the torture of a group of former friends). In Rwanda, I investigate the extralethal violence committed by a regional official and ardent supporter of the genocide, a man I call Joseph. Joseph actively participated in the genocide, but also engaged in violent displays of his own.

Chapter 6 examines the immediate aftermath of these displays. I find that violence did not simply end with the killing of the victims, but continued through the dumping of bodies, the taking of souvenirs, and continued narrativizing of the event. In Rwanda, the displays continued through official commemorations of the dead, which involved exhumations and reburials of alleged victims of the genocide. In reality, these reburials were a hoax. Through official genocide reburials, the government was able to recategorize many dead bodies, transforming victims of RPF killings and even *génocidaires* into victims of the genocide. In the Eastern Shore, the violence continued through the next days and weeks, with tourists descending on Princess Anne to find out what they missed and others bragging about what they saw and did during the lynching.

Chapter 7 returns to the theoretical contributions of the book. It argues that despite perpetrators' best efforts, violent projects—including violent displays—failed to harden or shore up group boundaries, even when terror tactics diminished people's room for maneuver. Even under the most threatening circumstances, people in each locale continued to violate the precepts of the nationalist, ethnic, or color line, laying bare the fragility of race- or ethnicity-based claims and racial and ethnic categories to order and direct people to act in specific ways. The dividing line (whether it be race or ethnicity), in a word, resists attempts at fixing its content and meaning, including violence put on display.

What do these fine-grained studies of violent displays teach us about the power of collective violence to embolden citizens, coerce neighbors, and inspire others to do things they would not normally do? Understanding the power of collective violence to transform not only political hierarchies, but also shared notions of belonging can help to lessen the allure of putting violence on display.

FIXATIONS
The Making and Unmaking of Categories

> **As deployed by the powerful, race serves as a rationale for brutality, and its history is ultimately a local one, best understood through the lives of individual men, women, and children.**
> —Jacqueline Jones, *A Dreadful Deceit*

> **Well-known journalist covering the war: "Are you a Muslim or Serb?"**
> **Local man: "I'm a musician."**
> —E. Filipović, personal communication

The starting point of this book is that violent displays are a powerful way of reordering society and political hierarchies and rewriting the basis for belonging in that order. By putting violence on display, actors are telling the world "who they are" and by extension, who everyone else is not. To contextualize how violent displays transform the basis for belonging, this chapter explores what came before. Through a brief survey of category making in all three countries, I make three arguments. First, fixity is a fiction. Variability in meanings and usage is the norm, even during conditions of violence. Second, state institutions do not reflect existing relations between "groups"; they are mechanisms for creating uniform categories, fitting everyone into them, then arranging those categories in a hierarchy of rights, privileges, and entitlements. Third, despite states' best efforts, meanings remain not just variable, but also ambiguous. It is this ambiguity that becomes a potent force for those who put violence on display.

By emphasizing the ambiguity of who is who, I mean to push back against a tendency to begin studies of nationalist or racial violence by sorting actors into broad racial or ethnic categories conceived of as clearly bounded, internally homogenous, stable, unitary, invariant "things" in the world. Such a groupist view is a fiction, as Rogers Brubaker (2004a, b) reminds us. No such entities exist, because meanings vary over time and space. What it means to be Muslim in Bosnia is very different than what it means in Bangladesh (Roy 1994) or Sierra Leone (Ferme 2001). Even within Bosnia, what it means to be Muslim or Serb in rural areas differs from what it means in urban centers (Bringa 1995; Judah 2009;

Lockwood 1975), just as what it meant to be Bosnian in 1982 is not the same as what it came to mean in 1992.

It is this variability in meaning and usage that makes social categories so adaptable to violent projects. Categories provide a familiar vocabulary that political entrepreneurs can repackage, reharness, and deploy. Which categories become salient depends on the context, for there is nothing intrinsic to any social label—be it ethnic, racial, national, religious, or political—that makes one more suitable than another. As Robert Hayden (2000) notes, Bosnian Muslims could have been Bosnian Buddhists and still have become the target of violent expulsion, mass killing, and mass rape by Bosnian Serb forces. John Mueller (2000) argues similarly that perpetrators in Bosnia and Rwanda could have chosen left-handedness or right-handedness as the basis for targeting their victims instead of "nationality" or "ethnicity." The outcome would have been the same. Forensic anthropologist Clea Koff (2005) concurs. After working on the excavation of mass graves in Kibuye (Rwanda), she concludes that killing people because they were Tutsi is "about as arbitrary as attempting to kill everyone wearing a long-sleeved shirt on a given day."

It is the very malleability and flexibility of social categories—not their permanence or fixity—that makes them useful to political actors who seek to mobilize followers or invoke ideas or ideologies. This is not to imply that people automatically follow elite proclamations. Far from it. It does mean that elites as well as nonelites can harness social categories to their political projects in many different ways because lines of difference can be made to bend in almost any direction. It also means that people have their own ways of marking, minimizing, and overlooking difference.

Histories of Group Making

In this section, an all too brief glance at the history of group making in all three regions reveals how flexible meanings can be in a given context and how closely tied they can be to changing patterns of politics and power.

Moving Lines in Rwanda

There is no better illustration of how ambiguous social categories can be than Rwanda. In the local language, the word *ubwoko*, commonly translated as "ethnicity" in English, means a type of a person, thing, or animal. The term can apply just as easily to trees and cars as it can to groups of people. To speak of ubwoko is to raise questions about what marks the line of difference between so-called Hutu and Tutsi. As Claudine Vidal (1995, 9) explains:

> None of the usual criteria used to define ethnicities or ethnic groups apply to Rwanda. Geographic space? No, because Hutu and Tutsi have lived in the same territory for centuries. Religion and culture? No, because they share the same religious beliefs, whether traditional or Christian. Language? Contrary to the usual pattern in Africa, the inhabitants of the region have long shared a common tongue.

David Newbury (1980, 1995) concurs, pointing out there is no "corporate" history of "Tutsi" or "Hutu" as unified, cohesive groups. Rather, the history of these terms hews closely to the expansion of state power in the precolonial era and European intervention in the colonial period. Meanings shifted with the politics.

Before the arrival of Europeans, meanings and usage of Hutu and Tutsi varied by region and changed over time. In some places, the terms signaled a person's place of origin. For example, in southwest Rwanda, people living on Ijwi island (in what was then Zaïre) referred to all Rwandans as "Badusi," a local derivative of the Kinyarwandan term *Abatutsi*, or Tutsi people (Newbury 1988). In other regions, the labels signified social status, with the term *Tutsi* denoting someone with higher social status than those designated as Hutu. When a person's situation changed, so, too, could his or her classification. A Hutu man who married into a rich family could become Tutsi. Similarly, a Tutsi family that had lost its wealth might henceforth be known as Hutu (de Lame 1996; Fujii 2009; Gravel 1968; Newbury 1988; Newbury and Newbury 1999).

Meanings changed further with state expansion. Under the *mwami* (king) Rwabugiri, the central court began to expand its reach outward and downward into the lives of ordinary Rwandans (Des Forges 2011). As state power began penetrating new regions, many ordinary Rwandans who had never before had contact with the royal court began to associate the term *Tutsi* with a person's "proximity to power" (Newbury 1988).

Meanings continued to shift with the arrival of the Père blanc (White Father) missionaries at the turn of the twentieth century, followed by the Belgian colonizers who took over the territory from Germany after its defeat in World War I. It was European intervention that inaugurated the process of racializing social categories. This process was an attempt by Belgian colonizers and missionaries to affix uniform category rules to labels that were fluid and changing. Europeans' assumption that Hutu and Tutsi were *racial* designations was rooted in a specious, race science theory called the Hamitic hypothesis, which posited that "everything of value ever found in Africa was brought there by the Hamites, allegedly a branch of the Caucasian race" (Sanders 1969, 521). The Belgians used the Hamitic hypothesis to make sense of the highly developed and centralized political system they encountered in Rwanda. They attributed such "advancements" to a superior race, which they deemed to be the Tutsi. C. G. Seligman expressed the prevailing view of Europeans in 1930: "The incoming Hamites were pastoral 'Europeans'—arriving wave after wave—better armed as well as quicker witted than the dark agricultural Negroes" (Seligman quoted in Sanders 1969, 521). The Tutsi "race," the Belgians believed, were descendants of the original Hamites and were therefore of European stock. As a "European" race, Tutsi were born to rule, they believed, while the "negroid" Hutu were only born to serve.

This view of Rwandan society was not based on any actual knowledge of the country's political history. This history was a complex tale of palace intrigues and assassinations, nobles currying favor with the mwami, and various independent kingdoms that refused to be absorbed by the central court. Given the uneven authority the mwami exercised throughout the territory, he and his nobles did not try to dissuade the foreigners from their distorted view of Rwandan society because the Europeans were useful, at first, in helping the mwami to consolidate his power and establish his claim over the entire country (Des Forges 2011).

The Belgians proceeded to realize their racialized view by establishing institutions that reflected their imagined reality. Some of these changes the mwami approved of, but others he fiercely resisted precisely because they threatened to undermine his power, authority, and standing among the nobles at the court, who were starting to see the Belgians as the apex of power and no longer the mwami (Des Forges 2011). All the interventions had lasting and profound effects on Rwandan society and the direction of the country's politics.

The Belgians began by upending the existing system of customary authority, which involved a complex tripartite assignment of chiefs, each of whom had authority over different aspects of local life, from military organization to the oversight of land and cattle. Because the distribution of power among the three chiefs overlapped across the same territory, the system made no sense to the Belgians, so they began establishing one that did. As Filip Reyntjens (1985, 75–76) explains,

> In the context of their attempts to "rationalise" the Rwandan political and administrative organization, it was difficult for the Belgians to accept that parts of the territory escaped effective control by the Mwami. Such a situation of incomplete and diversified sovereignty was, of course, alien to the European concept of the State and contrary to the Belgian desire to bring about unity of authority and uniformity of administration.

The Belgians began applying a "racial" logic to every administrative structure. They began by removing all Hutu chiefs and subchiefs and replacing them with Tutsi chiefs who had sole authority over a single, contiguous territory. This change had wide-reaching ramifications. Many of the newly appointed chiefs had no ties to the local community. They could abuse their power at will because there were no longer other local authorities to keep them in check. This new system of rule, based solely on the appointee's "racial" classification helped to invest the labels "Hutu" and "Tutsi" with even more marked associations to power (Lemarchand 1970; Reyntjens 1985, 113–16). In the new system, to be "Hutu" meant being vulnerable to the whims of local authorities; to be "Tutsi" meant—for a very select few—a newfound basis for unchecked political power and authority.

The Belgians did not stop there. They instituted other systems that further transformed the terms *Hutu* and *Tutsi* into immutable, racial categories. One of the most significant was establishing a system of identity cards that all adults would be required to carry. The cards bore the person's name and that of his or her parents and spouse, *colline* (hill) of origin, and the person's "race," of which there were three possibilities: Hutu, Tutsi, or Twa (a pygmy group that accounts for less than 1 percent of the population). These identity cards slotted every Rwandan into a permanently affixed category, one that would not change under any circumstances. Other institutions reinforced the process of transforming social categories into racial markers. In the education system, for example, the Belgians and Pères blancs gave preference to the sons of Tutsi chiefs in order to groom the next generation of local rulers. This left Hutu, rich and poor alike, with very few avenues of advancement, even for those who managed to obtain an education (Lemarchand 1970; Linden 1977).

Postindependence regimes continued many of the practices that Belgians had instituted, including the system of identity cards. The first two presidents also introduced forms of favoritism that cut across European assumptions about racial unity. For example, Grégoire Kayibanda, the country's first president, directed the benefits of state power toward people from his home region of Gitarama, in the center-south of the country, effectively shutting out Hutu from all other regions. In 1973, when a young army officer named Juvénal Habyarimana overthrew Kayibanda, he redirected state largesse to his home region of Gisenyi préfecture in the north. So intense were regional rivalries that Habyarimana developed a policy of *équilibre* (balance), ostensibly to ensure that no region would receive preferential treatment. He fulfilled the regional quotas, however, by appointing Tutsi from the south. This guaranteed the loyalty of his appointees and kept Hutu rivals from the center-south in check (Gasana 2002).

By 1980, regional divisions were more salient than so-called ethnic ones. Habyarimana's most dangerous rivals were not Tutsi, but other Hutu elite and particularly those who came from Kayibanda's home region. As James Gasana (2002, 54) notes:

> By the end of the 1980s, the biggest problem in Rwandan society was not ethnicity. Nothing can be further from the truth than the claim that Habyarimana was anti-Tutsi. Even though the main problem in Rwanda was rural poverty, the most acute political problem was clearly regionalism. This one factor completely outweighed the ethnic factor in the policies of the Second Republic from its inception. From 1973 until October 1990, the victims of persecution and political assassination were not Tutsi but Hutu dissidents from the South.

Regional divisions meant that Habyarimana's biggest enemies were not Tutsi at all, but Hutu from other regions. This situation changed little in 1991 with the dawn of multiparty politics. The biggest opposition party to Habyarimana's MRND (Mouvement Révolutionaire National pour le Développement) became the MDR (Mouvement Démocratique Républicain), the successor party to Kayibanda's, whose base of support continued to be rooted firmly in Gitarama.

This brief glance at the political history of Rwanda reveals a complex constellation of competing centers of power before and after the colonial period. What it meant to be Hutu or Tutsi varied by region during the precolonial period, then shifted as a result of state expansion under Rwabugiri, then changed in more radical ways under Belgian rule. In the postcolonial period, the most potent political force became regionalism among competing Hutu elites battling for regional dominance. In this period, ethnicity was by no means the only or main line of division that shaped Rwandan politics.

Crossing Lines in Bosnia

In Bosnia, meanings, too, changed as quickly as the winds, particularly with the emergence of nationalist politics in the late 1980s. By the beginning of the Bosnian war in 1992, nationalist definitions of "Serb" and "Croat" included Bosnian Muslims. Serb nationalists were publicly declaring that Muslims were simply "lapsed" Serbs. Croat nationalists were making the same claim, declaring Bosnian Muslims to be "really" Croats (Bringa 1995, 30–31; Malcolm 1996, 127; Silber and Little 1997, 86; Toal and Dahlman 2011, 51). As Serb extremist Vojislav Šešelj told a journalist in 1991: "The Muslims of Bosnia are in fact Islamicized Serbs." Šešelj went on to make the same case for "so-called Croats," maintaining that they, too, were "Catholic[ized] Serbs" (Grmek, Gjidara, and Simac 1993,

305; Malcolm 1996, 226–27). Bosnian Serb nationalist leader, Radovan Karadžić, went a step further, telling a journalist from a Belgrade magazine that "our Bosnian Muslims are Slavs, of our same blood and language, who have chosen the European life along with their Muslim faith" (Maass 1996, 159).

This brotherly construction of Bosnian Muslims would shift markedly in a short period of time. By October 1991, during a session of Parliament where he had no official standing, Karadžić would declare: "We cannot live with the Muslims and the Croats, for there is so much hatred, centuries old hatred" (Bringa 2002, 197, 221n11). And by January 1992, Croatian President Tuđman would be telling US ambassador Warren Zimmerman that Bosnian President Alija Izetbegović was "just a fundamentalist front man for Turkey" (Tesser 2013, 143). What explains this about-face in discursive constructions of "Serb," "Muslim," and "Croat?"

The answer lies in recent politics, not distant pasts. Contrary to nationalist claims that the region has been marked by "ancient hatreds," Bosnia's history is one of conquest, competition, migration, and co-optation. The region's history makes any references to centuries-old hatreds nonsensical. The period of Ottoman rule, for example, which began in the mid-fifteenth century, was not marked by mass conversions to Islam or the rise of an Islamist strain that Tuđman was claiming had afflicted Izetbegović. The reverse was actually the case. As Noel Malcolm (1996, 49) explains: "Although Bosnia was ruled by Muslims, one could hardly call it an Islamic state. It was not state policy to convert people to Islam or make them behave like Muslims; the only state policy was to keep the country under control and extract from it money, men and feudal incomes to supply the needs of the Empire further afield." Ottoman-ruled Bosnia resembled a Weberian state in a Tillyian world: the imperial authorities focused on collecting revenues and conscripting men for its army, not converting the population to any particular religion (Tilly 1985). Converting to Islam did have its benefits; slaves captured by Ottomans could apply for their freedom if they converted (Malcolm 1996, 66–67). But those who were converting were not only choosing to become Muslim; some were converting to and from Orthodoxy and Catholicism (Malcolm 1996, 57).

With or without conversion, religious practices remained syncretic. Followers of all religions continued to combine and borrow practices from other traditions. As Malcolm (1996, 59) points out, "We not only find Muslims kissing the most venerated Christian icons, such as the one at Olovo, or entering Christian churches to pray; we also find them, in the early nineteenth century, having Catholic Masses said for them in front of images of the Virgin in order to cure a serious illness." There is similar evidence of Christians inviting dervishes to read the Koran over them in the hopes of being cured from serious illness (Malcolm

1996, 59). This type of borrowing continued well into the twentieth century. As William Lockwood (1975, 25–26) observed in the 1970s: "The religion of these 'Islamicized' peasants was a mixture of Islamic, Christianized pagan, Christian, and heretical Christian elements." Following any particular religion encompassed a wide range of practices, such that no single, monolithic understanding of what it meant to be Catholic, Muslim or Orthodox prevailed.

Fast forward to the late nineteenth century, after the Ottoman retreat and takeover by Austria-Hungary. Under the new authorities, the terms *Muslim*, *Catholic*, and *Orthodox* continued to take on variegated meaning. As Max Bergholz (2016, 33) explains, "These labels continued to exist [but] . . . often in confusing and contradictory ways, alongside newer more 'national,' or more 'ethnic' understandings of 'Muslim,' and especially of 'Catholic Croat,' and 'Orthodox Serb.'" These newer "national" understandings, however, did not mean people's actions followed a "nationalist" logic. When Austria-Hungary declared war on Serbia in 1914, for example, following the assassination of Archduke Ferdinand by a Serb nationalist, congeries of so-called Serbs, Croats, and Muslims fought on the side of the imperial state. Indeed, some 25 percent of the Austro-Hungarian units were comprised of Serbs (Judah 2009, 98).

The onset of World War II also failed to produce evidence of "ancient" hatreds or even clearly drawn national loyalties. Shortly after invading Yugoslavia on April 6, 1941, the Nazis declared the new "Independent State of Croatia," known by its local initials as the NDH (Nezavisna Država Hrvatska). At the head of the new collaborationist state was Ante Pavelić, a Croat nationalist who had been living in Italy (Bougarel 1996, 34). Almost immediately, NDH authorities began trying to recruit Croats and Muslims into its armed militia, called the Ustaša (Ustaše, pl.), but they encountered numerous obstacles in Bosnia, which was declared part of NDH territory. In a meticulously researched microhistory of the war's onset in the region of Kulen Vakuf in northwest Bosnia, Bergholz (2016, 133) found that mass support for the new Nazi-aligned state was tepid at best: "Many of those whom the authorities considered to be "Croat" were, in fact, appalled by the violence." When violence against non-Croats began, many so-called "Croats" and "Muslims" did not join in; instead, they took action to save a significant number of their Orthodox neighbors (Bergholz 2016, 136).

What Bergholz's research also reveals is the highly subjective approach that the NDH used to define a "Croat." The NDH relied on a multiconfessional conception of the term, which made it possible for a person to be "Muslim" and "Croat" at the same time. Pavelić himself declared Bosnian Muslims to be "Croats of the Islamic faith" (Bergholz 2016, 63; Bougarel 1996, 35). NDH conceptions of what constituted a "Serb" were also highly subjective. Official policy was to "remove" all non-Croats from NDH territory but this did not necessarily mean, at the least in the beginning, murder them. One method of "removal" was conversion. By converting to Catholicism, so-called "Serbs" could be transformed into "Croats" and indeed, some "former Serbs" took this option to ensure their security (Bergholz 2016, 81–82). The very possibility of turning "Serbs" into "Croats" through religious conversion indicates that the NDH treated these terms as socially constructed, rather than fixed at birth.[1]

The larger multipronged war that consumed the region also failed to produce clear "ethnic" lines or loyalties. So-called Serbs, Croats, and Muslims fought on all sides. After the Nazi invasion of Yugoslavia, two major resistance movements arose: the Četniks led by Draža Mihailović and the Communist Partizans led by Tito. From the beginning, the two Axis powers backed different movements. The Italians found an ally in the Serbs because they shared a common enemy in the NDH. The Germans, by contrast, saw all Serbs as an enemy to be eradicated (Redzic 2005, 7–10). At the same time, both resistance movements focused their efforts on defeating the other and yet, nevertheless collaborated at times (Malcolm 1996, 181; Ramet 2006, 8). In Bosnia, for example, the two groups fought together against the Ustaša until November 1941, at which point Partizan leaders began distancing themselves from the Četniks partly in response to massacres of Muslim civilians (Bergholz 2010, 9). By 1943, Četniks were collaborating with the Nazis instead of fighting against them, while the Partizans were enjoying Allied support. By this point, the Allies, too, had changed sides. They had originally backed Mihailović's Četniks but then switched their support to the Partizans after learning about Četnik collaborations with the Axis armies (Donia and Fine 1994, 153).

Membership in the various armed groups also belies the idea that "ethnic" loyalties trumped all others. Until 1943, Serbs dominated the ranks of both the Partizans and Četniks (Hoare 2013, 4). In 1943 and 1944, Bosnian Croats and Bosnian Serbs who had once been loyal to the NDH were switching sides to join the Partizans, further shifting the numbers (Malcolm 1996, 184). So-called Muslims also fought on all sides. Some joined the Ustaša while others joined the Partizans to fight against the Četniks. In other areas, Muslims joined Četnik fighters against the Partizans. By December 1943, four thousand Muslims were among Mihailović's Četnik forces (Malcolm 1996, 188).

Just as in Rwanda, a brief excursion into Bosnian history shows little evidence of a centuries-old hatred among so-called Croats, Muslims, and Serbs as nationalists were proclaiming in the late 1980s. There is also little evidence of the kind of "national" unity and allegiance that nationalists such as Šešelj or Karadžić were trying to assert and establish. During World War II, the exigencies of war and occupation created opportunities for many to profit from their newfound power and authority, a pattern that would emerge again in the late 1980s with the rise of Slobodan Milošević. Most people during this period, however, as Bergholz (2010, 3) points out, were on "no side." They were simply trying to survive. That pattern, too, would repeat itself in the 1990s.

The "Muddled Middle" in the United States

In the United States, the same race science tenets that shaped Belgian polices in Rwanda were informing responses to the "Negro question" both before and after the Civil War. Even before the end of war and the emancipation of the slaves, white politicians and intellectuals were claiming that black people were inherently inferior to whites. These claims, however, were confounded at every turn. In fact, it was largely because racist tropes about "black" and "white" were so often rebutted by the reality of black achievement and success that white supremacist politicians had to go to ever greater lengths to keep "white" and "black" in a strictly hierarchical relationship.

The history of race in America is not a simple binary between "white" and "black." The United States was born from chattel slavery, but the salience of "white" and "black" did not begin with this system of human bondage. Slavery did not depend on the racialization of any group, enslaved or free. As Jacqueline Jones (2013, 42) points out: "In 1656 the idea that all black people belonged in slavery, a notion that would come to dominate American public life, was hardly a foregone conclusion." The distinctions that settlers in colonial America made centered not on race, but other lines of belonging, such as religion (Protestant versus Catholic; Puritan versus non-Puritan), country of origin (Dutch versus English), colonial boundaries (Maryland versus Virginia), and political alliances (Indian allies versus Indian foes) (Jones 2013, chap. 1).

The racialization of slaves and slave owners occurred as a response to the Christianization of slave and Indian populations. As slaves converted to Christianity in ever larger numbers in the seventeenth century, slaveholders needed a justification for keeping their fellow Christians in bondage. The answer was race. By viewing Africans as people who were "preordained for slavery" (Sanders 1969, 523), slaveholders could Christianize their slaves while maintaining their fellow believers in a state of human bondage (Jones 2013, 44). Eventually, the process of enslavement would homogenize differences in culture, language, and religious practices among enslaved peoples, creating a new class of people called "slaves" (Hale 1999, 15; Jones 2013, 44).

What complicated the relationship between slavery and race was the existence of blacks who were free, rather than enslaved, and slave owners who were black rather than white. As Hale (1999, 4) notes, "The existence of free blacks as well as black slaveholders made the antebellum dynamic of power one of slave versus citizen, dependent versus independent, rather than white versus black." Race and enslavement, in other words, did not always go hand in hand.

Perhaps because of these complexities, many "learned" white men were invoking the same race science tenets that Belgian colonizers were applying in Rwanda. The American version of the Hamitic hypothesis predicted that emancipation would not make any difference because those deemed racially black lacked the intellectual and moral sense that only so-called whites possessed. This is the logic that US senator Robert Goodloe Harper of Maryland was using when he wrote in 1817 that "you can manumit the slave but you cannot make him a white man" (Dorsey 2011, 100; Papenfuse 1997, 58, quoted in Smith 2008, 22). According to Senator Harper, even if a slave were made free, he would still not possess—and indeed could never possess—the attributes of whiteness that make whites superior to nonwhites, such as industriousness, morality, and reason.

Many others were making similar statements in the postbellum era. Former British ambassador to the United States, James Bryce, wrote extensively on the incapacity of freedmen and freedwoman to participate in democracy, including voting. For Bryce, black men were not only incapable of taking part in democracy, they were a "danger to society" (Hawkesworth 2016, 36). Similarly, John W. Burgess, a professor at Columbia University, claimed that democracy was a singular achievement of the "Teutonic" race. Burgess, too, saw the very presence of black people as a threat to democracy and called for deporting "the ethnically hostile element in order to shield the vitals of the state from the forces of dissolution" (Hawkesworth 2016, 38–39). In short, even before Belgian colonizers were taking over the territory of Rwanda, leading American thinkers were harnessing the tenets of race science to construct black people as "threats" to the republic. In their view, black people were unqualified to be or act as full citizens—not because of their previous status as slaves, but because of their innate abilities that were supposedly circumscribed by race.

It was this belief in the *racial* inferiority of "blacks" that animated the cause of white supremacy in the North and South. The end of slavery required building new foundations to keep whites in a position of superiority over all blacks, including those who had never been enslaved. Segregation was but one solution to the "Negro question" among many that various political actors proposed (Cell 1982; Marx 1998; Woodward 1955). There was nothing inevitable or "natural" about the emergence of such a system. As John Cell (1982, 17) points out, segregation "had to be made to happen."

Segregation was a northern innovation that was oriented toward the peculiarities of urban life, where blacks could circulate and move about with more autonomy than in rural areas, and where the "mixing" of races occurred more frequently and in closer confines than in the less densely populated rural regions

(Cell 1982, 134; Marx 1998, 42; Ritterhouse 2006, 51). As a legalized system of racial hierarchy, it was flexible enough to bend with complex, interpersonal relations that varied by region, neighborhood, and household (Barnes 2006; Cell 1982, 18). As Cell (1982, 18) argues, "Segregation triumphed for the very reason that it *was* flexible and sophisticated."

Ironically, however, a system of spatial segregation presumed a clear line between "black" and "white." The problem for segregationists was that the color line had always been fuzzy at the edges. As in Rwanda and Bosnia, meanings about "black" and "white" varied over time and place. What it meant to be "Negro" or "mulatto" before the Civil War differed from what it meant during Reconstruction (Hale 1999). Meanings and classifications also varied by state. Some states recognized the space "in-between" categories by legally recognizing the category "mulatto," while others did not (Davis 2001, 34–37).

The very indeterminacy of race in many cases led the courts to issue rulings that declared a person *legally* one race and not the other. In *Plessy v. Ferguson*, for example, the Supreme Court ruled that a man like Plessy, who was light-skinned and mixed race, could not be both "black" and "white" at the same time. The court declared him legally black, even though he was socially white (Hale 1999, 23) when it upheld a Louisiana law that required black passengers to ride in a separate car from whites. *Plessy* exposed the essence of the problem—schemes that presumed "black" and "white" as neatly separable and mutually exclusive categories had to confront a vast, muddled middle at every turn. In this space of ambiguity, people could be both black and white and neither at the same time.

Like the race-based institutions that Belgians established in Rwanda, segregation did not reflect existing realities but was established to remake society according to the race science beliefs to which many whites subscribed. But this effort always fell short. As Hale (1999, 8–9) explains:

> The whiteness that some Americans made through segregation was always contingent, always fragile, always uncertain. Positing an absolute boundary and the freedom to cross only in one direction, segregation remained vulnerable at its muddled middle, where mixed-race people moved through mixed spaces, from railroad cars to movies to department stores, neither public nor private, neither black nor white.

What segregation did manage to do was render invisible the very class of people that white supremacists like Burgess, Bryce, and Harper claimed would never come to be—an educated, well-heeled, and "properly" dressed, coifed, and mannered black middle class. By relegating this rising middle class of freedmen and women to the same waiting rooms, train cars, bus seats, and restrooms as poor blacks, segregation simultaneously pushed all whites to the front—both literally and figuratively. Regardless of economic background, all those who could claim they were white would benefit from what David Roediger (2007) aptly calls the "wages of whiteness," that is, the privileges bestowed by racial status alone, regardless of how poor or unlettered a given white person was. Segregation placed poor, illiterate whites "above" educated, professional blacks in all public spaces, from courthouses to public waiting rooms, from restaurants to train cars.

Segregation, however, did not build on what already existed. It was a means for transforming postbellum society in ways that would ensure white supremacy without the institution of slavery. Just as the Belgians' elevation of Tutsi as a racial category did not reflect society but rather remade it in the image of race science beliefs, so too did segregation remake society according to the same tenets. Segregation, put simply, was a means for creating and maintaining racial difference in a postslavery world, for only by making and maintaining a boundary between "white" and "black" could two different races exist at all. As J. William Harris (1995, 388) writes, "It was not the presence of two races in the South that created a boundary between them, but the presence of a boundary that created two races." Segregation established such a boundary in spatial terms in order to create the illusion of difference between so-called "blacks" and "whites" in biological terms.

Official Categories and Local Deviations

As the foregoing discussion indicates, states have always put much effort into making racial and ethnic difference "real" and making society fit into its own sanctioned grid. Societies, however, do not necessarily follow official edicts. Where the state seeks uniformity in rules and practice, people prefer their own ways of doing things, which often contradict or deviate from official policy. These deviations and contradictions highlight the impermanence and incompleteness of state projects and the ambiguity inherent in all categorical schemes (Scott 1998). In addition, people learn who they are by doing. Through play, interactions with adults, and schooling, people learn to embody the meanings they attach to social categories.

Learning Social Categories

Tito inherited a country that had been devastated by war. The tally of dead was 1 million, the majority of whom had died at the hands of fellow Yugoslavs (Malcolm 1996, 174; Ramet 2006, 8). The challenge for Tito was to create state institutions that recognized national rights without allowing the (re-)emergence of nationalist movements, such as Mihailović's Četniks. To cobble together a cohesive state out of the ruins of a multipronged civil war, Tito promoted the slogan of "Brotherhood and Unity" (*Bratsvo I jedinstvo*). He established a "three-tier system of national rights" that was unique in the postwar Communist world. He then tried to make the new system a reality.

One of the main institutions that states use to establish official categories is the census. In Yugoslavia, the first census results revealed the extent to which people did not see themselves in the two dominant categories the state recognized, that of "Serb" and "Croat." In the 1948 census, 72,000 declared themselves Serb, 25,000 Croat, and 778,000 "undeclared" (Malcolm 1996, 198). Over time, the state provided additional options. While initially refusing to offer "Yugoslav" as a category (Yankovitch 1971), the 1953 census featured the next closest thing: "Yugoslavs of undeclared nationality" (Bringa 1993 86). This became the new catchall category for those who did not wish to mark any other on the form. In the 1981 census, the state finally added "Yugoslav" as a "national" category. That year, 5.4 percent of the population or 1.2 million people identified as such; many were the offspring of so-called mixed marriages (Bringa 1995, 27; Ramet 2006, 8–9). Other changes followed. The option to declare oneself "Muslim in the ethnic sense" appeared for the first time in 1961; ten years later, in 1971, Muslim in the sense of "nation" (*narod*) appeared on the form. Obtaining "nation" status was important for political, not religious, reasons (Malcolm 1996, 199–200). Such recognition meant "guaranteed numerically equal political and administrative representation with Serbs and Croats" (Bringa 1995, 9).

"Facts on paper," however, do not always match the "facts on the ground," as Scott (1998) points out. A system of official categories rarely covers all the ways that people self-identify. Different people used different strategies to respond to the menu of census categories on offer. Before 1971, for example, when it was not possible to check the box for Muslim in the national sense, Bosnian Muslims used a variety of ways to identify themselves on the form. Tone Bringa's (1995, 29) rich ethnographic data reveals that personal friendships drove some people's choices.

> When I asked my Bosnian Muslim friends how they identified themselves at censuses, the replies varied from person to person. Furthermore, the same person would slot into different national or ethnic categories at different times, particularly as census categories changed. Many would identify themselves as Yugoslavs when this was an option. Otherwise, they would identify themselves as a Croat or Serb according to personal experience: if you had a good friend or neighbor who was a Serb, you would "write yourself" as a Serb.

Various individual strategies made for interesting results. As one journalist observed just before the 1971 census, "It is not unusual to find three different nationalities—Croatian, Serbian and Moslem—represented in the same family" (Yankovitch 1971). One example of this very situation is the sociologist, Esad Ćimić, a Muslim. Just before the 1971 census, a reporter asked how he would mark the form. He replied he was going to be a Croat while his brother was going to be a Serb [Bra #1/2].

Some Bosnian Muslims refused to mark any of the categories and opted to remain "unspecified" or later, chose "Yugoslav" when that category became available. One man summed up his own experience while testifying during the trial of Duško Tadić at the ICTY:

> Up until 1974 when a new constitution was adopted, to us, Muslims, we were not allowed to declare ourselves as Muslims, but we were forced by political measures to be either Serbs, Croats, Montenegrins, Slovenes or, if we did not want any of those, we had the possibility to be unspecified. After 1974 it was possible to be a Muslim, not as religious belonging, but as a National belonging. The only difference was that the religion was with a small letter; whereas the National belonging was with a capital "N". Neither theoretically nor practically did I agree with the use of a name of a religion for a national group, so I decided to be a Yugoslav. [Tadić 1209]

Others went further in their refusal to identify with "national" categories. A reporter for *Oslobodjenje*, the Sarajevo newspaper that published daily throughout the war, recalled her mother had always "marked *0*" on any official document that asked for nationality (Gjelten 1995, 51). The zero expressed the woman's rejection of *all* official categories on offer.

Censuses are not the only mechanism that states use to create uniform categories. States also inculcate official forms of belonging through educational systems. In all three countries, children learned at a young age "what" they were, even if they did not know what belonging to a given category actually meant. During a visit to a school in Bosnia, for example, Bringa observed the teacher ask the students to show by raise of hands if they were Serb, Croat, or Muslim. As Bringa (1995, 4) recounts: "Most of the children were confident in their knowledge of whether they were Serbs, Croats, or Muslims, but some hesitated or got it wrong and had to be instructed by their friends." One man I interviewed had a similar recollection of his childhood: "We did have children who had absolutely no idea what they were. I knew because of my father. These things were genuinely not important. Until someone told me, I just disregarded it. I understood that we were Muslim and Muslim was a religion but I didn't understand why it was different than anything else" [Bra #1/2]. The very possibility of not knowing indicates the extent to which children learn "what" they are at home. Across different homes, such talk varied, which, in turn, produced different understandings about national categories and their importance or lack thereof in people's daily lives.

In Rwanda, people evinced similar variation in how they learned to embody social categories. As in Bosnia, teachers sometimes made students line up by "ethnicity," with Hutu children instructed to go on one side of the classroom and Tutsi on the other.[2] Those who did not know which side of the room to go to were subject to taunting by the other students as well as the teacher. As one interviewee recalled, teachers "would ask why this or that student did not know her 'ethnicity.' They would make fun of him. They would say he was like an idiot" (Fujii 2009, 109). Jennie Burnet's (2012, 52) interviewees recount similar experiences of teachers asking students to stand up "according to their ethnic category."

At home, people's experiences learning "what" they were varied by household just as in Bosnia. For a variety of reasons, some young people in Rwanda did not learn their ubwoko until they were older. Some students, for example, only learned they were Tutsi when they earned high scores on national exams but were still denied a coveted place in secondary school or university because they were Tutsi.[3] Officials often passed over these students and awarded the spots to Hutu students with lower scores (Burnet 2012, 52). One of Burnet's interviewees, who had a Tutsi mother and Hutu father, explained her upbringing this way: "In my family, the subject never came up. We were Banyarwanda [Rwandan people]. My mother and father never talked about Tutsi this or Hutu that. We [the children] didn't even know what we were, and we didn't care. We were simply children of a love [whose political implications] had nothing to do with us" (Burnet 2012, 51). This woman had grown up in Zaire so the relevant category for her and her family there was "Banyarwanda" (Rwandans) as opposed to Zaireans (Burnet 2012, 51).

In the former Yugoslavia, it was also possible to learn at a later age because of government policy that sought to socialize people toward identifying as Communists or, at the very least, *not* identifying primarily through national categories. One reporter for the newspaper *Oslobodjenje*, for example, who grew up in the 1970s, only learned that her father was Serb when she was sixteen. Since her father was born in Croatia, she had always assumed he was a Croat (Gjelten 1995, 51).

In the United States, the process of learning race also occurred through state institutions like the census and school system. At a very young age, white children learned both inside and outside the home that being white meant having power and authority over anyone black. These lessons included, for example, how to address adult men and women in ways that clearly marked the person's race. White children learned, for example, to reserve terms like "lady," "Miss," and "Mrs." for white women and to use a different vocabulary for black women in order to deny all black women the designation of "lady" (Harris 1995; Ritterhouse 2006).

These lessons of racial hierarchy were reinforced when black and white children went to separate churches on Sundays and separate schools during the week. As in Rwanda and Bosnia, schools were powerfully socializing institutions that reinforced the power-laden meanings of "white" and "black." White children learned to enact their power both inside and outside the classroom. One story clearly illustrates this process. As a young girl, famed black educator, activist, and leader Mary Church Terrell attended a mostly white school in Ohio. One day, she happened on a group of white girls doing poses in front of the mirror in the girls' restroom. The young Terrell responded by trying to join in their play. "Haven't I got a pretty face too?" she asked the others, to which one of the white girls responded, "You've got a pretty black face" as she pointed her finger "derisively" at Terrell (Ritterhouse 2006, 115). Ritterhouse (2006, 116) analyzes this encounter by noting Terrell's rejection of white standards of beauty and assertion of the beauty of her "black" complexion, which, as Ritterhouse notes, "was not much darker than Walter White's or, presumably, than those of the other girls in the cloakroom." In other words, even when so-called black children looked nearly the same as their "white" counterparts, white children knew better and made sure their black classmate did, too.

Children also learned the power-laden meaning of whiteness from observing adults. Historian John Cell (1982, 126–27), for example, recalls his own childhood growing up in the American South:

> Until after World War II, a child such as myself, growing up on the outskirts of the capital of the South's reputedly most liberal state, North Carolina, became accustomed to chain gangs, supervised by guards with shotguns, working only a few feet from the front door. The guards were always white. The convicts were segregated. Sometimes they were white; more often they were black. The association in the child's mind between black males, crime, and forced labor at gunpoint was inescapable.

For Cell and, no doubt, countless other white (and black) children, the color line was visibly etched in the spatial arrangement of black and white bodies. The physical line of bodies in a chain gang or at a restaurant or lunch counter did not simply emphasize white from black; it also created a visible hierarchy of power in which whites were always over and above blacks no matter the context.

Encounters with the Color Line

Life under Jim Crow was not monolithic, however. Practices and norms in Maryland were not the same as those in Alabama or Mississippi; similarly, life under Jim Crow in Baltimore was a different experience than segregated life in the rural Eastern Shore (Chafe, Gavins, and Korstad 2001; Krech 1981; Moody 2011; Smith 2008). As William H. Chafe, Raymond Gavins, and Robert Korstad (2001, 3) write:

> Children's experiences . . . varied. Those who lived in or near cities often remember the physical signs of segregation—placards over water fountains, separate platforms at the train station, the often-shifting terrain of racial separation on the street car or bus. In the rural South, children's memories of learning about racial difference are sometimes more subtle (rural children played together) and sometimes brutally stark (in the countryside, white violence tended to be even less restrained).

These experiences depended not only on the laws in the place (which varied by state), but also on the cultural norms and practices within a given community.

Add to this variation the fact that the Eastern Shore was a place unto itself. As one observer wrote in 1950, the region is not just a place; it is a state of mind (Phillips 1950, 991). The region's past is one of slaves and plantations, tobacco and grain, but also of abolitionists and freedom seekers. Two of the most famous sons and daughters of the Eastern Shore are former slaves who escaped to freedom—Harriet Tubman, the fearless "conductor" of the Underground Railroad, and Frederick Douglass, tireless opponent of slavery and one of the earliest advocates for women's suffrage. In addition to Tubman and Douglass, Maryland produced other luminaries in the same period, including Roger Brooke Taney, a lawyer who rose to become chief justice of the US Supreme Court. It was Taney who, in 1857, penned the infamous decision in *Dred Scott v. Sandford*, which found that black people were not entitled to the most basic rights of citizenship (Smith 2008, 5).

Change came in fits and starts. The 1864 state constitution officially abolished slavery, but slavery on the Eastern Shore was already in decline by the 1850s (Wennersten 1992, 130). Emancipation still came as a shock. As John Wennersten (1992, 140) observes, "Of the numerous social and economic adjustments confronting the Eastern Shore in the Civil War era, none would be so painful as emancipation." As newly freed slaves began to migrate north from the Deep South, white fears of a growing black "menace" increased. It mattered little if the black body belonged to a native-born Eastern Shoreman or a new arrival from outside the region. The economic downturn of the 1890s, which turned former proponents of black franchise and civil rights into fear-mongering "Negrophobes," increased tensions further; this crisis, according to C. Vann Woodward (Woodward 1955, 60), was "a more profound upheaval of economic discontent" than the Great Depression.

When the Depression hit, the effects were not uniform across the South (Brundage 1993, 137), but they hit both white and black families hard (Woodward 1955, 105). The Eastern Shore was already one of the poorest regions in the state (Wennersten 1992, 146). The closure of businesses, such as canneries, affected entire communities. As the situation worsened, people became increasingly desperate (Brugger 1988, 500–503). In 1932 in Somerset County, for example, 89 families asked for relief; by the following year, the number had grown to 625 (Brugger 1988, 506; Smith 2008, 73). As always, racist practice shaped who was able to obtain relief. According to Wennersten (1992, 146), "Those few blacks who received flour from the local Red Cross had to perform domestic service in white families to pay for it." Fourth-term Maryland governor Albert C. Ritchie did not help matters. Sticking doggedly to his platform of self-help, Ritchie refused assistance from Washington (Brugger 1988, 504). As Smith (2008, 73) points out, "People were hungry but Ritchie clung to principle."

Even with economic upheaval and the passage and expansion of Jim Crow, blacks and whites in the Eastern Shore continued to live and work in the same spaces, though in an explicitly regulated hierarchy. Black women worked as maids and cooks in white homes, while black men worked as waiters, bus boys, or dishwashers in white-owned restaurants. Black and white children went to different schools that were wholly unequal in salaries and conditions. White janitors at white schools were paid more than black teachers (Wennersten 1992, 148). White children also had the privilege of riding to school in a bus, while black children had to walk [interviews]. Riding the bus allowed white children to engage in risk-free taunting. The man who grew up across the street from the family of Norman Dryden, a deputy sheriff for the town of Princess Anne, remembers that as he walked to school, white children yelled at him from the bus, "Glad you got to walk, Nigger" [interview].

The petty practices extended to the corner drugstore, where black customers were served their drinks in paper cups, while whites were served theirs in a glass. Black customers had to take their sodas off the premises to enjoy them, while white customers could stay and drink theirs [interview, 11 Oct 2011]. Most interviewees, both black and white, do not recall a life straightjacketed by Jim Crow, but rather adapted to it. Like people in other parts of the segregated south, most interviewees grew up knowing "the ways of the segregated world" (Smith 2008, 7) without necessarily finding it utterly defeating. Many did not give it a second thought. It was, as many told me, just the way things were.

When interviewees from the Eastern Shore remember this period, they remember it within the confines and spaces of their own lives. Throughout the Shore, communities were small, families large, and networks tight. The result was a web of relations that linked people to one another in multiple and overlapping ways. As one white "old-timer" explained to me, "In lower Mt. Vernon, you can't be raised down here without knowing everybody" [interview, 19 May 2010].

Within this web of multiplex relations, social hierarchies remained important. Everyone knew who was rich and who was poor, just as everyone knew who the local elites were. As Dorothy, a white woman who grew up in the 1920s, explained, "There were well-to-do people and there were poor people like I was." She described her hometown of Princess Anne as "small" and "thriving." Dorothy rattled off the various businesses that populated the small downtown during those years: "A dress shop, a men's store, theatres, two dime stores—5 & 10 stores—all that" [interview, 9 Dec 2009]. As is typical of people from the region, Dorothy took pride in her ability to make a living through hard work and self-reliance, despite humble beginnings. As she told me during one interview, "Honey, we grew what we ate, made what we wore, and manufactured the rest" [interview, 9 Dec 2009]. She contrasted the independence of "back then" with the global interdependency of "right now" when nearly everything bought and sold in the United States is manufactured overseas. Jim Crow and economic hardship did not define people's lives so much as push them in some directions and not others.

Proximity also meant that white and black children who lived near one another played together as well, and, as one interviewee quipped, they also fought together [interview]. Yet, play was also a way that children learned and enacted race. As Jennifer Ritterhouse (2006, 13, 128) notes, white children learned from "doing." They learned "to inflict [racial subordination], often first on black nurses and playmates." Play was an important domain in which white children learned to *embody* race and their own emerging sense of power over black children and adults.

One white interviewee's story clearly illustrates Ritterhouse's point. During one interview, the interviewee recalled a scene from her childhood in the Delaware part of the Shore. Born in 1911, she grew up in what she called the "horse and buggy days." She related this story in 2010, using the language she grew up with.

> We were quite accustomed to the dark people. We didn't have slaves. We played together. I had an older brother and two older sisters. One day they were whitewashing the trees, we had an apple orchard, to reduce bugs. I guess they got tired of playing with the black boy so they whitewashed him. I remember they even painted his hands. They painted his whole face but I remember they painted his hands. The parents got angry. My parents did, too.

Even as she related this story decades later, the woman seemed especially struck by the fact that her siblings had "even" painted the black boy's hands, as if painting his face with a substance meant to keep bugs off of trees was not bad enough. The enduring salience of this one detail suggests her own uneasiness with the layered meanings of her siblings' actions. Her brother and sisters were not just playing with a black neighbor boy; they were also using the privilege of their whiteness to change the terms of play unilaterally. Once the white children began to paint him, the black child ceased being their playmate and became instead their play *thing*—the *object* of the white children's amusement. As the white children undoubtedly knew, painting a black boy's skin "white" might momentarily change the child's *physical* appearance, but it did not make the boy white in the *social* sense, for whiteness was not about the hue of any person's skin, but about the power that people in one category could exercise over those in the other. This incident also highlights the relative powerlessness of the black boy in the company of white children. He could not refuse to go along. Neither could he share in the joke. The children were playing, or rather performing, the adult game of race and power.

Playing with Difference

While people in all three sites, not just Maryland, learned race, nationality, and ethnicity "by doing," differences alone did not determine the types of relationships people had with one another. Even in the Eastern Shore, black children had warm memories of certain white adults (just as they had memories of cruel or mean black teachers and other adults [interview]). The daughter of a black maid, for example, remembers her mother's white employer with great fondness. "She was so nice to me. I'd love to go by there. She'd give me something.... Candy or cookies. She was so nice to me" [interview]. Another interviewee about the same age recalled growing up across the street from Norman Dryden, a deputy sheriff for Princess Anne. This man, still bitter about the racism he grew up with when I talked with him decades later, recalled the Dryden family with genuine fondness. "They weren't bad people ... they were white but they were our friends." He recalls playing on their property as a child and going over to their house for eggs, milk, and other staples whenever his family needed them. "I don't remember being treated any differently," he mused. One of his earliest memories was when Sheriff Dryden came across the street to take his mother to Crownsville, a mental hospital outside Annapolis. The moment left an impression on the young child. As he related the story to me as a man in his eighties, there was no rancor in his voice toward Sheriff Dryden for taking his mother away. If anything, Dryden seemed to have performed the task professionally.

Friendships across the ethnic divide were also a fixture in Bringa's (1995) site of Dolina, a mixed Croat-Muslim village that included one "stray" Serb married to a local woman. There (as elsewhere) understandings of difference were *shared*. Everyone largely agreed on what distinguished Muslims from Catholics, just as they agreed on what makes Dolina—as a whole—different from other villages in the same region and what made people in the countryside different from those who lived in cities (Bringa 1995, 66). Even in the ambit of "ethnic" categories, Dolina villagers distinguished those who lived in their community from those who did not. They expressed this distinction by referring to their Catholic neighbors as "Catholic," but to Catholics in Croatia as "Croats" (Bringa 2002, 87).

Residents of Dolina also agreed on the basis for ethnoreligous difference. What makes a person Catholic and not Muslim are precisely those things that Catholics do differently than Muslims. When a Catholic woman served coffee to a mixed group of visitors that included Bringa, for example, the hostess gave each person her own spoon. The Muslim guests insisted they could share one spoon. But the hostess replied, "Among us" (*kod nas*), the custom is to serve a spoon to each guest (Bringa 2002, 83). Bringa does not interpret the hostess's gesture as an indication of prejudice or social distance—to the contrary. As Bringa (2002, 83) explains: "Paradoxically, then, it is the acknowledgement of the fluidity of collective identities which makes it necessary to invoke an 'ethnic boundary' through frequent statements of 'what customs are and are not.'" Cultural difference requires constant making and remaking on the part of Dolina villagers, lest those differences dissolve completely.

Cultural differences did not prevent Catholics and Muslims from forming long-standing and close friendships. Neighbors acknowledged and participated in each other's holidays and paid visits to one another during important life cycle events, such as the return of a son from military duty or the birth of a child (Bringa 1995, 55).[4] People also worked side by side in the field or at the factory; they served together in the reserves; they helped each other build their homes. They did these things not because difference did not matter, but because through shared activities, people could jointly express social ties and distinctions that constituted a shared sense of community.

In addition to marking difference, Bosnians also, at times, choose to play down difference, as the various responses to census categories indicates. Another domain where Bosnians sometimes chose to play down national categories was in the naming of their children. As Bringa (1995, 19) writes, "In Bosnia your name tells people who you are," yet some names are more "telling" than others. Parents could choose to play down their ethnic category by giving their children "neutral-sounding" names. In the 1950s, for example, many parents chose "folk" names, such as Zlata/Zlatko. These names did not denote the parent's ethnoreligious category, but instead indicated that the parents came from two different ethnoreligious groups (Bringa 1995, 19).

Some last names, however, are already ambiguous. Owing to the region's history of conquest, conversion, invasion, and movement of peoples, many last names are shared by all groups. For example, the takeover of the region by Austria-Hungary placed families on two sides of an international border. Despite members of the same family converting to different religions, some surnames remained intact, such as "Osmanić" or "Abdulić" (Bergholz 2016, 27). One man from Prijedor explained the ambiguity of names and nationality while testifying at the trial of Duško Tadić. The prosecutor asked the man if it was possible to tell a person's nationality by his or her name, to which the witness replied: "Yes, one could know that according to their names and first names, much less according to the last names. The Muslim names were very characteristic and different than the first names of Serbs and Croats. But when one came to last names, there were many cases that the same last name was to be found among the Serbs, the Croats and the Muslims" [Tad 1213–14]. Some distinctions in names might also be quite nuanced. The same witness quoted above went on to explain that differences in nicknames, which are common in Bosnia, are sometimes indistinguishable even to him. He had a Serb friend named Blažo, whom he called "Blaž" for short. His friend finally corrected him, saying that Blaž is a Croat nickname, whereas Blažo is for Serbs [Tad 1214].

Additionally, "Muslim" names may be well-known because an individual or family is well-known in certain quarters and not because the name itself is Muslim. For example, the name "Filipović," which contains a Christian patronym, is associated with a well-known Bosnian Muslim scholar (Bringa 1995, 19). This ambiguity in names underscores the importance of other markers, such as character, social class, reputation, and education level.

Ambiguity is also the norm in the racialized contexts of the United States and Rwanda, despite the state's attempt in both contexts to slot everyone into an unchanging racial category. The various ways people express (or ignore) difference confounds the uniform meanings that states seek to establish and enforce through various institutions. In contradistinction to Bosnia, neither names nor religion signify whether a person is Hutu or Tutsi in Rwanda or black or white in the United States. And ironically, physical traits such as skin color or height—the very traits that should constitute the biological basis for racial categorization—are also unreliable markers of "race."

In the United States, physical markers of "white" and "black" are often unreliable because of the long history of slave owners raping enslaved women and the equally long history of consensual relations between so-called blacks and whites. This produced generations of people who "looked" white, but were black according to the law (Davis 2001). Some black people even chose to live as white or moved back and forth across the color line when it served a certain purpose. Civil rights leader, educator, and race theorist Mary Church Terrell, for example, gave a speech at the International Congress of Women in Berlin in 1904. Many of the German conference goers assumed she was white; on discovering she spoke German, several began asking her about *die Negerin*, not knowing that the so-called "Negress" they were expecting was Terrell herself. As Brittney Cooper (2017, 78) explains, "Terrell's choice not to identify herself as Black effectively, if not intentionally, rendered her a white woman." It also rendered Terrell an instant confidante of the German attendees.

In another well-known case of intentional passing, Walter White, long-time president of the National Association for the Advancement of Color People (NAACP), used his seeming appearance as a white man to visit communities right after a lynching in order to investigate what happened. Because most local whites assumed he, too, was white, they did not hesitate to share details of the lynching with him.

Yet another example of strategic passing comes from the Eastern Shore. While covering the Matthew Williams lynching that occurred in Salisbury, Maryland on December 4, 1931, an *Afro* reporter interviewed a black man whom the reporter described as "fair of skin and may be colored or white *as he pleases*" (emphasis added) ("Eye Witness" 1931). The phrase "as he pleases" suggests that the man could pass as white whenever he chose to or could be easily "mistaken" as white by other whites. And indeed, that was just what happened. As the man explained to the reporter, "A white man mistook me for one of them . . ." while he was reading a newspaper bulletin posted by a local (white) newspaper about Matthew Williams's state ("Eye Witness" 1931).

Because skin color is an unreliable indicator of a person's race, behaviors became the ultimate signifier of "whiteness" or "blackness." As James F. Davis (2001, 56) writes: "Behaving like blacks or willingly associated with them were often treated as more important than any proof of actual black ancestry." There is no better example of this than the Irish. When poor immigrants escaped the old country for the new, they were "in danger" of becoming "black" because they took the most menial, low paying jobs and lived in the poorest neighborhoods; in a word, they acted like "slaves." Only by working hard at becoming "white"—such as joining in violence against blacks—did the Irish manage to become "white" (Roediger 2007; Walker 1997).

Even Southern whites sometimes acknowledged that behavior trumped biology when it came to racial classification. Though most subscribed to the race science beliefs about the biological basis of white superiority, some still worried that white children who worked in textile mills alongside black children and adults might lose some of their "whiteness" (Ritterhouse 2006, 65). Needless to say if proximity to black people made a white person less white, then racial classifications and white status, in particular, were always in danger of coming undone.

The inherent ambiguity of what constituted people as "white" as opposed to "black" was "mystifying" to both black and white children (Ritterhouse 2006, 118). Novelist Richard Wright, author of *Black Boy*, himself had relatives who looked white. So unremarkable was this state of affairs that when Wright heard the news of a white man having badly beaten a black boy, he automatically assumed the white man must be the boy's father (Ritterhouse 2006, 119). When his mother told him the white man was not the boy's father, he became confused and began to ruminate about what it meant to be "white." He sought clarity from his mother about the whiteness of his grandmother, for example. "Did Granny become colored when she married Grandpa?" he asked. But his mother refused to indulge his childhood logic (Ritterhouse 2006, 120).

Similar forms of confusion arose in Rwanda, both before and during the genocide. Here, too, ambiguity abounds. As in the United States, physical traits are unreliable indicators, contrary to Belgian beliefs that Tutsi were distinguishable by their so-called "Caucasoid" physiognomy. Not all Tutsi are tall and not all Hutu are short. Cultural stereotypes are also often misleading because many Tutsi are poor, while many Hutu are rich. Indeed, one of the most prominent families in Ngali was that of Jude, the man who became the genocide leader. His family owned many cows, a signifier of wealth and social status. Other indicators of a person's ethnicity, such as region, are equally unreliable but these markers suggest that just as in the United States where behavior was as important as biology, in Rwanda, region could also serve as a proxy for identifying others. As Des Forges (1999, 353) writes, "Hutu from the northern part of Rwanda sometimes used to say there are no Hutu in Butare, meaning that the Hutu population there was so fully integrated with the Tutsi that it had lost any distinctively Hutu characteristics." The personal experiences of Rwandans from the center-south who self-identified as Hutu also attest to how often their region of origin led others to assume they were Tutsi (Fujii 2009; Kabagema 2001; Karemano 2003; Umutesi 2000).

Even the system of identity cards that the Belgians established did not succeed at removing all ambiguity because people could subvert the system by obtaining a new card. One woman from Ngali told me her father had done just that. In the transition to independence, when she was still a young girl, he purchased new identity cards for the family. The new cards instantly transformed her family from "Tutsi" to "Hutu" (Fujii 2009, 115–16).

As this chapter argues, the starting point for understanding so-called racial or ethnic violence should not be the groupist assumption that races or ethnic groups are naturally occurring entities and that difference inevitably eventuates in conflict and war, for the historical record says otherwise. While states work hard at creating uniform categories to administer populations, people's own practices and understandings do not always align with the state's grid. People do not always see themselves in the grid of official categories; and even when they do, one type of classification does not determine with whom people will be friendly or distrustful. As with all social relations, it depends. This was equally true in the more racialized contexts of colonial Rwanda and the post-Reconstruction United States where state institutions decidedly shifted power and privilege toward one racial category ("white" in the US context, "Tutsi" in the Rwandan) than in the former Yugoslavia. In sum, when it comes to racial or ethnic categories, fixity is a fiction and ambiguity is the norm. No one knows this better than nationalists seeking to reorder society by redrawing the ethnic and color line through violence and force.

REHEARSAL

**The Serbs had always been a people on the move
and some moves were better than others.**

—Tim Judah, *The Serbs*

**It is only by exaggerating the difference between within and without,
about and below, male and female, with and against,
that a semblance of order is created.**

—Mary Douglas, *Purity and Danger*

Staging order, as in ritual, would make order happen.

—Diana Taylor, *Disappearing Acts*

While histories of ambiguous, varying, and changing lines of difference do not tell us what leads actors to put violence on display, more proximate processes can. What preceded the main attractions and sideshows in each locale was a period of rehearsal, during which actors began to challenge and in some cases, overturn the existing political order, displacing those in power. Scholars often assume that radical political change is a function of brute force from above which leads to compliance from below. This assumed convergence, however, overlooks important parts of the process that are not reducible to top-down capabilities or bottom-up acquiescence. Key to establishing a new political order, with its distinct rules, organs, and personalities, is not just the capacity to enforce new precepts and structures or to install new individuals in positions of power, but rather, the co-optation of bodies that will enact the new order and bring it to life. Carrying out road blocks, night patrols, manhunts, and other collective activities give the new order visible, three-dimensional form. In some cases, enactment helps to insert the new order into the fabric of day-to-day life; in others, it leaves its mark through dramatic breaks from the ordinary. Whichever the pathway, the process of enactment transforms how people see and experience power, hierarchy, and belonging.

I identify three components to the process of enacting a new political order. They are neither sequential nor determinant of one another. Depending on the context, they may unfold in different ways and in different order, with more emphasis on some than others. Much like Kirk Fuoss's (1999, 10) theory of lynching performance cycles, the process of enactment is "less a timeline with a fixed beginning, middle, and ending than . . . a wheel that keeps turning over." The following analysis focuses attention on what people do, or more specifically, what they are *seen* to do. Every new political order prescribes and proscribes ways of acting in order to distinguish itself from what came before, for without such distinctions, what is to mark the end of the old and the start of the new? Enactment helps to render this new formation visible and concrete.

The first component of the enactment process is the destruction or abandonment of normal ways of relating to and acting toward neighbors, friends, co-workers, and acquaintances. These "old" habits might include greeting co-workers, gossiping with neighbors, and frequenting certain restaurants or bars. Such habits mark the boundaries between belonging and exclusion and create and sustain various types of social ties. Breaking these habits is particularly significant in communities that put a premium on regular, face-to-face interactions. In such communities, any rupture in the norms of sociality is immediately noticeable.

The second component of the process is the adoption of new habits to take the place of the old. By new habits, I mean acting in novel, and even previously unthinkable, ways toward neighbors and friends. A new habit might be as small as avoiding eye contact or no longer engaging in small talk with certain co-workers. It might also involve more shocking transgressions of existing norms, such as robbing a neighbor's home or joining in violent abuse of former acquaintances. It matters little whether people adopt these new habits out of fear or insecurity, or whether they support the larger project of forcible takeover. What matters is that they enact these new habits and *are seen doing so by others* not just one time, but over and over again such that the actions become the norm.

The third component is inhabiting new roles. Political change and upheaval provides ample opportunity for people from all social backgrounds to become someone "new." Not everyone will take this opportunity but those who do may be able to raise their own status or profile in the community in an instant. Nobodies can become somebodies. Experiencing a new perch of power, authority, or belonging—however temporary that perch might be—can be enticing and thrilling in and of itself, a reason to continue playing such roles as long as possible. Indeed, in all three sites, specific actors did indeed succeed at becoming "new" men.[1]

Focusing on how people act out the new order helps to explain how embodied actions, large and small, are vital to bringing about and constituting the new order. This move also moves the analytic lens away from outcomes toward processes. In all three sites, the enactment processes shared similar elements even though their contours and contexts differed. While enactment does not guarantee a particular outcome or ensure the durability or legitimacy of a particular order, it does show everyone what the new order looks like.

Nationalists on the March in Bosnia

War in the former Yugoslavia allowed actors at all levels of society to become someone new, from former Communist apparatchik Slobodan Milošević to small town dentist Milan Babić in Knin (Croatia) to a pair of unemployed men in Selo. By 1987, Milošević was busy rebranding himself a nationalist, shedding former friends and mentors. The reason was strategic. As a nationalist, Milošević could become supreme Serb leader. He would no longer be subordinate to Serbian president Ivan Stambolić. He would no longer have to vie for support with the reform-minded Federal prime minister Ante Marković, who by 1990, was the most popular politician across all Yugoslav republics, including Serbia (Gagnon 2004, 91). Milošević was busy putting his nationalist brand of politicking on display. He decried the state of Serbdom in neighboring Kosovo and organized mass demonstrations in Serbia and Kosovo (Glenny 1996, 34). The visibility he gained through these showboat tactics pushed Milošević to continue them. Stambolić's old-style politics could not compete. He quickly fell victim to Milošević's maneuverings.

War started first in Slovenia, but lasted only briefly. The Yugoslav National Army (JNA), under Milošević's control, withdrew after ten days of "fighting." The withdrawal was yet another calculated move by Milošević who was counting on Slovenia's departure from the Yugoslav federation to push Croatian president Franjo Tuđman to follow suit. Milošević vowed that Croatian independence would mean war since he would never allow Croatia to secede with large Serb communities within its territory. Croatia did indeed declare its independence as Milošević expected, but what he did not expect was the reluctance of JNA soldiers to fight against fellow Yugoslavs. The process of enacting Milošević's new nationalist vision was off to a rocky start. During the brief war in Slovenia, levels of desertion and draft dodging remained extremely high (Gagnon 2004; Milicevic 2004; Sikavica 1997, 141–42). Among the soldiers the Slovene army captured, for example, were thousands who had "either deserted or given themselves up without a struggle" (Silber and Little 1997, 166). The situation changed little during the longer and more brutal war in Croatia.[2]

War fighting became part of Milošević's strategy to turn the JNA into the official army of his Greater Serbia project. He was learning quickly how to stage-manage his nationalist project. Milošević used an array of measures to transform the organization. Beginning in 1991, he implemented forced recruitment of "volunteers." In the officer corps, he carried out a series of purges, sacking those officers who remained committed to the idea of a multirepublic Yugoslavia, while sparing those loyal to him (Sikavica 1997, 148). He also awarded officers who "fought" in places like Vukovar with promotions and a hero's welcome when they returned to Serbia, even though the "fighting" consisted of large-scale attacks on civilians and destruction of their homes (Sikavica 1997, 144).

The war in Croatia provided a blueprint for many of the tactics Milošević would use in Bosnia. (Not to be outdone, Tuđman also used similar methods in his cleansing of Serbs from the Krajina in 1995 and during a period of the Bosnia war when Croatia was fighting against the Bosnian government instead of alongside it.) The Croatian town of Knin, which local Serbs took over with Milošević's blessing and steady supply of arms, provided a model in miniature. Former dentist and self-styled nationalist, Milan Babić, became the new "big man." For Babić, the war was a boon. He suddenly enjoyed a level of martial power and authority that his previous life did not provide. He used intimidation and terror to recruit "volunteers" for the Croatian Serb army, which would defend the newly declared (Serb) state within a state.

Not everyone in Knin was ready to jump aboard the Greater Serbia ship, however. Many residents, Serb and non-Serb alike, did not approve of Babić's methods of coercion and threats. Journalist Misha Glenny (1996, 20) talked to one couple who "described how the followers of Babić and [his chief henchman] Martić would knock on the door of recalcitrant Serb males at all hours to demand why they had failed to volunteer for duty on the *straža* [patrols]. They painted a convincing picture of the general fear which Babić had created to guarantee his order." That Babić had to resort to terror tactics to elicit "volunteers" underscores the importance of enactment in establishing a new political order with new rules of belonging, advancement, and survival. People did not have to believe in the idea of a Greater Serbia or in Babić; but they did need to *be seen* going out on patrol if they wanted to avoid harassment or worse.

This pattern of intimidation of both Serbs and non-Serbs would achieve new levels of brutality in Bosnia. Even before the last of the JNA troops pulled out of Croatia, plans for carving up Bosnia were well under way (Silber and Little 1997, 185). In March 1991, Milošević and Tuđman were relaxing at Tito's former hunting lodge in Karađorđevo, figuring out how to "ditch" both the idea of Yugoslavia and its institutions (Maass 1996, 27). They met in secret but quickly made their agreement public (Gagnon 2004, 103). The two planned on getting rid of Ante Marković, the Federal prime minister, who continued to work toward maintaining a multiethnic Yugoslavia (Silber and Little 1997, 212, 131–32). They also agreed on which parts of the territory each would control (Malcolm 1996,

231). In Bosnia, the two would operate less like foes and more like partners with closely aligned interests and mutually reinforcing goals.

The reordering of "who was who" in Bosnia came through territorial claims backed by force. Dismemberment of the territory began in the spring and summer of 1991, when Bosnian Serb nationalists had begun proclaiming "Serb Autonomous regions" (SAOs) (Gagnon 2004, 104–5; Silber and Little 1997, 214). It was similar to the strategy Krajina Serbs had used earlier in Croatia. Bosnian Serb nationalists would declare certain areas a distinct and separate political entity, then move to consolidate control and authority in those spaces. Once they declared the SAO, the SDS, the Serb nationalist party in Bosnia, under Karadžić's leadership, began creating the administrative organs that would operate the newly declared Serb state-within-a-state (Malcolm 1996, 224).

After declaring the Bosnian Krajina its own Autonomous Region (ARK), SDS authorities created various crisis staffs (*Krizni stab*, sing.) to carry out the new policies set by Karadžić. Regional crisis staffs exercised authority over municipality crisis staffs. In July 1992, Karadžić ordered all crisis staffs to become war presidencies (or war commissions). As Dorothea Hanson (2009) describes, "By ensuring this crucial coordination at the municipal and regional level, the Crisis Staffs were the mechanism by which the Bosnian Serb leadership seized and maintained control of territory in the initial months of the war."[3]

To Serbianize a territory and people, the new authorities had to reconfigure social and physical spaces from the ground up. First, they had to redefine what it meant to be Serb. Prior understandings put a premium on maintaining good relations with all neighbors, regardless of their putative identity. Karadžić and Milošević, however, were intent on creating an entirely new basis for Serb identification.

The first step in the enactment process involved removing all non-Serb workers from their jobs and replacing them with Serbs (Glenny 1996, 77). The new authorities also used violence to terrorize local Serbs into submission and non-Serbs into mass flight. This process of expelling or mass murdering non-Serb residents followed a similar path across the Krajina. As the human rights organization Helsinki Watch (1992, 63) reported in 1992: "The 'cleansing' of such areas usually involves the execution, detention, confinement to ghetto areas, and the forcible displacement and/or deportation of non-Serbs. . . . Hundreds of thousands of civilians have been the victims of "ethnic cleansing" practices."

In some locales, the new authorities used a two-pronged approach, with paramilitaries entering a particular town first, to kill and rob residents. A few days later, the JNA would arrive to help the paramilitaries consolidate power. The violence not only caused non-Serbs to flee, it also forced local Serbs to abandon any old habits of relating to their Muslim and Croat neighbors as friends and neighbors. No longer could local Serbs acknowledge their non-Serb neighbors or greet them as they had before. This rupture in how neighbors acted toward one another constituted a crucial step in the reordering process.

Takeover in the Bosnian Krajina

Throughout the Krajina, takeover followed a similar path.[4] One of the first acts that marked the transition to the new Bosnian Serb order was the summary firings of all non-Serbs. Dismissals took place in all public sectors: police, army, courts, schools, media, and hospitals. The only people who avoided losing their jobs were those with close ties to Serbs through marriage or family [Brdj 1461–66].[5] In addition to summary firing of all non-Serbs, authorities sometimes forced elite-level employees to do menial forms of work so that everyone could see them being humiliated. As Muharem Krzić explained in testimony at the ICTY: "So you could be a director of the greatest company in Banja Luka, and you would end up cleaning the streets" [Brdj 1461]. To keep their jobs, Krzić explained, people had to change their names and be "rechristened" [Brdj 1462].

Serbs who did not tow the nationalist line were treated as if they were no longer Serb. For example, according to Krzić, Serb journalists who were unwilling to write in the new nationalist "fashion" were also dismissed from their jobs, along with their non-Serb colleagues. Some Serbs saw what was happening and chose to leave before being fired. Some also offered succor to their non-Serb friends by helping to hide or feed them [Brdj 1464–65].

In the town of Ključ, sixty-four kilometers south of Prijedor, takeover followed the same pattern. As elsewhere, the process began with the firing of all non-Serbs from their jobs. The dismissals were abrupt and came as a shock to those who suddenly lost their jobs. As one factory worker explained: "That day I was at work. We had a break at ten and we went to our restaurant. We came back at noon. We heard them telling us 'go home.' Before, in big companies, there were loudspeakers everywhere for announcements. I didn't know what was happening." [Comp].[6] Another interviewee described the experience in similar terms: "You came to work one day, they told Muslims and Croats there were no jobs for them" [Coll]. Those working in small, private businesses were also told not to come to work anymore [Sue]. Another resident recalled, "The first thing they did was kick out Muslims and Croats from the police. They also fired people from companies. It was the policy. That was when we realized that something…" [Toll]. The wholesale removal of all non-Serbs from their jobs made it impossible for everyone, including Serbs, to continue as before. No longer would Serb and non-Serb co-workers take coffee breaks together. No longer would they share a laugh or cigarette. No longer would they exchange gossip or news. The summary firings ended all comingling and daily interactions at work.

In addition to making it impossible for co-workers to interact as before, authorities also required people to act in radically new ways in and outside of work. The factory worker quoted above said she experienced sudden changes in her co-workers, whom she had known for years. These were co-workers with whom she never had any problems. Even children started to behave differently toward Muslim adults and children, no doubt following their parents' lead [Comp; Bra].[7]

New ways of acting toward former friends and co-workers also involved instituting new norms of segregation in spaces previously open to everyone. The "unmixing" of shops, restaurants, and bars led to new forms of abuse. When a Muslim woman tried to buy flour in town (a rare commodity after the war started), the shop owner refused, saying "No Muslim can buy here." This, in turn, led to rent-seeking on the part of Serbs willing to buy flour for their Muslim or Croat neighbors at considerable markup. As one woman explained, "So Muslims with money gave two to three times the amount to Serbs to buy something they needed" [Comp]. This new form of "exchange" was one of many new habits that some local Serbs were beginning to adopt.

Unmixing also involved barring Muslims from places they once frequented.[8] This, too, abruptly changed existing habits, enabling local Serbs to act in ways that would have been largely unthinkable before the war. As this same woman explained: "One Muslim man went to a restaurant and went in. They took him outside because that that time, Muslims didn't go out late and didn't go to bars and restaurants. They kept a low profile. It was really tense. They tried to avoid problems. This man—he was a little drunk and wasn't scared—and they killed him" [Comp]. It may have been this man's lack of fear that led others to kill him, for failing to show proper deference to the new rules of the newly installed political authorities constituted an act of defiance.

Other opportunities arose to try out new habits as authorities tightened control over the non-Serb population. This included forcible detention of non-Serb men in Ključ. On May 28, 1992, the new authorities issued orders over the radio that all Muslims were to gather at two nearby collection points. Local Muslims assembled as ordered, then awaited further instructions. After six or seven hours, another announcement came over the radio, saying that women and children could go home but the men had to stay. Authorities detained the men for one or two nights; during that time, they encouraged local residents to harass the prisoners. The detention was an opportunity for local Serbs to be seen abusing people with whom they had recently been sharing coffee and a cigarette. According to one interviewee, even women came to "beat them up" [Comp]. Such displays demonstrated people's willingness to go along with the new nationalist order and in doing so, make it come to life.

Nobodies Becoming Somebodies in Selo

Takeover followed the same pattern in the rural community of Selo, just outside Ključ.[9] The shift in how people related to one another began around the period of the referendum on Bosnian independence. The vote took place on February 29–March 1, 1992. Karadžić had instructed Serbs all over Bosnia not to vote. Even in Selo, local nationalists tried to enforce the boycott through intimidation. One local Serb woman received threatening phone calls. "They told me if I vote for this referendum, they were going to burn my house down" [Bito]. Summary firings began shortly after the referendum. In mid-March 1992 authorities fired all non-Serbs from the police force. The removal of non-Serbs from other jobs began on May 20, 1992.[10] As in Ključ, these firings quickly put an end to prior forms of daily interaction among co-workers.

During this same period, the new authorities started putting up roadblocks (*blokade*). Those tasked with manning them were locals. Their job was to check the papers of all passers-by, who were also their neighbors and former co-workers. This activity, like the detention of men in Ključ, seemed to be less about containing threats and more about enacting the new order. According to one local man, "There was no need to do this [check papers], because they had known each other for about twenty years or so" [Brdj 9051–52].

In Selo, just as with small town dentist Milan Babić in Knin (Croatia), the process of enactment also featured a select few becoming new men. For two lifelong residents of Selo, "Milan" and "Dino"—one Serb, one Muslim—the war was a chance to grab their moment in the spotlight. Before the war, the two had very low standing in the community. Neither had jobs. Both lived off family, one off his mother's earnings and the other, his wife's. By all reports, the two spent most of their days drinking together. When the takeover occurred, they enlisted in the newly established Bosnian Serb army. Joining conferred instant authority on the men. The two became armed and with guns in hand, they instantly reconfigured the terms of their prewar relationships. No longer could people ignore them as they had before the war.

The men took quick advantage of their new found power. Interviewees said nights were the worst. The lack of electricity and a strict curfew made the whole village vulnerable to their nocturnal "visits." Since the men were local, they knew who owned what. Drinking bolstered their bravado. One resident said they would come between 11:00 p.m. and midnight and take gasoline, alcohol, or money [Bouc]. But stealing was not their only activity. The two also raped women. One interviewee said the two had raped his cousin, who was old enough to be their mother [Hum #2/3]. Another said the two had also raped a pair of sisters [Aus].

The two men also used their newfound power to even personal scores. One woman described a night when Milan came to her house with a local Muslim man named Avdo in tow.

> Milan was looking for Avdo's brother who already left through the mountains, and was outside Bosnia. He used Avdo to go to houses to look for [Avdo's] brother and terrorize people. One day he came to our house. He told us to sit and sing. All the time he was acting like he was going to kill us. He was asking for cigarettes. He stayed like this for two hours.

> *What did he ask you to sing?*

> Milan wanted to know where Avdo's brother was and Avdo had a coffee shop and he wanted to know if there was alcohol.

> *Did I understand that right, that he asked you to sing?*

> I asked him what are we going to sing; if it's not the right song, he could kill us. He asked for a cigarette. We had cigarettes. But he was just asking Avdo, just him. My grandmother was in another room and was already blind. . . . She didn't understand what was going on. Something happened. On the table was hand cream and then Milan was asking Avdo to put cream on his [Milan's] eyes because they were red. God knows why—alcohol, drugs, whatever he was taking. Avdo's hands were shaking. He took too much cream and put it on his eyes. It was funny; maybe that saved us. Milan couldn't see anything and Avdo just ran away and left me with Milan. But I knew Milan very well because his sister-in-law was a school friend. Then he said to me—I was so scared, my hands were shaking—and he said, "Don't be scared. I'm just interested in Avdo's brother. I'm not going to do anything to you." And then he left. [interview]

Such encounters were terrifying, even when no one was hurt. They also forced residents to act in entirely new ways toward Milan and Dino. They had to acquiesce to their night time raids because they had no way to resist them.

The two men did not restrict their marauding to Muslim households. One of Milan's Serb neighbors said he used to shoot at her flat from his own house next door [Bito]. Milan also spread rumors that she was actually a Croat, a claim that made the woman a target for expulsion, killing, or both. It was the men's marauding of Serb households that prompted their superiors to send them to the frontline in Bihać. Before their removal from Selo, the two had indeed made a name for themselves. Virtually every person whom I talked to mentioned Milan and

Dino. When I asked who the two men were before the war, one interviewee said of Dino: "No one noticed him before. He didn't work. Can't remember any time when he had a job" [Aus]. Milan seems to have had a similar reputation. Needless to say, the enactment process in Selo radically changed how people talked about and saw the two men; it also radically changed how they interacted with them. Joining the new Bosnian Serb army turned these former nobodies into terrifying somebodies.

Takeover in Bosnia followed a similar pattern at every level, from national maneuverings to the Serbianization of small, mixed villages. The process was not simply about removing non-Serbs through mass detention, firing, or expulsion. It was also about transforming how people—including and especially Serbs—acted toward one another. People had to be seen acting in particular ways and *not* acting in other ways. They had to be seen abandoning prior forms of neighborliness, friendship, and collegiality and replacing those old habits with new ways of relating to former neighbors and friends—checking their papers at roadblocks, beating captive men, shunning co-workers, and harassing and threatening neighbors. The war also provided opportunities for a few to "rise" above their prewar selves and inhabit entirely new identities, as Milan and Dino tried to do.

Extremists on the Rise in Rwanda

In Rwanda, the enactment process took a different form because of the political context, which, in many ways, was the reverse of that in Bosnia. Rather than trying to upend the status quo, the extremists in power were trying to maintain it. They sought to prevent any political reforms that would unseat them or force them to share power. Their plan was simple—to forestall the transition to multiparty rule enshrined in the Peace Agreement that President Habyarimana had signed in Arusha (Tanzania) in August 1993. To do so, they sought to eliminate all political enemies, Hutu and Tutsi alike.

Habyarimana had been in power since 1973, when he and fellow army officers overthrew Rwanda's first president, Grégoire Kayibanda. Like the previous regime, Habyarimana and his inner circle enjoyed unchecked power. For a time, they also enjoyed widespread popularity because Habyarimana restored order and put an end to the violence that his predecessor, Kayibanda, was using to prop up his failing regime. Habyarimana's popularity lasted until the late 1980s when multiple crises presented multiple threats: the global price for coffee, the country's main export, dropped precipitously creating a serious economic crisis and worsening a famine occurring in the south; the fall of the Berlin Wall created a governing crisis when donors began to tie bilateral aid to Rwanda's progress toward democratization; this, in turn, led to a political crisis when opposition parties began forming in 1991; finally, the invasion by the RPF rebel group on October 1, 1990, created a massive security crisis and an ongoing guerrilla-style war, for which the Rwandan government army, known by its French acronym FAR (Force armée rwandaise) was ill-equipped to fight.

Unlike in Bosnia, where the initial international response to the wars of dissolution was largely mute, the RPF invasion on October 1, 1990, prompted multitrack negotiations right away. Formal and informal talks led to numerous ceasefires, most of which were violated, usually by the RPF, which was a much more effective and seasoned fighting force than the FAR. On August 3, 1993, under intense pressure from regional heads of state, Habyarimana finally signed the Arusha Accords, which brought fighting to an end and stipulated the terms for integrating the two armies and transitioning the country to a power-sharing arrangement through multiparty elections. What came next was politics by other means: the UN authorized a peacekeeping force to oversee implementation of the agreement, Habyarimana found numerous ways to drag his feet, and the extremists ratcheted up their bellicose rhetoric, which they had begun even before the accords were signed. Indeed, by summer of 1993, extremists were criticizing Habyarimana for having given away the farm. The peace process, they believed, had turned Habyarimana into yet another political enemy (Des Forges 1999; Jones 2001; Prunier 1995).

Throughout the summer and fall of 1993, political moderates continued to support the peace agreement and the introduction of multiparty politics. An event in neighboring Burundi, however, would profoundly transform the political landscape. On October 21, 1993, only two and a half months after the signing of the Arusha Accords, Tutsi army officers in Burundi assassinated President Melchior Ndadaye, the first democratically elected Hutu president of Burundi.[11] The assassination and resulting flood of Burundian refugees into Rwanda pushed moderates into the extremists' camp and led extremists to unite under a common banner of "Hutu Pawa" ("pawa" being the local version of the English word, "power") (Des Forges 1999; Jones 2001; Prunier 1995).

Following the assassination, radical wings began to emerge in all the main political parties. These radical wings, in turn, united behind a common set of goals and interests, not unlike the meeting between Tuđman and Milošević in which the two men agreed on how to divide Bosnia between them. On October 23, 1993, supporters of the largest opposition party, the MDR, came together with members of the MRND and CDR, the two parties aligned with the president (the latter of which was more of a radical appendage of the MRND than a separate political party). These former rivals held a joint rally in Kigali to deplore the assassination of the Burundian president, a very public and important instance of collective *enactment*. One MDR leader took to the stage, claiming that the RPF had been behind the assassination. At the end of a rousing speech, he shouted to the audience in call and response fashion: "Hutu Power! MRND Power! CDR power! MDR Power! Interahamwe Power! JDR Power! All Hutu are One Power!" (Des Forges 1999, 103). Thus was born the unifying cry that would wed all extremists to a common goal—preventing the RPF from seizing power. In this single moment of political theater, former rivals became friends. Each party's Pawa wing was henceforth united with the Pawa wing of all other parties. Old foes became new friends.

On the evening of April 6, 1994, the next shock occurred. As President Habyarimana was returning from a meeting of regional heads of state in Dar es Salaam, unknown assailants shot down his Falcon jet as it was about to land at the airport in Kigali. Everyone on board died instantly. Within hours of the crash, militia assassinated Prime Minister Agathe Uwilingyiamana, the next in line to lead the country after Habyarimana's death. A new political order was forming at a rapid pace, not only through brute violence but also through a process of enactment. The new regime ordered roadblocks to go up throughout the city to prevent movement and escape. Those manning the roadblocks stopped people to check identity cards. They killed anyone whose card read "Tutsi" as well as those who "looked" Tutsi or claimed they had lost their card (Des Forges 1999).[12] Roadblocks were not simply execution sites, however. They were also spaces for unemployed, powerless youth to become "new" men, in the fashion of Milan and Dino in Selo. The consequences in this case, however, were much deadlier than in Selo, for the young men with machetes were not just controlling movement; they were determining who was who. It was they who decided who "looked" or "acted" like Tutsi—regardless of what the person's identity card said—and it was they who executed people on the spot.

The morning after the plane crash, organized killings started throughout the capital. Soldiers, police, and Presidential Guard (an elite force trained by the French) went door-to-door with lists of targets. The names on the list included journalists, human rights advocates, opposition party members, and anyone who was not firmly in the extremist camp. Needless to say, such organized killing was not the norm before the plane crash, though organized massacres of Tutsi had occurred as early as January 1991 in regions where Habyarimana's party enjoyed the greatest support. The door-to-door killings in the capital, however, were without precedent. Killers not only executed those on the list, but also anyone who happened to be at home, including children, housekeepers, spouses, and relatives. The majority of these victims were, in fact, Hutu, underscoring the political rather than ethnic nature of these killings. As with Serbs in Bosnia who were not willing to support the new Bosnian Serb regime, any Hutu who defied or challenged the extremists were now part of the problem; they were to be eliminated immediately.

Outside the capital, killings began at different times in different regions. The first mass killings began in the regions that were the biggest supporters of the president's party, the MRND (Straus 2006). Outside these MRND strongholds, the process of enactment depended largely on local officials; those who preached calm were able to stave off violence until the genocidal regime bussed in outsiders to "jump start" the killings. By contrast, those communities where local officials encouraged and pressured people to kill tended to see a rapid escalation of violence carried about by people in the local community (Des Forges 1999; Kimonyo 2008; Longman 2011a; Straus 2006).

Out with the Old, In with the New

The resumption of the civil war and onset of killing provided opportunities for many to realize new ambitions. In some cases, there was a changing of the guard through intimidation and force. In other places, the current officials were able to play the role of "big men" in new ways. In yet other instances, leaders used their authority to enact the genocide according to their own "preferences," which did not necessarily jibe with the "master narrative" of the genocide (Kalyvas 2003). The sum of these shifts shows how contingent the process of enactment was across rural communities throughout the country. The process did not guarantee that everyone would react the same way or enact their newfound power for the same ends.

In many provinces, like Gitarama, support for the genocide was uneven among the various *bourgmestres*, officials in charge of an administrative unit called a *commune* (akin to a county in the United States). Some, like Jean-Paul Akayesu, only began going along with the genocide when it became impossible to remain on the fence (Straus 2006). Others needed no prodding. Such was the case with "Joseph," the bourgmestre for the commune where Ngali is located. In the same way that war was a boon for small-town dentist Milan Babić in Knin, the genocide was an opportunity for Joseph to realize new ambitions and goals.

Even before violence began in his community, Joseph was an active supporter of the extremist wing of the president's party [Chau #7/8 22; FL2 #4/4 13]. A former medical assistant, he became bourgmestre after the introduction of multiparty politics in June 1991 [Fl2 #4/4]. His active support of Habyarimana's MRND party likely explains his rise to the post of bourgmestre, one of the most powerful positions in the country's administrative hierarchy (Wagner 1998).

This office came with many privileges, not the least of which was a vehicle, a luxury that only the most elite social class in Rwanda enjoyed.

Following the plane crash, local officials acquired yet more power and authority by supporting the genocide. Joseph wasted no time. The morning after the crash, he ordered everyone to stay home and not to gather in groups of more than two or three people (Fieldnotes, Dec 2011). This single order marked a rupture in existing habits of relating, where the rhythm of rural life often involved gatherings of more than three people, whether for social, work-related, or other reasons (de Lame 1996).

Joseph then proceeded to organize the mass murder of Tutsi in his commune. At night he held meetings with subordinate officials, where he relayed orders. The first order he issued was to burn and loot Tutsi homes; several days later, he gave the order to kill all Tutsi [Vns #1/3]. Joseph then drove around to various parts of his commune to make sure that his orders were being carried out and that the killings were going as planned.

Joseph and subordinates such as Jude, the leader of Ngali *secteur*, also used a ruse. They used old habits to "trick" Tutsi into gathering at a single spot to facilitate their own mass murder. At one of his nighttime meetings, for example, Joseph instructed officials to have all Tutsi gather at the commune office for their "protection." He then went to a nearby military camp which housed Burundian refugees who had fled their country in October 1993, following the assassination of President Ndadaye. Joseph instructed the refugees to kill the Tutsi who had gathered at the commune office. The Burundians agreed. They came in the dark of night, encircled the building, and threw grenades inside, killing everyone inside.

The swift and murderous actions of Joseph, however, took place in a larger context of enactment that did not steer actors in only one direction. While Joseph relished playing the role of big man, other local leaders were using the same newly acquired power to protect certain Tutsi. For example, the Interahamwe leader for the *sous-préfecture* (which comprised five communes, including Joseph's) was using his power to protect Tutsi women and girls. According to an interviewee who worked as a driver for this leader, the man's position as president of the local Interahamwe made him superior to all other local officials. It was he who organized everything; it was he who decided everything, and it was he who gave orders to the bourgmestres. He also had his own car and his own team of Interahamwe. The bourgmestres were afraid of him, which made it easier for him to save or kill whomever he pleased. The interviewee believes this leader's desire to save Tutsi women and girls stemmed from his efforts to save his wife, who was also Tutsi [Lam #6/8].

The data do not provide as clear a picture of embodiment at the commune- or sous-préfecture-level as there is for the Bosnian Krajina and town of Ključ, but a look at the process of enactment in Ngali shows that it followed a similar path as that which occurred in Selo.

Star Turns in Ngali

Just as in Selo, the war and genocide in Rwanda provided ample opportunities for people at all levels of society to become new men.[13] In 1993, there had been elections for the position of *conseiller* (the head official) for Ngali. The man who won the most votes died of illness shortly after the election. The sous-préfet and bourgmestre decided that Paul should be the new conseiller since he had the next highest number of votes. As Paul recalled, "Afterward, the bourgmestre and the sous-préfet gave me the flag and I took the oath before the population" [#1/7].

On April 15, 1994, nine days after the plane crash that killed the president, Paul was usurped. That day, Jude, a *responsable* for one of six cellules in Ngali, proclaimed himself the new conseiller. This was a Pawa coup at the local level. At a central spot along the main road that runs through Ngali, Jude announced that Paul was no longer conseiller, and that the authorities in Gitarama, which, by then, was comprised of the self-proclaimed, interim government which had fled Kigali on April 12 (Prunier 1995, 235–37), had just named him the new conseiller. This act vested all power in Jude.

In his new role as leader of Ngali, Jude quickly began to remake the community. Like the process of takeover that unfolded in Ključ and Selo, the transformation of Ngali began through summary "firings" of the old guard. Jude ousted all current responsables (cellule-level officials) and replaced them with people whom "he could trust." All the newly installed authorities were MDR party stalwarts [Paul #2/7]. Many also came from Jude's large and prominent family, including brothers, uncles, sons, nephews, and other male relatives.[14] Most went along eagerly and were at the forefront of the violence from the very beginning. Interviewees repeatedly identified members of Jude's family as leaders of the road blocks as well as the attack groups called *ibitero* (*igitero*, sing.).[15] Needless to say, this changing of the guard marked a momentous transformation in local power hierarchies. These abrupt changes seemed to be more about individual initiative on the part of Jude rather than institutional overhaul. Regardless, Jude's handpicked lieutenants claimed instant status and authority. Many used that newfound authority to lead the killings. As one interviewee described one particularly violent génocidaire: "No, he never led this cellule but during the killings, he had suspended the responsable and it was he who was leading [it]" [Em3 #1/2]. Existing forms of authority no longer counted once Jude took over.

Part of the process of remaking Ngali also involved requiring local residents to enact the new order just as residents had done in Selo. The first step was enacting new forms of communal activity. One of the first secteurwide activities that Jude organized was night patrols (*amarondo*). These patrols involved small groups of men who roamed the secteur at night presumably to prevent attacks from outsiders. Initially, even Tutsi took part. As one local man explained: "At the beginning, Tutsi also had to be in the night patrol and after a week, we didn't see them any more" [Alp].

The patrols began right after the plane crash that killed the president [Naf #2/2; Sa, #2/2; Alp]. All men over eighteen were required to participate [Tar #2/2].[16] Anyone who refused or caught shirking was forced to pay a fine or suffer a physical beating [Naf #2/2; Sa #2/2]. The night patrols followed a regular schedule. They started at nine o'clock at night and ended around five in the morning, shortly before the sun came up [Leo]. The men were armed with small sticks or clubs that they had to gather themselves [Naf #2/2]. I asked interviewees if it was possible to get out of amarondo duty by paying someone. One man said that was not allowed. There were other risks as well. Failing to show up for amarondo duty drew suspicion and made the person vulnerable to accusations that he was an *icyitso*, or accomplice of the RPF [Cl #2/2; El, 22 Dec 2011; Vi #2/7]. As one interviewee explained: "I didn't go one time and around three o'clock in the morning, they came to my house looking for Tutsi" [Alp]. Another said he was beaten for not showing up for his assigned duty [Vi #2/7].[17]

Officially, the patrols were aimed at ensuring the security of the secteur from attack by outsiders, such as the RPF whose supporters, extremists claimed, included *all* Tutsi. When I asked several interviewees what the amarondo were for, the answers focused on the threat posed by *inyenzi* ("cockroach") or *inzoka* ("snake"). These were derogatory terms that extremists used to refer to Tutsi. As one man explained, patrolling "was for keeping track of people's movements, arresting people, asking to see people's identity cards and if they were Tutsi, it meant killing them straight away" [Em #5/6]. Another replied, "We had to yell out when we saw any *Inkotanyi* soldiers from Uganda" [Jn #1/1]. Yet another man explained: "To assure the security of the nation against the infiltration of *abacengezi*" [Na #2/2]. When I asked who were the *abacengezi*, he replied, "The inyenzi." When I asked another man what they were supposed to do with the sticks and clubs, he replied: "They were for defending ourselves in case we encountered an inzoka" [Naf #2/2].

Like roadblocks in Selo, night patrols were important forms of enactment in their own right, beyond whatever *actual* security they provided. The patrols forced men to take part in bringing about the new genocidal order and, more importantly, to be seen doing their part. These patrols also enabled Jude to perform his newfound power as leader of Ngali by monitoring compliance and punishing shirkers. He could take note of who was absent and why. He could show up at the door of anyone not "seen" on his scheduled patrol at any hour, day or night. He could levy fines. In using these patrols to help constitute the new order, Jude also made his own power highly visible.

In addition to night patrols, Jude ordered road blocks to go up all over the secteur. Road block duty was also mandatory. Each man took his turn according to a set schedule [Cee #2/2]. Those manning the barricades were instructed to check people's identity cards [Tar #2/2]. The task was meaningless insofar as those doing the checking already knew who their neighbors were, as was the case in Selo. It was not meaningless, however, from the standpoint of enactment. As in Bosnia, organizing road blocks led residents to act in new ways toward people they had known all their lives. These roadblocks also forced residents to see who was manning them and to see the new political order literally taking shape before their eyes.

In addition to roadblocks and night patrols, there were other forms of enactment. Jude held meetings during which he and his subordinates extolled people to join the MDR, which had become the dominant political party in the region [Cee #1/2; Fii #3/4].[18] These meetings were part motivational exercise and part opportunity to pressure people to support the takeover of their community. Participating in these meetings and joining the MDR were demonstrations of support for Jude. The meetings were also another platform for Jude to perform his new role as leader of the genocide in Ngali (Alexander 2011).

When orders came to start the violence, Jude knew what to do. He held meetings at his home where he issued orders to his lieutenants. The first orders were to loot and burn Tutsi homes. Torching Tutsi homes forced inhabitants to flee which, in turn, allowed Jude's men to pillage the victims' property. Like the other collective activities he organized, Jude took an active role. He often oversaw the pillaging and controlled the looted goods. Women were allowed (perhaps even encouraged) to loot household items, such as cooking materials, food, and clothing, while the men were tasked with stealing larger items, such as roof tiles, mattresses, furniture, and livestock. Jude gave explicit instructions that all looted goods be transported to his house, where he later divvied everything up [Cee #2/2]. Looting also constituted a significant break from peacetime habits of relating to one's neighbors. Stealing would have been unthinkable before the war and genocide. Thefts did occur but there was shame and stigma attached to the act. With the start of genocidal violence in Ngali, stealing became de rigueur—not only as a way to enrich oneself, but also as a radically new way of relating to one's neighbors.

The theft of cows provided additional opportunities for enacting the new order. After attackers stole a cow, they butchered and ate it. Everyone was expected to partake in eating the stolen meat, even those who did not participate in the attack. As one man explained, "Everyone in the cellule had to eat the [stolen] meat; whether you were present at the attack or not, you had to do your part, including the weakest and poorest." One man refused and his refusal led to accusations that he was an *icyitso* (an accomplice of the RPF). He also suffered beatings and constant threats as a result (Fujii 2009).

The sharing of stolen meat extended enactment outward, to those who would not necessarily be recruited for violence or may have managed to avoid roadblock or night patrol duty. Eating is something anyone can do; it is a form of participation that can be easily secured. The fact that most Rwandans can rarely, if ever, afford to eat meat would have been an added bonus for those who went along. Eating stolen meat is not necessary for any genocide, but in this case, the shared activity was yet another part of the larger process of enactment that leaders like Jude were directing at the local level to create the new political order.

After a week of looting and burning Tutsi homes, the orders came to kill all Tutsi—men, women, and children. As with the other activities, enforcement was strict. The consequences for avoiding participating in an *igitero* (attack group) were almost immediate [Tar #2/2]. As one man explained, "During the war, we were beaten by the Interahamwe [local killers] for having refused to go to the road block to kill Tutsi. We even had to pay a fine" [Ias]. Another said that refusing to join the igitero resulted in forty blows from a cane or stick [Alm].

In theory, the ibitero were tasked with killing all Tutsi. In the beginning, however, Jude issued orders to spare Tutsi women married to Hutu men [Cee #2/2; Lon]. The reason may have been practical since many of the men in the ibitero had Tutsi wives. As one man explained, "Martin wanted to proceed with hunting down Tutsi women married to Hutu men starting with the wife of Emmanuel.... they didn't get along . . . As Emmanuel was part of the ibitero, he said that if his wife were killed, he would go kill Martin's wife and children" [Cee #2/2].[19] These clashes among men in the same *igitero* over who should be killed and who spared shows the limits of Jude's authority and that of the extremists more generally. Many who were active in the killings went to great lengths to protect their Tutsi wives and their wives' families.

In Ngali, the process of enactment resembled that in Selo in Bosnia. Through threats or enticements, people stopped acting as they did before and quickly began adopting new ways of relating to their neighbors, which constituted radical departures from prewar norms of neighborliness and sociality. Many of these changes were quite sudden and unexpected, as they had been in Selo [Rem #2/2; Cla]. Indeed, many people were quite shocked at the sudden change in the way their neighbors, friends, and acquaintances began acting. As one interviewee remarked, "Martin [a member of an attack group] completely changed during this period, even though he was a good guy before" [Cee #2/2]. As in Bosnia, these new ways of acting toward neighbors and friends were clear rebukes of prewar norms and helped to bring to life the new political order, one predicated on assaults on Tutsi property and later, the annihilation of Tutsi as a group.

The resumption of the civil war and the start of the genocide also enabled ambitious local officials like Joseph and Jude to inhabit new roles. By becoming genocide leaders, they claimed new forms of authority and power that went far beyond peacetime standards. In their new roles, both Joseph and Jude organized collective activities that led people to embody the new order. It mattered little whether residents believed in Project Genocide; what mattered was that by following orders, they were giving the new genocidal order three-dimensional form. The process of enactment did not bring monolithic compliance, however. Even among local leaders and members of the attack groups, there were those determined to protect their Tutsi wives, even if that meant killing other génocidaires. In this way, enactment was not a totalizing process.

Rough Justice in the Eastern Shore

While conditions of war in Bosnia and Rwanda provided ample opportunity for men and women to shed old habits, adopt new ones, and in some cases, become someone new, it is also possible for the same process to emerge in peacetime. Absent war, a new political and social order can also arise quite suddenly, in ways similar to Bosnia and Rwanda. In the Eastern Shore of Maryland there was no regime change as in Bosnia or a regime fighting to stay in power as in Rwanda, yet a process of enactment unfolded in the years before the lynching of George Armwood. In two major confrontations, mobs claimed the right to usurp the legal authority of the state and to take matters into their own hands. This process began in early October 1931 when people dropped their normal routines and adopted radically new ways of acting toward others. Here, the process did not turn old foes into new friends, but rather made old friends into new foes.

The Near Lynching of Euel Lee

The weekend of the tenth and eleventh of October 1931 began like most others. The Green Davis family ran a produce stand from their property, located not far from Ocean City, a tourist destination along the Atlantic Ocean. Neighbors recall seeing the family's usual activity in front of the house on Saturday. On weekends, the family sold produce from their front lawn. On Sunday, however, they saw no one. This was unusual, so unusual that by Monday, when the two Davis daughters failed to turn up at school, neighbors went to check on the family. What they found was a horrific sight. All four family members were lying dead in their beds; someone had shot them as they slept ("Eastern Shore Family" 1931; Ifill 2007, 50–51; Moore 2006, 13–14).

News of the killings spread fast, marking the start of the enactment process. Local neighbors talked to police and to one another. Very quickly, attention turned to a sixty-something-year-old black man named Euel Lee, who also went by the alias Orphan Jones, a nickname he received from the white family who raised him (Ifill 2007, 50). White neighbors knew Lee as someone who had done occasional farm work for Davis. They also recalled that Lee had had some kind of argument with Davis over unpaid wages. Whites often claimed disputes over money as the motive for black-on-white crime. Lee would tell a much different story to police, however, after his arrest. Police found Lee at the boarding house where he lived in Ocean City. They also found belongings from the Davis family in Lee's room and $70 that he was carrying on his person ("Family" 1931). During his interrogation, where he suffered extensive beatings at the hands of police, Lee told interrogators that he had given Davis $250 and a gun for safekeeping, but when he asked for both back, Davis claimed he had lost the money at a local bank and threatened to have his daughters tell authorities Lee had attacked them if Lee did not let the matter go. Lee claimed that Davis was trying to cheat him out of his own money (Ifill 2007, 51–52; Moore 2006, 232–33). The contradictory versions of the story mattered little to whites in community, most of whom had no doubt that Lee was the murderer of the Davis family.

The process of enactment continued with Lee's capture. Local police initially took Lee to the nearby jail, but a crowd of angry whites had formed in response to news of the arrest. The formation of a mob is an important form of enactment precisely because mobs do not arise "naturally"; they are made to happen. People must drop what they are doing and jump in their vehicles to congregate at a central point; those who show up do not start out as a cohesive unit, but become so through the process of assembling, waiting, watching, milling, and talking. Whites in Worcester County and beyond did just that. As the *Afro-American* reported, as soon as news of the murder and arrest spread, excited bands of armed men converged on the courthouse. "But for last minute change in plans . . . [Orphan Jones] would have in all probability been a lynched victim Friday morning" ("Sho' Mob Waits" 1931). Police responded in kind. To avoid the mob, State Police continued on to the larger and more secure jail in Snow Hill, Worcester's county seat, but the crowd followed. State Police then decided to take Lee to Baltimore, a five-hour drive away ("Eastern Shore Family" 1931).[20] Police knew that if they did not take Lee off the Shore, the mob would surely wrest him from their custody and lynch him on the spot.

Despite police actions that prevented Lee's lynching, the mere act of coming together with the intent to lynch a black man was important from the standpoint of enactment. Assembling in large numbers and pursing police were assertions of an alternative authority and an effort at realizing an alternative form of justice. Coming together to pursue police was a clear act of repudiation of the existing order where only agents of the state—police and courts—had the authority to take prisoners into custody. In this case, local whites were claiming their right to enact "rough justice," a right that trumped the existing legal rules and procedures (Pfeifer 2004). By joining the crowd, people were enacting this alternative authority, regardless of whether they succeeded in lynching Lee or not.

Local whites continued to enact rough justice in the week following Lee's arrest. On the streets of Berlin, the town closest to the scene of the crime, local mobs were attacking and beating black residents, people who had no connection to Lee, the murdered family, or the crime itself except their status as "blacks" (Ifill 2007, 53). These attacks constituted a moment of rupture from the usual way that whites interacted with blacks. Even under the strictures of Jim Crow, normal modes of interaction, even among the most prejudiced whites, did not include random physical assaults on black people going about their daily business.

What further increased tensions over the next several weeks was the intervention of a lawyer from the International Labor Defense organization named Bernard Ades. To most local whites, Ades came with a trifecta of negative attributes: he was a Jew, a communist, and an outsider. Worse, he wanted to defend Lee, a man whom most believed to be guilty of the most heinous crime in the county's history (Ifill 2007, 85; Moore 2006, 8). To whites across the Shore, Ades's involvement represented everything that was wrong with the legal system. To many, the system was "rigged" precisely because it accorded the same rights to black as white defendants. In doing so, it failed to uphold the primacy of white supremacy.

So strong was sentiment against the legal system that three weeks after Lee's arrest, a local mob attacked Ades and his two companions, both women, in Berlin. (The trio had traveled there to press the question of Ades representing Lee in lieu of Lee's court-appointed attorney.) The group suffered two different attacks that day. The first occurred inside the courthouse lunchroom; the second took place when the group tried to leave the courthouse, at which point a mob beat all three. To keep Ades and his party from being lynched, the local sheriff stepped in and took all three to the county jail to keep them safe. The party finally left town in a sheriff's car "under guard of three deputy sheriffs and a member of the State police force" ("Snow Hill Mob" 1931). All these attacks—those on black residents and those on Ades and his two companions—were important to the process of enactment. It did not matter that the mob did not in fact succeed in lynching Ades and the two women with him. What mattered was the attempt. Similarly, it did not matter that the black residents who were assaulted had no connection to Euel Lee. What mattered was the act of coming together to assault anyone and everyone who represented an obstacle to rough justice for the alleged killer of a local white family.

Tensions increased further in the following months as Ades put his skilled lawyering on display in his defense of Lee. After the assaults in Berlin, he managed to win a change of venue off the Shore completely. Shore whites took extreme umbrage at this maneuver because of the powerfully symbolic line that Eastern Shoremen drew between the Eastern and "Western" Shores. Nevertheless, Lee's first trial took place in Towson in Baltimore County. A jury quickly convicted him on all charges. Ades then appealed the verdict on the grounds that there were no blacks in the jury pool. The Maryland Court of Appeals, the highest court in the state, found in Ades's favor and granted Lee a second trial. A second Towson jury found Lee guilty. Despite the two convictions, Ades managed to keep Lee alive for two years after his arrest and to set legal precedents that were far ahead of their time (Ifill 2007, 52–54). He also managed to keep Lee from being lynched.

These legal victories made Ades a hated man in Worcester County. It also provided the basis for Shore whites to continue dropping old habits and acquiring new ones. An opportunity to try out these new ways of acting would arise only six weeks after Lee's arrest. This time the scene was Salisbury, a town located in neighboring Wicomico County.

The Lynching of Matthew Williams

Matthew Williams was a young black man who worked at a box factory in Salisbury, twenty-five miles from where the Green Davis murder had occurred. On Friday, December 4, 1931, Williams walked into the office of his employer, Daniel J. Elliott. What happened next is contested. In one version, Williams shoots and kills Elliott in a dispute over wages, at which point, Elliot's son, James, happens on the scene, picks up Williams's gun from the floor, and manages to shoot Williams as he tries to escape. In another, it is Elliot's son who has just shot and killed his father, possibly over a dispute about money, when Williams unwittingly walks into the office. In this version, the young black man was simply in the wrong place at the wrong time. As soon as he enters the office, James, the son, shoots Williams as the latter tries to flee, wounding Williams badly.

Howsoever the crime unfolded, word spread quickly that Matthew Williams, a black man, had murdered Elliott, a prominent white business owner. The process of enactment had begun. People dropped what they were doing.

Many headed to the office of the local daily, the *Salisbury Times*. They talked amongst themselves, referring to the bulletin that the newspaper had posted announcing that Matthew Williams had died from gunshot wounds. One out-of-town eyewitness, who was light enough to pass as white, was part of the group reading the bulletin. As people stood there reading the latest notices, one white man remarked to the witness, "Ain't that a damn shame that nigger died so soon. There was going to be some fun here tonight." Almost immediately, the newspaper posted a revised bulletin that said Williams was not dead but was "improving." The eyewitness described what happened next ("Eye Witness" 1931).

> The men stood there for about five minutes. They stood talking in groups; more persons read that bulletin, and the crowd grew ever so thick, Almost like an explosion, some one [*sic*] yelled, "Let's go to the hospital and get this nigger and lynch him."
>
> Almost as though it was a military command, the crowd started toward the hospital. I followed along to see what was going to happen.
>
> The white man who was walking along side of me said: "Its [*sic*] going to be good to see that nigger swing." ("Eye Witness" 1931)

As in the Euel Lee case, this type of "talk" was an important form of enactment. It helped to socialize whites to heed the call to action as several men began shouting "Let's lynch Williams!" "Shore Mob Lynches" 1931). This served as a rallying cry for all those who had begun to assemble.

The mob proceeded to the Negro Ward at the local hospital. The police chief and deputy sheriff were guarding the main entrance so several men entered through a side door. The nursing superintendent on duty that night did not try to dissuade the men but implored them to go about their business "quietly" ("Lynchers in Salisbury" 1931; "'Shore Mob Lynches" 1931). The group quickly seized Williams and threw him out the window to the crowd waiting on the street. As Williams lay on the pavement, someone threw a rope around his neck. The mob then marched their victim three blocks to the large tree in front of the courthouse. Someone hoisted a small boy up so he could pull the rope over the branch. The lynchers then hanged Williams repeatedly, pulling his body up and down. As this same light-skinned eyewitness reported, the body would fall to "within two inches of the ground and suddenly be jerked back." The man added that "This was done three times. The leader each time would say, 'Pull him up, boys,' and then, 'Give him the works, boys'" ("Eye Witness" 1931). The large crowd cheered with each rise and fall of Williams's body ("'Shore Mob Lynches" 1931). The fun and games lasted about twenty minutes ("'Shore Mob Lynches" 1931) with call and response accompanying every move. Every time someone yelled out the names of the mayor and chief of police, the crowd booed in response, but "cheered" the mob leaders as they carried out the violence ("Eye Witness" 1931). This collective naming and shaming of state agents—the mayor and chief of police—was a clear rebuke of the legal system. Mob members were quite literally telling officials that the state's authority had been usurped and mob justice was the new order of the day. Needless to say, this was not the way that upstanding white citizens of Salisbury usually acted toward law enforcement or state agents, more generally.

Next, mob leaders dragged Williams's body "a quarter of a mile through the business section" to an abandoned lot in the Negro part of town. Someone in the group tried to force the station attendant to hand over gasoline. The attendant refused so the mob helped itself to forty gallons. The men first spread newspapers over the body then doused it with the fuel. Someone lit the paper, which instantly produced flames that "leaped into the air." The crowd cheered. Mob leaders kept the flames going by pouring more gasoline ("Eye Witness" 1931; "'Shore Mob Hangs" 1931; Ifill 2007, 42–50). All these antics prolonged the spectacle and kept the mob engaged and active.

Newspaper reports estimated the crowd to have been two thousand or more ("Eye Witness" 1931; "'Shore Mob Hangs" 1931). It included men and woman, young and old, all determined not to miss the event ("Mob Described by Brockman" 1931). A nurse on duty that night recalls vividly that her brother, who was driving her to work that evening, was anxious to get to town because he wanted to see the lynching [7Ho]. Talk was not simply an instrumental act; it was an expressive form of enactment that made people excited and willing to drop old habits and quickly adopt new ones. As people assembled, whether in front of the newspaper offices or the courthouse, they continued to share rumors and details and to maintain an atmosphere of expectant excitement. When a group of men suddenly shouted "Let's lynch Williams!" ("'Shore Mob Lynches" 1931), the violence began in earnest, marking an even bigger break from normal routine and creating opportunities to become new men and woman. Once the murder was under way, people could fully inhabit their new roles as enforcers of justice. The enactment process did not depend on what mob leaders did; nor was it reducible to those few who were inflicting physical violence on the body of Matthew Williams. The process involved all those who gazed and gawked at the violence and cheered every time mob leaders pulled up Williams's body then let it fall, when they doused the body with gasoline and lit it on fire, and finally when they hanged the body on a lamppost at the edge of a black neighborhood. From the standpoint of enactment, all these actions were crucial for realizing the new political order, where the justice of the mob took precedence over that of the state.

In all three settings, political transformations were occurring at a rapid pace. Takeover occurred largely through the deployment of violence and coercion. Equally important, however, was the process of enactment or the ways that people began to bring the new order to life through collective activities, whether organized by specific leaders or arising more spontaneously. The first step generally involved people abandoning old ways of relating to neighbors. Ordinary men and women in Bosnia, for example, suddenly stopped exchanging greetings with longtime neighbors or friends. The process continued with people acquiring new ways of acting toward neighbors. These new ways of acting did not necessarily involve violence, nor did they necessarily serve any larger purpose beyond the act itself. For example, going out on night patrols in Ngali might have brought very little added security to the community, but such actions were crucial to the process of takeover by Jude, the newly proclaimed authority.

The process of enactment continued with actors at all levels of society becoming "new" men and women. In Bosnia, nobodies became somebodies when they acquired guns and uniforms, as in case of Milan and Dino. In Rwanda, local elites achieved new heights of status and power through acts of usurpation, as when Jude declared himself the new conseiller for Ngali. In the Eastern Shore, ordinary white citizens were transformed when they became part of a large collective called a "mob" that began acting in concert to bring about a form of justice that the legal system denied them.

While takeover unfolded differently in each locale, the process of acting out the new order followed a similar pathway across all three sites. Bodily enactment rendered the new order visible. It made it real and concrete to those forced to watch and go along, however imperfect or temporary that new order was. The process of enactment was also an important prelude to the more elaborate displays of violence that would come later. It is to these displays that we now turn.

MAIN ATTRACTION

Mostly our conversations underscored that to be a kamajor was a performance.

—Danny Hoffman, *The War Machines*

It was an uneasy landscape, the early twentieth-century South, a small-town, small-city world of ice companies and beauty parlors, soda fountains and gas stations. It was a world where people who went to church on some days and watched or participated in the torture of their neighbors on others.

—Grace Elizabeth Hale, *Making Whiteness*

How and why do people end up putting violence on display? And what do these displays communicate and signify? While the previous chapter drew attention to the importance of embodied action in bringing to life a new political order, this chapter continues the investigation to ask how and why people of diverse backgrounds end up participating in violent displays. To answer this question, I develop and apply a theory of casting.[1] This theory is less about individual nobodies becoming somebodies and more about the diversity of people who help to constitute a violent display as such, including those who happen on the scene unwittingly or unwillingly. The casting process does not guarantee anyone a particular role; some might try but fail to grab a starring role, for example. What it ensures is that everyone becomes part of the show, whether they want to be or not.

Casting is the process by which actors take on roles and roles take on actors. These roles give the display its form, content, and meaning. They push the action forward and bring the display to "life." The process is dynamic and interactive. As people take on roles, the display begins to emerge. As the display begins to take shape, new roles become available as others fade. At each step of the process, roles make possible new ways of acting. No matter their duration or prominence, the roles combine to make the show what it is—to turn a murder into a lynching, for example, or prison detention into pornographic fun and games.[2]

The main roles involved in displays are leads, supporting roles, bit parts, and spectators. What it means to inhabit any of these roles depends on the display itself. What it means to play spectator at a public lynching in 1930, for example, differs markedly from playing spectator at a state execution in 2017. The former calls for boisterous and vocal engagement while the latter involves somber and silent witnessing. Which roles make up the display also depends on the form the episode takes. Some displays highlight a single star, while others showcase an ensemble cast.

Casting is a constitutive process. Roles do not exist separate from action. Roles and actions coconstitute one another such that one begets the other. The process is emergent. Roles are always in the process of becoming, of being made and remade through action, never arriving at or existing as an endpoint. As such, they can be fleeting or sustained, singular or overlapping, played by one or many. Ordinary citizens might jump in their cars to chase a suspect, for example; that action, in turn, casts them in a collective activity called a manhunt. Being cast in these roles vests these actors with police powers to pursue and capture—powers they would not have outside this role and powers that quickly end when the chase is over.

Roles are not usually scripted ahead of time, but they generally carry implicit prescriptions for how to act. In doing so, they invite participants to do things they would not normally do. Joining a manhunt, for example, might mean driving at high speed and running over anyone who gets in the way, including small children (Jolley 1933b). If the display is part of a repertoire—that is, if actors are already familiar with the form of collective action—participants might already know what to do. Those who assembled in Newnan, Georgia, to burn and torture Sam Hose to death, for example, may have never seen a lynching before, but most were likely familiar with the general form that a mob execution of a black man takes. Roles also force unwitting and unwilling participants to do and see things they would not normally see. When viewers turned on the evening news to see images from the videotaped beheading of American reporter, James Foley (Davis 2014), they, too, became unwitting participants in ISIS's display.

Casting is also an embodied process. People perform roles with their own and others' bodies. Embodiment may involve inhabiting a role to the point of becoming someone new, if only for a moment. Taking on a role involves much more than "pretending" to be an arresting officer during a manhunt; it means experiencing firsthand the kind of authority, status, and power that being a police officer entails. For some, that experience might be novel and thrilling. When the guards at Abu Ghraib, for example, forced detainees to strip naked and enact degrading positions, they may have been experiencing unbridled power and authority for the first time (Fisher 2004). For others, the experience might be powerfully socializing, overcoming individual actors' reluctance or hesitations (Fujii 2017).

Embodied action also enables actors to feel part of something bigger than themselves, as part of a special team, unit, or community, regardless of the extent or type of their own individual involvement. Feeling part of a larger social body might add to the excitement and singularity of the experience. Or, it might force unwilling or reluctant actors to go along, out of fear of going against the group or collective (Berezin 1997; Fujii 2009; Taylor 1997). By going along, these actors, too, help to bring the display to life.

Casting is also a contingent process. Who gets cast in which role depends on the rest of the group. Others must accept that person in that role. No man or woman can be a star, for example, without the collective affirmation of a supporting cast. If the rest of the crew, gang, or unit accepts the person in the role, their actions will help to uphold the person's status in the lead role. If they do not, the casting fails.

Casting is a process of continual inclusion, in which all-comers are brought into the show. By including everyone and anyone, casting helps to ensure that no one stands outside the bounds of the display and that everyone takes part, whether they want to or not. In this way, casting not only enables the most eager or willing to take part; it also pushes and pulls in the unwitting and unwilling.

Spectacle in Princess Anne, Maryland

On the morning of Monday, October 16, 1933, a work crew found Mary Denston, a seventy-one-year-old white woman, alongside the road. She was alone, nearly naked, and in obvious distress. Later that day, she explained to the state's attorney that she had been walking to her daughter's farm when an assailant dragged her into the woods and tried to rape her, tearing off her dress in the process (handwritten notes in Robins 1933). Suspicion turned immediately to George Armwood, a twenty-two-year-old black man whose mother and sister lived nearby ("Officers" 1933; "Rush" 1933).

A manhunt for Armwood quickly ensued. This activity constituted an important first step in the casting process. Local and state police led the chase, while hundreds of local whites jumped into their cars, trucks, tractors, and other "machines" to join in the hunt (Jolley 1933b). The *Baltimore Sun* estimated the size of the "posse" to be around two thousand people ("Negro Admits" 1933). So numerous were the reinforcements that they "jammed" the main road connecting Salisbury to Princess Anne as well as all the side roads and lanes. In addition to those in vehicles, local men armed with guns and rifles made their way to stores, gas stations, and anywhere police had gathered to show their support.

The sheer size of the citizen posse indicates people's determination to be part of the show. By joining in the manhunt, these actors became part of a large supporting cast of "self-deputized" law enforcement. Becoming part of the cast conferred instant status. Ordinary citizens were suddenly vested with police powers to pursue, stop, and arrest—powers they would not have outside the context of a manhunt and powers that would quickly end as soon as the chase was over. Joining the manhunt also placed ordinary men and women above the law. They no longer had to obey traffic laws; they could drive however they saw fit, including careening down the wrong side of the road, barreling through stop signs and traffic lights, and even running over pedestrians who got in the way. As one white woman drove down the wrong side of the road, for example, she hit a seven-year-old black girl as the child was alighting the school bus. After hitting the girl, the woman stopped, then quickly returned to her car and rejoined the chase after leaving "instructions" for the girl to be taken to the hospital (Jolley 1933b).[3]

Police and posse scoured the county for hours. The extended search gave nonstate actors the opportunity to inhabit their new roles as citizen-police. By the time police located Armwood some twenty miles from the spot where the road crew had found Mary Denston, "there were so many machines trailing theirs, authorities said, that the Sheriff and police had to halt to hold them back" ("Negro Admits" 1933).

Authorities arrested Armwood at the home of the brother of John Richardson, a white man with whom Armwood used to live and work. Armwood's mother had "given" him to Richardson, most likely out of desperation for someone to feed and clothe her son.[4] Many whites suspected that it was Richardson who drove Armwood to his brother's house to hide him from the search party ("Negro Admits" 1933; "No Fear" 1933). After arresting Armwood, police beat him with their fists and handguns, according to one eyewitness (Jolley 1933a).

With Armwood in custody, State Police headed first to the jail in Salisbury, which they believed would be more secure than the smaller building in Princess Anne. When they arrived, however, they encountered a large crowd so they continued on to Baltimore ("Maryland Prisoner" 1933; "Negro Admits" 1933; "Rush" 1933), in the same fashion as they had done two years prior after arresting Euel Lee in Worcester county. By removing Armwood from Princess Anne, State Police brought a temporary halt to the casting process by denying local whites access to the person *and body* of Armwood.

What happened during this offstage period was police business as usual. State Police arrived in Baltimore in the early morning hours of Tuesday, October 17, 1933. Later that morning, at 9:30 a.m., detectives began interrogating Armwood, asking about his timeline the morning of Monday, October 16, 1933, and details about the assault. They questioned him a second time later that afternoon, at 4:30 p.m. This time the detectives, which included at least one who had been involved in the interrogation of Euel Lee exactly two year before, focused on Armwood's drinking before the alleged assault. Armwood answered all their questions, though some responses contradicted others.[5] Despite these inconsistencies in his statements, local newspapers reported that Armwood had "confessed" to the crime ("Negro Admits" 1933; "Police" 1933; "Woman's Assailant" 1933).

Sometime after this second interrogation, state's attorney John B. Robins and Judge Duer asked State Police to return Armwood to Somerset County. The two did not bother to inform the governor about this request ("Governor" 1933), an indication, perhaps, of their desire to keep the matter in local hands. Baltimore authorities acceded to the request. At ten fifteen that same night, a procession of cars carrying twenty-five State Police and Somerset County officials left Baltimore with Armwood. "An advanced guard" of fourteen State Police joined the group when it reached Salisbury. The entire party arrived at the jail in downtown Princess Anne around three o'clock in the morning on Wednesday, October 18, 1933 ("Police" 1933; Robins 1933). The jailer placed Armwood in the Negro section on the second floor of the small, two-story building. Along with Armwood were a dozen or so other prisoners, both black and white, spending the night in jail.

The return of Armwood to Princess Anne marked the resumption of the process of putting violence on display. As the sun rose on the morning of Wednesday, October 18, 1933, rumors began circulating about a possible lynching later that evening. Officials for both the black and white schools took the rumors seriously enough that they let students out early. Some black teachers explained to the students what was happening. As one black interviewee who was fourteen at the time recalled, "[The teacher] told us there was going to be a lynching." Other students did not need an explanation. A white man, who was thirteen at the time, said no one needed to tell him why they were being let out early—he knew why [interviews].

Like joining a manhunt, passing on rumors was an important step in the casting process. Participating in such talk began to mark off the moment as special. It also cast people in a "happening" that was starting to take shape. A white man from out of town detailed what he saw and heard that day to the *Afro* newspaper. Frank Spencer was a thirty-nine-year-old, unemployed white man from California who was visiting a friend in Princess Anne. While running errands in the small downtown around noon, he overheard people talking about plans to lynch Armwood that evening. People were talking openly, even in front of local police. Spencer also overheard different individuals make reference to the Matthew Williams lynching, which had occurred in December 1931. He was standing with a group of men, for example, when another walked up and said, "We'll have a bigger lynching here than when Williams was lynched two years ago" (Spencer 1933).

In addition to local, face-to-face talk, local radio stations were also announcing the upcoming lynching on air. As Clarence Mitchell and three other reporters from the *Afro* headed to Princess Anne, they continued hearing updates on the radio (Mitchell 1986, cassette I, side 1:11). All this talk—in person and over the radio—helped to propel the action forward. By participating in listening, commenting, and circulating news and rumors, people began taking on roles; and taking on these roles led them to act in new and novel ways.

By mid-afternoon, talk was turning into more concrete action. People began to gather in front of the jail. A light rain began to fall but still more came. The crowd included men, women, and children of all ages and backgrounds ("Ritchie" 1933, 334, 415). Assembling was another step in the casting process. It situated those present within a larger body of like-minded actors. Gathering in one place, however, does not by itself turn a diverse collective into a single-minded mob. The process of transformation is always contingent.

Some twenty or so State Police maintained a thin line in front of the jail. From their vantage point, the officers could closely track the activity of individuals in the crowd. The men and women who had assembled did more than simply stand quietly. They milled and talked. They watched and waited. A few tried to cast themselves in lead roles by testing the resilience of the line. Their pushing and shoving had the effect of momentarily dislodging the entire crowd. As one officer described the scene:

> One man would break away or step over the line and would have to be pushed back, and then another man would break away and step over the line and have to be pushed back. It was this crowd that forced Officer Bohler and myself back to Captain Johnson's car. . . .
>
> The mob at this time was jammed up close, so close that those in front kind of leaned back so that they were not pushed through. As one would go across the officer would grab him and push him back. [Police Statement, 324][6]

Those who kept trying to push through the line were would-be leaders of the mob. These were individuals who were interested in steering the scene in a particular direction. In addition to these individuals, a few men seemed intent on grabbing a supporting role. One man, for example, drove his truck up to the alley next to the jail, announcing that he had "eight cases of dynamite, if they needed it" [Police Statement, 236].

Among the would-be stars were several relatives of Mary Denston, the white woman whom Armwood allegedly raped. One of the first people police noticed was her brother. The man was dressed in "baggy" clothes that "looked like he had been working in them." He also appeared to be drunk [Police Statement, 429, 435]. To goad people into acting, the man pushed his way to the front and tried to urge the crowd to act by appealing to their moral outrage. Despite his best efforts, the crowd did not respond. As one officer described: "He was standing around hollering, "Come on, you yellow sons of bitches, haven't you got a sister, haven't you got a mother," and he attempted to be a leader, and he said, "'If you follow me I will get into the jail.' At that time no one followed him. He would walk out a little ways, and then we would push him out in line again" [Police Statement, 393]. The crowd did not heed the man's appeals. His attempt at becoming a star failed.

In addition to Denston's brother, her son also came to the jail, having traveled all the way from the Philadelphia mainline where he worked as a patrolman. One Maryland State Police officer who talked with the son recalled him saying, "My mother is alone in the large old home, and I am doing this to protect her" [Police Statement, 436]. Denston's son assumed wrongly that his fellow officers would simply let the crowd through. As the officer who spoke with him observed, "He went up and banged on the [jail] door, some conversation ensued, and in substance he said, 'Well, if you won't let us in, why, we will break in'" [Police Statement, 436]. Several times the officer had to push the son off the front steps of the jail. The son, like Denston's brother, was unable to grab a starring role.

A female relative also showed up at the jail. She was very young, about twenty years old according to Frank Spencer, the white man visiting from San Francisco. "She was the worst of the bunch," he noted. Yet, despite her efforts to mobilize the crowd into action, no one followed her. This lack of support meant that she, too, failed to cast herself in a lead role (Spencer 1933).

Other actors also arrived at the scene. These men were trying to steer the action in a different direction than the would-be stars from Denston's family. Early in the evening, Circuit Court judge Robert F. Duer, a well-known local elite who lived in Princess Anne, stopped by to address the crowd.[7] He stood atop one of the police cars [Police Statement, 348; 446] ("Mob Storms" 1933) and implored the crowd to go home and let the courts do their job. He assured everyone that Armwood would be tried quickly ("Mob Storms" 1933). One man yelled back, "Euel Lee cost our county $20,000 and you people don't want to have to do that" [Police Statement, 431].[8] Another officer recalled the comment in more vivid language, quoting the man as saying, "You are a God damned liar, you told us that in the Euel Lee case" [Police Statement, 446–47].

After giving his first speech, Judge Duer drove "through the mob and turned around and came back and stopped at the north end" where he addressed the crowd once more [Police Statement, 447]. He spoke directly to a few individuals whom he recognized. He asked one man, for example, "Why don't you go home and take a lot of these boys with you." The man replied, "Well, there is a lot of fellows here, police here, and I guess they want company so I think I will stay with them.... They will have a lot of fun throwing gas, etc. and I think I will stay with them." The officer who observed this exchange said that the man "practically ignored" the judge [Police Statement, 402]. As one of the most prominent members of the community, Judge Duer was used to people doing what he told them. But these were not normal times. Being part of this assembly on this special occasion enabled people to respond to an important man in a new way—some, by talking back and others, by ignoring him altogether.

After Duer left, the confrontation with police continued. Other individuals tried to assert their leadership. One man was William H. Thompson, the owner of a local drugstore in Princess Anne [Police Statement, 414]; another was Rusty Heath who was so drunk "he could hardly stand" [Police Statement, 422, 426–27, 430]. Another was Irving Adkins, a farmer who "jumped in the centre of the crowd and had his hat in his hand, and with his hand up in the air, and he hollered, 'Follow me,' or, 'Go get him,' or words to that effect" [Police Statement, 426]. Yet another was Shelburn Lester who worked as a meter man for a local public utility [Police Statement 448].

The multiplicity of people attempting to take charge is striking. The crowd, however, was not easily moved. And without its support, most of these individuals failed to cast themselves as stars. Eventually, a clear leader did emerge, according to police. He was a large man, better dressed than the others, who kept yelling, "Come on, let's go" [Police Statement, 385, 389, 391]. The well-dressed man turned out to be William P. Hearn, the owner of a trucking business from nearby Salisbury. Like Denston's brother and Rusty Heath, Hearn, too, appeared to have been drinking heavily, his breath reeking of alcohol [Police Statement, 391–92). "He was standing back talking to the crowd. I remember him saying positively—telling the crowd to come on, that they could not shoot you. The next thing I saw of him the crowd had closed around and he was right at the head of the step [of the jail] and he was what you might call number 1 man in that bunch" [Police Statement, 390]. Despite his ability to command attention, the crowd did not automatically follow Hearn. Its hesitation underscores how contingent the casting process can be. Police, too, did not stand idly by when Hearn and his followers tried to break through the line. At one point, they responded by throwing tear gas to repulse those in the front ("Mob Storms" 1933; Player 1933b).[9]

Hearn persisted. He continued trying to break through the police line and finally succeeded with the help of some other men willing to follow his lead. As one officer recalled:

> This man [Hearn] was the first leader of the crowd out at that point. He would go back sometimes quite a distance back in the street, get together a crowd up to around 50, and would lead them on to the police line. He would continue to holler, "Let's go", and would lead this crowd right up against the police, and would step over, apparently expecting the crowd to follow him, and when he saw no crowd was following him he would go back in the crowd behind, being grabbed by the officer, and then would proceed to organize another crowd, yelling, "Let's go", and lead them. Up until the time I saw this man did not appear to have any leadership. He and his crowd were the ones who finally, by their activities, broke through the line and caused Officer Bohler and myself to fall back. He assumed leadership of the entire crowd at that point. [Police Statement, 325–26]

A short while later, around eight thirty, the crowd did act (Player 1933a). Every action cast people in big and small roles. Hearn took the lead. He and his men grabbed a fifteen-foot pole from a nearby lumberyard to break through the police line. One officer standing in front of the jail door refused to budge. A small confrontation ensued, indicating that even at this point, the lynching was not inevitable. As the officer explained in his affidavit:

> I was directly in front of the door with my back to the door, down one step from the door, when a ram was brought up. I would recognize the first man on this ram. The ram extended out in front of me. This man said, "Are you going to get out of the road?" Down the line several people yelled, "Aren't you going to get out of the road?" I said, "No," and the next thing I know, I was rammed in the stomach with the ram. I reeled and kind of turned to get up a step when I was rammed in the back and in the legs. [Police Statement, 424]

Frank Spencer, the man from San Francisco, remembered the scene differently: "I was within 200 feet of the mob when they rushed the jail door and I saw that battering ram pass in between the policemen, merely brushing their uniforms." According to Spencer, the officer's claim that he was struck by the battering ram was false (Spencer 1933).

Using the battering ram, the crowd broke through the police line and entered the jail [Police Statement, 378, 414]. As the action moved forward, numerous supporting roles and bit parts were becoming available. Most were fleeting but

they enabled specific individuals in the mob to grab their moment in the spotlight. Someone grabbed the keys from Deputy Sheriff Norman Dryden (Player
1933b). As many as could fit rushed up the metal, circular staircase to the second
floor. The men headed directly to the "murder cell," where the worst offenders
were locked up (Inquest 1933, 20).[10] Mob members knew which prisoner was
Armwood because someone had come earlier in the day to find out who Armwood was and which cell he was in ("Blonde" 1933).

It was at this point that Sheriff Luther Daugherty arrived from Crisfield, a
town about twenty-five miles away. He went inside the jail and made one last
plea; he implored those who had broken into the jail not to take Armwood, but
his words fell on deaf ears (Player 1933b). He and Duer would be the last people
to try to bring the process to halt. Both failed.

The crowd packed itself into the small space. As one prisoner explained at the
Coroner's Inquest: "Just as many as could get up there. They kept coming one
after the other as fast as they could come up" [Inquest, 26]. The crowd assured the
other prisoners that they were after only one man, George Armwood [Inquest,
40]. One black prisoner, who, like the others, kept his head down the whole
time, testified at the Inquest that he heard "hollering." As the man explained:
"I don't know hardly what they were saying. I heard them saying, 'let's go get
him'" [Inquest, 28].

Once the crowd had seized Armwood, it dragged him down the metal staircase and out the front door. One prisoner heard Armwood crying out, "Oh,
Lord," at which point someone "stabbed [Armwood] in the back and he shut
up" ("Blonde" 1933). According to the *Baltimore Sun*, Armwood did indeed "put
up a fight in his cell, for he was gashed about the chest and head, and appeared
only semi-conscious when they got him outside" (Player 1933b). Once the action
moved outside, more bit parts were becoming available. A young man jumped
on Armwood's back and cut off his ear; another knocked him to the ground; a
woman ran over and kicked him in the stomach (Spencer 1933). These roles were
fleeting but they enabled these individuals to stand out for a brief moment and
claim bragging rights later.

As the action continued, more bit parts emerged. Someone threw a rope
around Armwood's neck, others tied him to the back of a car, and someone began
driving the vehicle that dragged Armwood through downtown streets (Spencer
1933). The crowd moved in concert, cheering their approval and delight.
A reporter from the *Baltimore Sun* described the scene this way: "Two blocks
up the main street they dragged him at a run, turning into the business section,
pursued by a mob of four or five thousand men and women, shouting and howling. 'Here's what we do on the Eastern Shore!' they cried" (Player 1933b). The
mob headed directly to the home of Judge Duer, the same man who earlier that

evening had urged the crowd to go home. Lynching Armwood on Duer's front lawn would have been a graphic rebuke of his earlier admonitions to the crowd to let the courts do their job. A woman came out of Duer's house and begged the group not to hang Armwood there. Mob leaders paused, conferred, and decided to hang Armwood from a tree at a nearby house [Police Statement, 443].

Bit parts continued to emerge. People shined flashlights on the tree to light up the branches; someone boosted a young man up the tree, who then threw the rope down to the those on the ground [Police Statement, 443–44] (Player 1933b). Others untied Armwood from the car; someone had to prop him up because he could no longer stand.[11] About half a dozen men pulled on the rope to hoist Armwood's body up (Spencer 1933).[12] The police who followed the crowd recognized the men holding the rope; one was Rusty Heath, who earlier that evening had tried to break through the police line [Police Statement, 395, 410]. Despite not being able to rally the mob earlier in the evening, Heath still found a way to be front and center once the violence began, thereby casting himself in a prominent supporting role.

As Armwood's body hanged from the tree, he appeared lifeless. The lack of any signs of life mattered little to the crowd. The action continued unabated. One officer recalls the mob "pulling the negro's body up and down several times" [Police Statement, 444]. Frank Spencer, the man from out of town, also witnessed a woman who "rushed in and hit [Armwood] in the stomach with a big stick" as he hung from the tree (Spencer 1933). One woman who was present at the lynching recalled that someone pulled Armwood's pants down, which struck her as "a funny thing to do" [Py 9 Dec 2009]. The *Baltimore Sun* also reported that "the Negro's trousers had given way" (Player 1933b).

After about five minutes, the crowd took Armwood's body down. The show was far from over, however (Player 1933b). As the action moved forward, more supporting roles and bit parts became available. Those with initiative grabbed an opportunity to get in on the action. As one officer recounted: "The colored fellow had been laid down on the ground and they were standing there holding the rope before the crowd pulled it out of their hands and pulled the fellow up the street again" [Police Statement, 397]. The mob dragged Armwood several blocks back in the direction of the jail, and stopped at the main downtown intersection near the courthouse. Someone threw the rope over one of the wires [Police Statement, 439]. The crowd then strung up Armwood a second time, and, as an additional flourish, threw gasoline on the body and lit it on fire. A burning body against the dark, nighttime sky would have been a sight to see. In the only photo of the event, it is possible to just make out the profile of a large crowd, heads all turned in the same direction, their gaze trained on a single point of focus, with car headlights shining in the background.

After the mob burned the body, Armwood's corpse dropped to the ground. As it lay on the street, Frank Spencer recalled the macabre behavior that followed: "After, while his burning body lay in the street, filling the breeze with the stench of burning flesh, the mob, men, women, young girls and boys, joined hands and danced around and around his prostrate body, singing 'John Brown's Body' and 'Give me Something to Remember You By'" (Spencer 1933). Spencer left the scene, sickened by all he had heard, seen, and felt. Unable to sleep, he returned about forty-five minutes later, at which point the crowd was beginning to disperse. Eventually, a police officer dumped the body in a nearby lumberyard (the black undertaker having refused to take possession of the body). Clarence Mitchell, one of the *Afro* reporters who covered the lynching, would find it the next day—mutilated and burnt. He would place burlap sacks over the body before taking a photo, perhaps to cover up the blistered flesh and obvious signs of mutilation. The photo appeared on the front page of the *Afro* under a six-inch, red-hued headline that read simply "BURN."

Why kill Armwood so publicly and with so much extralethal violence? Why go through all the trouble? Why not take him out of the jail and simply shoot him and go home?

Viewed as a strategic act, the violence served as a deterrent. The extensive violence showed local blacks the consequences of violating the color line. While seemingly "obvious," this explanation falls short on multiple levels. First, black residents of the Eastern Shore were already familiar with the violent folkways of Jim Crow and the consequences of violating its precept of white supremacy. Segregation structured how black and white people lived from the moment of birth (when black and white mothers gave birth in separate wards at the hospital). Second, this explanation is troubling for another reason. It parrots pro-lynchers' justifications for their acts—that lynching was "necessary" to prevent other black "beasts" from raping white women or killing white families. To proffer such an explanation is to side with the mob.

Third, even if the lynching *did* function primarily as a deterrent, the question remains why send the warning through a lynching rather than some other form of action? A spectacle lynching, after all, was exactly the kind of act that prompted condemnation of the county and the Eastern Shore from the rest of the country. Why risk besmirching the county's good name with such an act?

Another possible explanation comes from Amy Louise Wood (2009, 11), who argues that lynchings were about restoring a sense of order. Yet, the order that lynch mobs were "restoring" went far beyond the status quo. It was based on a fantasized world where whites, blacks, police, judges, and the governor all knew their place when it came to punishing black men accused of having committed crimes against whites. In this imagined world, police turn over black suspects to white mobs rather than protect them; judges back mob justice rather than try to stop it; state officials do not interfere with local matters; and black citizens do not enjoy the same legal rights and protections as whites. And because this imagined order was not in existence, it could not be a reference point for "restoration." It had to be created.

I argue that the answer to the question "why go to all the trouble" lies in the power of the casting process to ensure that no one stands outside the display. This power worked in multiple ways.

First, the process allowed for widespread and sustained participation. Quick execution would not. The route the lynchers took covered a lot of ground. The distance they covered totaled almost twenty blocks and the festivities took more than ten hours, from the spreading of rumors in the early afternoon talk to the dispersal of the crowd sometime around nine or ten o'clock at night. The more time and distance the display took, the more opportunities for various people to grab leads, supporting roles, and bit parts, and the more opportunities for the unwitting and unwilling to be pulled in at the same time (more below).

Second, participation itself was transformative. Roles conferred instant status on the most willing and eager. To use Arthur Raper's (1933, 9) words, the lynching enabled the "obscure and irresponsible" to play the roles of judge, jury, and hangman. Participating also elevated everyone above the law, including the hundreds or thousands who played the crucial role of spectator by gazing, moving, yelling, cheering, clapping, and screaming. But for these spectators, there would have been no show. Participation also conferred status on those individuals who took on bit roles. The young teenager who cut off Armwood's ear, for example, was seen later "dart[ing] about wildly waving a severed ear of the lynch victim" (Player 1933b). Such acts ensured these actors could boast of what they did later and to show off their prized souvenirs.

Third, the process also cast unwitting and unwilling actors. These were people forced into the role of spectator because of their physical proximity to the scene. Among the unwilling (though not unwitting) were the other prisoners inside the jail that night—both black and white. All these men could hear and see the action on the street as well as that inside the jail after the mob broke in. One white prisoner described the scene to an *Afro* reporter: "For hours the mob was howling outside and it kept growing louder and louder and we kept back out of sight for fear they might get all of us, but there wasn't any fear of that because they knew just who they wanted" ("Blonde" 1933). Even those who tried not to see, such as the black prisoners who kept their heads down the whole time, were nevertheless forced to hear and feel the mob as it came to seize Armwood from his cell (Inquest 1933). By virtue of simply hearing the action—whether they ever looked up or not—they, too, became cast in the show.

Among the unwitting participants was a prominent white man named Sidney Hayman who lived downtown. He recalled the event decades later in a 1992 interview for a television program on the Great Depression.

> Well, the night, the night of the lynching, . . . we went to play bridge on a street or two from the main street, and we heard all the ungodly yells, and we didn't know what was happening, so we broke up the bridge party and came out on the main street to see what was going on. There, about two or three blocks away, *I could see this mob coming towards us, and perhaps there were about three or four hundred people in the mob, and they were yelling and screaming, and oh, it was just horrible.* (S. Hayman, 1992, emphasis in original)

Hayman's account may have downplayed his prior knowledge and perhaps even his support of the lynching, but it nevertheless points to the vocal intensity of the crowd, which Hayman recalls as being "ungodly." Whether he meant to take part of not, he could not ignore the sounds. It was these sounds that made him look. And by looking and listening, he, too, became cast as a spectator.

In addition to the prisoners in the jail and downtown residents like Sidney Hayman, there were black families who lived near the small downtown. Their proximity to the lynching also forced them to play spectator. One black woman, who was a child at the time, said she would never forget the crowd's screams as it passed by the house where she and her parents were attending a revival. "I heard the tin cans. They were dragging him behind a car. The preacher said, 'There's a lynching. We have to get down on our knees and pray.' . . . There was yelling and screaming. The white people were cheering: 'This is great.' I could hear it. It was close by. I'll never forget that" [interview, 21 Oct 2011]. When I asked this woman whether she understood what a lynching was at such a young age, she responded, "I did. A six-year old could understand when someone was being treated badly. A six-year old can understand that" [interview, 21 Oct 2011].

Another black woman, who was seventeen at the time, remembered that her father was forced to spend the night in the courthouse because he worked downtown (J. Hayman, 1980). Given her father's proximity to the lynching, he, too, was likely forced to hear the sounds of the mob, feel its movements as it commandeered downtown streets, and smell the smoke of burning flesh from Armwood's body. These real-time experiences of the lynching cast these black men and women as spectators, albeit unwilling and unwitting ones.

In addition to pulling in one and all, the display also did important meaning-making work. First and foremost, it inscribed a brand of hyper-powerful whiteness, the kind that did not exist in regular, daily life. This brand of whiteness was vested with complete and absolute control over black bodies *where nothing was out of bounds.* What better way to show that lack of restraint than by going beyond the pale. All the extralethal acts, from mutilating to burning to skinning Armwood alive, were not extraneous to the action. They *were* the main attraction. They were the very reason people dropped their normal routine to come downtown in the middle of the week. They were also clear expressions of a limitless power that no white, even Judge Duer, could claim outside the context of a spectacle lynching.

While Jim Crow mandated unequal rights and privileges according to a person's status as black or white (Apel and Smith 2008; Harris 1995), it did not grant whites unlimited control over or access to black bodies. Indeed, one of the ironic consequences of legal segregation was the creation of all-black spaces in which black men and women could exercise autonomy and self-determination, the very kind of dignity and independence that Jim Crow was supposed to stifle and prevent (Hale 1999, 199–200). In addition to being an imperfect system of hierarchy, segregation was also a poor substitute for the institution of chattel slavery, which conferred on slave owners nearly unlimited power over their own slaves (Jones 2013). Lynching restored whiteness with the same kind of boundless power that slave owners had once enjoyed.

The whiteness inscribed by this display was also a vivid repudiation of the kind enforced by the police and courts. By protecting black prisoners from white mobs, the legal system was undermining white authority and privilege. And by according black suspects the same legal rights as whites—in theory—the justice system was also circumscribing white power and privilege. In the eyes of the mob, the legal system proved wholly inadequate at addressing the most egregious violations of the color line—the kind that threatened to expose the line for what it was: an imaginary wholly dependent on the constant reenactment of public subjugation of black bodies, both living or dead.

Politically, the display also constituted an act of usurpation of the state's legal apparatus. Far from rubber-stamping the status quo, the display repudiated and overturned it, if only for a single day. By enacting "rough justice" (Pfeifer 2004), the mob depicted *an alternative social order that rejected* the sterile justice of the court system—the same court system that kept Euel Lee, a black man accused of murdering a white family of four, from the lynch mob; the same system that enabled Lee to remain alive and well nearly two years after the crime through clever lawyering by an outsider, a Jew and a communist.[13] The lynching of Armwood helped to right that wrong. It reaffirmed white people's prerogative to take matters into their own hands regardless of what the letter or spirit of the law said. As one white interviewee told me, "[The Armwood lynching] was brought on by the other murder in Berlin. They didn't do anything about it. It was time to show who was who" [Py 9 December 2009]. And indeed, the mob was certainly showing *who they were*. The display broadcast the white community's claims to sovereignty far and wide—so far and wide that even those actors who were not on the scene, such as Judge Duer, who left the jail to go have dinner with friends, and Governor Ritchie, who lived on the "Western Shore" in Annapolis, would surely hear and read about it in the days to come.

From beginning to end, the lynching showed what this alternative order looked like. It enabled willing participants to experience a novel kind of power firsthand—through and with their own bodies. This display, like most spectacle lynchings, engaged all five physical senses. As Amy Louise Wood (2009, 11) explains:

> Spectators heard the speeches of the mob, the shouts of the crowd, the confessions of the victim, and most of all, his dying shrieks and cries. In cases where the victim was burned, to witness a lynching was also to smell it. And, in all instances, the feel and push of the crowd created the sense of belonging and commonality that sustained the violence. In this respect, spectators did not watch or consume a lynching as much as they *witnessed* it—that is, they beheld or experienced it with active engagement.

One need not have cut off an ear or pulled on the rope from which Armwood hanged to be part of the scene. It was enough to join the manhunt, pass along a rumor, show up at the jail, or cheer and clap at every act of violation to become part of the show. And to be part of the show was to experience and embody the brand of whiteness the lynching was inscribing.

The display also forced others to take part as unwitting spectators. Such is the power of violent displays to assign roles to everyone and everyone to a role. Even Frank Spencer, the white man who was visiting from San Francisco, was cast in the display, despite his opposition and initial attempts to find a way to prevent or stop the lynching. By showing up, he, too, became part of the show.

Parade in Selo (Bosnia)

Not all violent displays take the form of spectacle, however. In Bosnia, the display resembled a "parade." The parade lacked the sensational aspects of the Armwood lynching. The stagecraft was not the same, and the relationship between the what actors were putting on display and the spectators on the scene was much different than the lynching. And yet, this display, too, transformed how actors saw themselves; it, too, was rewriting what it meant to be part of the select group with power.

Friday, July 10, 1992, was a typically warm July day in northwest Bosnia (Samardžija Trial 2006).[14] Early that morning, so early that most people would still be at home, a group of soldiers knocked on the doors of all the Muslim households. As one man recalled, "They took us by surprise" [interview]. The soldiers informed the men in each house to gather at a meadow that locals called Jezerine.

The operation was straightforward. Unlike the lynching in Maryland, this display had a clear leader who embraced the role of star: former history and geography teacher-turned-company commander, Marko Samardžija. It was Samardžija who had sent the soldiers to knock on the doors of Muslim homes while the rest of his unit waited at the meadow.[15] With every order the soldiers carried out, they became part of a small but vital supporting cast, which affirmed Samardžija as star (Fujii 2017). Starring in the day's operation would solidify Samardžija's already high status in the community and perhaps even give him a place of prominence and visibility in the new, self-proclaimed, breakaway state of Republika Srpska.

The order to assemble was not new. On two previous occasions in June, just weeks before the current operation, army units from outside the region had carried out similar orders [Derviševič]. Sarmadžija himself recalled at his own trial that it was the Sixth Sana Brigade that had carried out these two earlier operations. He remembered the dates as June 16 and June 25 or 26 (Sud Bosne i Hercegovine 2006, 28 September).[16] Residents also recalled these previous actions. Soldiers had ordered all Muslim men to gather, then took them to a local school, but released them unharmed less than an hour later. According to one local man, these soldiers from outside the region had wondered why they had been told to come. Why were reinforcements needed to help herd a group of unarmed men to the local school and then set them free [interview; Muježinović]?

The operation on July 10, 1992, would unfold differently than the two previous, however. The night before, army officers had mapped out the plan at a meeting held at a local restaurant called Lovac. Lovac means "hunter" in the local language, an ironic moniker given what was about to take place. At the meeting, Samardžija received his orders. He was to lead the operation. The next morning, he was to have his soldiers instruct all Muslim men to gather at a central collection point, then march the captives to a local elementary school, where military police would question them. The pretext for the mission was a claim—unfounded but widely diffused—that local Muslims had been arming themselves and preparing for revolt or worse, a takeover. That evening, around 9:00 p.m., Samardžija relayed the orders to his men (Sud Bosne i Hercegovine 2006, 13 July).

At sunrise the next morning, the operation began. Samardžija had only a handful of men under his command, fifteen to twenty by one soldier's estimate (Sud Bosne i Hercegovine 2006, 13 July 2006).[17] One man in the unit testified at Samardžija's trial that the atmosphere at the meadow was low-key with Samardžija addressing the captives personally. "Marko [Samardžija] headed over, talking among them, the people were listening to him, no one was making any problems, not at all, they were even heading out to piss, and coming back. I'm saying that nothing bad was happening there" (Sud Bosne i Hercegovine 2006, 13 July). One older Muslim recalled Samardžija addressing the captives in a familiar but threatening tone: "Gentlemen, you are my pupils. The army is summoning you and whoever is guilty will be [held] responsible and who is not guilty will walk [go free]" [Dervišević, audiotape 2 of 3]. Samardžija was relishing his starring role and newfound power. Only in an operation that he himself was leading could he play the starring role.

The supposedly "relaxed" atmosphere may have been due in part to the fact that Samardžija's men were from the area (unlike the soldiers from the Sixth Sana Brigade who came from Drvar [Muježinvoć]). The men knew their Muslim captives, some as familiar faces and others as good friends (Samardžija Trial 2006, 13 July). Samardžija himself had close friends who were Muslim. His own *kum* (best man) had been a local Muslim. His father's *kum* had also been a Muslim. Such relationships were the norm in Selo and in many other mixed villages across the country (Bringa 1995).

The casting process, however, was placing erstwhile friends and neighbors in altogether different roles. Being part of the supporting cast enabled former social intimates to do things they would not otherwise do. The soldiers ordered their captives to empty their pockets, ostensibly to search for contraband (none was found). Soldiers then marched the men in two columns toward a local elementary school. As the men marched, the atmosphere continued to be relaxed, according to the same soldier quoted above. He testified that the prisoners walked normally, with their arms to their sides. At one point, one of the captives even asked Samardžija if he could go home to retrieve some heart medication to alleviate his breathing problems; Samardžija told him to go (Sud Bosne i Hercegovine 2006, 13 July).[18] One of the captives, however, remembers the scene differently, confirmed by others who testified at Samardžija's trial. Rather than being allowed to walk in a "normal" fashion, the prisoners had to march with their hands behind their heads with their eyes looking down so they could not recognize anyone. Meanwhile the soldiers remained "at the ready" to ensure that none of the captives tried to escape as they walked through cornfields.

Once Samardžija's unit reached the school, the military police, recognizable by their white belt buckles, took over (Weiss 2000). Unlike the civilian police who were also present, the military police were not from the area (Sud Bosne i Hercegovine 2006, 13 July). They immediately took charge of the captives. This changing of the "guard" recast Samardžija and his men as bit players in a much bigger show. The atmosphere changed precipitously. The police ordered the men to line up single file, then forced them to run through a gauntlet on their way to entering the school. As the captives ran through, military and civilian police beat the victims with their guns (Sud Bosne i Hercegovine 2006).

Once inside, the captors forced the men into classrooms, which were already crowded with prisoners from neighboring villages. The police searched the men's clothing and pockets. They took what they wanted and threw out the rest. They also took down the prisoners' personal information: name, date and place of birth. The prisoners then waited in the heat, fearful of what was to come next.

Perhaps to pass the time or to amuse themselves, the military police took groups of five men out of the classrooms and again forced them to run gauntlets in the hallways. As one prisoner recalled, "So you went through the *špalir* [gauntlet] and they were beating us with everything—feet, guns, whatever they had." As the police beat the men, they called them *balije*, a derogatory term for Muslims.

After several hours, buses pulled up in front of the school. The display was coming to an end. Military police swarmed the streets to make sure that none of the neighbors was peeking through curtained windows to watch what was happening next. The soldiers loaded the men onto the two buses. The vehicles pulled out, then stopped every five to fifteen meters, at which point soldiers off-loaded prisoners in groups of five and shot them. They continued until they had killed all one hundred and twenty men. According to one man who could hear (but not see) what was happening, the shooting lasted two hours [Derviševic, audiotape 2 of 3].

What was this display about? Why parade the men at all? Why not just collect the prisoners at the meadow and kill them there? Surely, that would have been more efficient. Then the soldiers could go home, drink coffee, and relax— mission accomplished. Why draw out the proceedings any more than necessary, especially if the plan was to kill the men all along?

As with the Armwood lynching, a strategic explanation might point to the utility of containing internal threats. Republika Srpska was newly established and rumors were circulating that Muslims had weapons. As Samardžija claimed in a 1999 interview with Dutch investigator Birte Weiss:

> We had to be very careful, though. We knew that, from 5 or 6 June, there had been a Muslim plan to cleanse the Serbs in Sanica. A list had been prepared of who should be killed by whom, the officers would be

killed first. And I had seen a list of 63 Muslim men who had orders to rape Serb women. Of course, the plan was never implemented, but it showed that we had to take our own measures. (Weiss 2000, "Traitor or Avenger")

And even if the rumors were not true, fighting age men could pose a serious threat to the new authorities if they tried to revolt or fight back. Making a show of rounding up such men and then killing them would send a powerful warning to the rest of the community.

Such an explanation would sound plausible but for the details of how and when this episode unfolded. By July 1992, the Republika Srpska (RS) had complete control over the entire region, including the major cities of Prijedor and Banja Luka (Helsinki Watch 1993, 30, 42).[19] As part of the takeover, the new authorities had established roadblocks along all the main roads, making escape extremely difficult. In addition, the captive men were unarmed; authorities had already confiscated all legally owned arms, which amounted to no more than a few hunting rifles that had been in the family for years. Even with such weapons, Muslims were no match for the new RS authorities who were armed by Milošević and the immense arsenal of the former JNA that Milošević controlled. And even if the new RS authorities wanted to send a message to local Muslims, it seems odd that they would do so by putting the actual killings out of sight and then removing the bodies and dumping them in vertical caves so they remained hidden from view. Surely, it would have been more terrorizing if the authorities had killed and left the dead bodies out in the open so that everyone would be forced to see them.

I argue that the parading of men had a different kind of power than killing them quickly. As in the Armwood lynching, the parade covered considerable distance. This was no quick traverse from the meadow to the school. Rather, the march would have taken at least fifteen to twenty minutes. As in the Armwood lynching, prolonging the activities over time and space enabled participants to cast themselves (or to be cast) in different roles at different points in time.

Extending the parade over space and time also allowed the actors *to be seen playing their roles*. The main star of the show was Samardžija, who was in his sixties by the start of the war and had long enjoyed the respect that someone with his level of education commanded in rural areas. Being a beloved teacher, however, may not have been enough for Samardžija. Putting violence on display would transform him into something more. It would perhaps make him a hero, someone others would talk about in heroic terms. Whatever he hoped to achieve, Samardžija, according to Weiss who interviewed him in the late 1990s, played the role of military commander with "great zeal."

He hectored his soldiers, a hotchpotch of youths, who had not yet done their military service, and experienced people with military training but lacking in preparation and suitable equipment. Therefore, they had to be motivated by calls to noble deeds, which in his universe meant the purging of neighbours and friends. He used alleged Bosniak [Muslim] murder plans, inflated Serbian heroism and references to events during World War II as his means of persuasion. When this verbal fortification proved insufficient, it was bolstered with slivovitz and other spirits. (Weiss 2000, The Bandits)

Whether or not Samardžija saw himself as the avenger of historic wrongs against the Serb people, he was playing the role of a lifetime by leading the day's operation. By playing the star, however briefly, he became someone much grander and more important than a local teacher. The display showcased his own marshal prowess.

No star works alone, however. To become a star, Samardžija needed a supporting cast who would affirm in that role. The mission guaranteed such a cast. By following his orders, all the men in his unit affirmed him as the star, including those who were reluctant to take part, such as radio operator Nikola Kuridža. The display ensured that all such men would be *seen in those roles*. By inhabiting their roles, Samardžija's men were also transformed, whether they wanted to be or not. They were no longer neighbors and friends of their captives; they were no longer "ordinary" men of a small rural village. They were now part of a much larger nationalist project called Greater Serbia.

Like the Armwood lynching, this display also did vital meaning-making work. First, the display inscribed the new nationalist brand of Serbness. This new brand did not accord with previous, shared understandings of what it meant to be Serb or Muslim (Gagnon 2004). Before the war, being Serb meant having an array of relationships to non-Serbs—as school-mates (*drugi skolški*), neighbors (*komšije*), friends, best friends (*kumovi*), and co-workers (*kolege*). Before the war, differences were a conduit, not an obstacle, to close and friendly relations among people living in the same face-to-face community (Bringa 1995). The new nationalist brand of Serbness, however, no longer countenanced mixed marriages and close friendships between Serbs and non-Serbs. To be a "real" Serb meant parading former friends and students as prisoners rather than sharing a cigarette or drink with them.

The display also made violence the basis for belonging in the newly redefined category of "Real Serb." This display showed everyone what it meant to be a "real" Serb under the new order. Being a "real" Serb involved going along with the organized mistreatment and killing of one's former neighbors and friends. Any Serb who refused to go along or tried to help their Muslim or Croat neighbors no longer qualified as a "real" Serb.

At a more general level, this display enacted a new political and social order. It showed what the new order looked and felt like. Serbs and non-Serbs alike experienced this new order through and with their bodies—when they knocked on doors, kicked and punched the men running through a gauntlet, or heard the shots from the guns of military police. They also summoned the new order into being with every knock, kick, and punch. The display also enabled the new authorities of Republika Srpska to communicate their power and authority far and wide—not only to non-Serbs, who needed no reminding that their lives were in peril, but also to the local Serb population who needed to learn firsthand what it meant to be a "real" Serb in the new RS.

Comparing Violent Stagecraft

Not all displays are flashy or dazzling. Not all feature extralethal acts. Both the Armwood lynching and Selo parade were much more steeped in stagecraft than the killings in Ngali during the genocide. Yet, even in a less showy display, the casting process unfolds in similar fashion.

In Ngali, some of the biggest displays were the killing of the children who came from one of the most prominent families in the community. Roland, the head of family, had sent his children to Ngali thinking they would be safer there than in Kigali. The central and southern regions of the country (where Ngali is located) had experienced little of the war since it began on October 1, 1990 [Ean: 16 June 2009; Eb: 24 June 2009]. In the aftermath of the plane crash that killed the president, these regions remained tense, but without violence, in contrast to Kigali, which was convulsed by mass killings in the days following the crash (Des Forges 1999; Guichaoua 2005; Kimonyo 2008). And while some Tutsi in the southernmost part of the country were already trying to cross into Burundi (Kabagema 2001, 16), most people in Ngali were staying put and adjusting to rapidly shifting lines of authority and power.

What occurred in this period was regime change at the local level. This "Pawa coup" was not only part of the process of takeover as discussed in the previous chapter; it also marked the beginning of the casting process. In declaring himself the new conseiller for Ngali, Jude made himself the star of the killing show. Becoming the "star" did not mean staging elaborate displays like the lynching in Maryland or the parade in Bosnia. It did mean organizing attack groups called *ibitero* (*igitero*, singular) and directing these groups to engage in various forms of

violence, including hunting down every member of Roland's large family, including his youngest children.

When the violence first began, some Tutsi, like Roland's mother, assumed
that the burning and looting *was* the extent of the violence, as it had been in
1973, in the waning days of the Kayibanda regime. So the first time an *igitero*
descended on her house, she urged the men to take some cows. As one man in
the igitero explained: "[She] was asking us to take three of the cows to eat so
that she could save the other seven. She looked at the situation as similar to the
events of 1973. She thought the attackers would just eat the cows but not attack
the people. We refused to slaughter these cows at first but then little by little, as
time went on, the war was turning into something else and the cows were taken
and eaten" [interview, 22 June 2009]. Many other residents of Ngali also thought
the violence would never escalate to killing Tutsi because that had never happened in the past. As one woman explained, "In our community, there were no
problems."

The looting and burning of Tutsi homes lasted a week. Then the killings
began. It was this violence that local level leaders like Jude put on display, not to
dazzle, but to force (and entice) people to enact the new genocidal order. Among
the targets were three of Roland's children, who ranged in age from around five
to twelve years old. The igitero that hunted them down was unusually large—
numbering well over one hundred men [E4: 22 June 2009]. It was ten o'clock in
the morning when the group located the children and brought them to a central spot. The children were made to lie face down on the ground. According to
one man in the igitero, the children were crying, knowing they were going to
die [E4: 22 June 2009]. According to another, they were silent, never uttering a
sound. Whichever version is true—and both could have been true at different
moments—Jude handpicked three individuals to act as executioner, one for each
child. Jude tended to pick men whose loyalties were suspect, either because they
had ties to the victim or because they had not been seen doing the "work" of
genocide, such as going out on night patrols or joining an igitero. In this killing,
Jude picked one man who was related to Roland's family through his mother.
That meant he himself was related to the child he was ordered to kill. In selecting
specific men to act as executioners, Jude was forcing them into key supporting
roles. Jude urged the men to get the killings done quickly. "Vite, vite, vite," he
yelled ("quickly, quickly, quickly"). The men bludgeoned the children with clubs
and hoes, killing them in a matter of minutes. Jude then ordered the group to
move on and leave the bodies where they lay. Later, he would tell two of his lieutenants to go back and have the bodies buried.

Why did the men not just kill the children on the spot, where they found
them? Why take the time and effort to bring them in front of the whole group

and then kill them? And why was the group so large when only a few men would have sufficed to kill three young children?

The murder of the three children was not unusual in its form. Most killings during the genocide took place in broad daylight and were carried out by groups that varied in size (Des Forges 1999; Fujii 2009; Mironko 2004; Straus 2006). I argue that the unusually large size of the igitero in this killing marked the moment as special. It turned the murder of three young children into a large-scale production wherein people were cast in different roles at different moments. Members of the igitero played dual roles. They not only constituted Jude's supporting cast (thereby affirming Jude as the star); they also played the role of spectator when it came time to kill the children. In this latter role, their job was to stand and watch the killings as they took place. The large-scale production also ensured that those living nearby would be cast as spectators, albeit unwittingly. Though many neighbors may not have seen the actual killing with their own eyes, most would have certainly seen and heard the large igitero hunting down the children and then gathering in a single spot to watch them be killed. By hearing and seeing, these residents, too, became cast in the show.

What is important in each of these episodes is not just the murder of a few or the killing of many; rather, it is the meanings that the displays inscribe. These meanings pertained to notions of belonging and hierarchy and were rooted in a specific context. They articulated, in three-dimensional form, what it meant to be a "real" Serb in Bosnia, to obtain "justice" in the Eastern Shore, or to be part of the new genocidal order in Rwanda. These meanings, however, did not jibe with existing understandings. Nationalist conceptions of what it meant to be a "real" Serb had no relation to how people had lived in mixed villages across Bosnia. In Maryland, the kind of whiteness lynchers were enacting was not the way most people on both sides of the color line lived, even under Jim Crow. In Rwanda, genocidal constructions of who was to live and who was to die bore little resemblance to the way people lived with one another prior to the war, whether Hutu or Tutsi.

In none of the three episodes did it matter whether people believed in the new brand of Serbness or whiteness or the new genocidal ideology that display makers were constructing and promoting. What mattered was the bodily enactment of those new orders. Each display assigned roles to everyone and everyone to a role. Even those who watched from behind curtained windows or heard the sounds from a nearby house became part of the show, albeit unwittingly and in many cases, unwillingly.

The displays also enabled many who took part to become someone new, as Rusty Heath did when he held the rope from which Armwood hanged, as Jude did when he organized the killings of Roland's children, and as Samardžija did when he led the mission that culminated in the killing of over one hundred Muslim men. These roles conferred instant status on these individuals, far beyond "normal" pathways to prominence or fame.

The displays worked by creating "scenes" that made the moment special. These scenes in turn drew an audience of active spectators, who, through their sheer presence helped to broadcast the power of the displays far and wide. Such is the power of display to upend the status quo by meting out violence on individual bodies and by doing so, violate and harm the larger social bodies those individuals represent. From one body to another, display makers transformed social reality.

INTERMISSION

Because almost no one in Gospić was innocent of the events in October 1991, everybody kept silent. And even if there were innocent people among them, they most certainly didn't dare to speak.

—Slavenka Drakulić, *They Would Never Hurt a Fly*

In this chapter, I pause the action to delve into questions about the challenges involved in researching violence. All researchers—no matter their foci—are inescapably tied to the present when conducting our studies. Present conditions structure what we can see and not see. Over time, stories about past violence might diverge in different directions; or they might crystallize around a singular, taken-for-granted "truth" (Malkki 1995). These latter versions might even help to foreclose alternative readings and divergent accounts. What should scholars do in these cases? How should we analyze stories that actively work to sideline other versions or render certain parts irrelevant to the "real" story actors continue to tell? I trace the sources of "silencing" narratives that arose in each research site. Silencing narratives are not simply "consensus" versions of events. They are stories that foreclose other possible accounts. As such, they are inherently political. Their circulation is also political. I argue that these accounts provide insight into what is at stake for certain actors to tell the story one way rather than another. By highlighting what is at stake, they not only inform researchers about the current research context, they help to constitute it.

In addition to investigating these narratives, I also discuss the methods and strategies I used to collect and generate data in each site. Research unfolded over several years (from 2009 to 2014) in three different countries. The research sites were all small, rural communities that had experienced violence. In each locale, I set out to do interviews with people who had lived through the violence. Only through interviews could I get a sense of the history of each community. I wanted to know not only about the violence, but also how daily life operated before the violence. How did people interact? What constituted neighborliness? Who was friends with whom? Who had power or status in the community? Who had none? From there, my aim was to situate the process of violence in a fine-grained rendering and tie those local processes to the larger regional and national context of politics.

In every site, I tried to talk with a wide range of people. I spoke with men and women from all "sides," however one defines those "sides." I talked to people as young as twenty-five (making them children at the time of violence) and two who were one hundred years old (making them grown adults when the lynchings of Matthew Williams and George Armwood took place). In addition to interviews, I had countless informal conversations during the course of fieldwork— at my guest house, in the local market, riding in a cab, or eating lunch with my research assistant. I also had more formal meetings with local scholars, journalists, people who worked for or ran local nongovernmental organizations or groups, and various other people who did not come from my research sites but came from the same region and knew it well. I also had countless personal experiences, which produced additional observations and allowed me to make sense of my own social location and vantage point as they shifted over time. I refer to all these encounters and experiences as "accidental ethnography" because the stories I overheard, the conversations I had, and my own, personal navigation of the sites were critical in helping me to see inside people's worlds and to understand the logics that ran through them (Fujii 2014).

Daytonized Realities in Bosnia

Silencing narratives and practices arose in each research site for different reasons. The end of fighting or violence did not always mean the cessation of politics about the violence. In Bosnia, vestiges of the nationalist politics that led to the war were still apparent long after the Dayton Agreement had brought fighting to an end. The agreement, named after the Ohio town where negotiations took place, established postwar Bosnia-Herzegovina as a federation with an autonomous region called Republika Srpska (RS). This arrangement amounted to an institutionalized spoil of war for Bosnian Serb nationalists. It also created ideal conditions for permanent gridlock and untrammeled corruption across the country as a whole, since those in power (at the federal and local levels) had little incentive to cooperate. The result has been a classic instance of Jean-François Bayart's (2006) "politics of the belly" (*la politique du ventre*), where a tiny few are able to gobble up all the resources and perquisites of government office, while the rest of the population struggles to reclaim what is left of their prewar lives (Toal and Dahlman 2011).

Vestiges of nationalist politics have also seeped into the language of everyday life—both literally and figuratively. In the postwar period, the language formerly known as Serbo-Croatian has taken on a bevy of names. In Bosnia, people refer to the local language as Bosnian (*Bosanski*), in Croatia, as Croatian (*Hrvatski*), and in Serbia, as Serbian (*Srpski*). And while it might seem logical or even quaint to name a language after the territory in which it is spoken, it is impossible to understand this change without reference to the nationalist politics that produced it.

One way that language has been become a domain of nationalist expression is through "linguistic engineering" where the aim to create difference where none existed before (Bugarski 2013, 164). Efforts have ventured into the absurd. At a screening of a film about Belgrade youth in Zagreb, for example, distributors made the decision to add subtitles—not because they thought a "Croatian-speaking" audience would not be able to understand "Serbian speaking" characters, but to satisfy a postwar policy in Croatia that mandates "translators" for any official documents coming from Serbia. As Tomislav Longinović (2013) points out, decrees that require officials to treat one language as two is a performative. Declaring makes it so. The audience, however, did not go along with the charade. At the screening of the film, "pandemonium" broke out in the form of laughter and knee slapping when the opening title of the film read "Beograd, jesen 1991" (Belgrade, spring 1991) and just below were the words, "Beograd, jesen 1991." As Ranko Bugarski (2013, 164) points out, four different political names for the same language do not make four distinct languages (the fourth being "Montenegrin" spoken in Montenegro, which declared itself an independent, sovereign state in 2006). While language games might provoke laughter in some quarters, they are nevertheless a lasting vestige of two nationalist wars and the dissolution of the country once known as Yugoslavia.

A much more serious vestige of nationalist politics has been the unmixing of formerly mixed communities. At the war's end, many Serbs whose homes fell on the "federation" side of Bosnia ended up selling their houses and moving away. Some moved to Serbia, others abroad, and still others ended up in the RS as "refugees" in their own country. This demographic upheaval made it impossible to interview Serbs and Muslims in equal numbers in Selo because most Serbs had moved away.

To find more Serbs from Selo to interview, I traveled to the town of Prijedor, about two hours away. With the help of a research assistant who had grown up there, we managed to obtain a list of refugees who had moved there from Selo. We began contacting people on the list but no one seemed eager to talk to us.

In one instance, a man broke down on the phone telling us he had lost his son in the war and it was too painful to talk about that period. In another, we managed to find a woman we were looking for as she was coming out of her house. She treated us like a nuisance and refused our request for an interview. On yet another occasion, we located the house of a different woman with directions provided by her neighbors. When we knocked on the door, however, the young man who answered said she was not at home, despite evidence that she was indeed inside the house.

When we did manage to find people who agreed to be interviewed, the conversation quite literally went nowhere. In one case, an older woman consented over the phone to meet with us, but when we arrived, she quickly made it clear that she did not want to talk about anything. The most telling sign of how unwelcome we were was when we were entering her apartment. Instinctively, my research assistant and I took off our shoes before going inside (a common courtesy in Bosnian homes), but the woman insisted that we keep them on. When we demurred and took them off anyway (so as not to dirty her spotless floors), she hurriedly brought our shoes inside. I surmised by this gesture that she did not want any of her neighbors to see evidence of strange guests in her house. The interview itself seemed to confirm that hunch. Our conversation did not go beyond pleasantries. We left after only fifteen minutes.

In another instance, our interviewee was much more open to talking to us. He had been in primary school when the war started. I asked him what he remembered from that time. He recalled one teacher with particular fondness. He had been suffering from an illness at the time and missed many days of school. This particular teacher, he explained, would visit him at home, bring him food, and check on him to see how he was doing. When I asked what happened to her, he mused offhandedly, "I think she went away. Maybe to Germany." I was struck by how blithely he talked about what became of his former teacher, who turned out to be a woman I had interviewed. As a young boy, he may well have had no idea whether she was Muslim, Serb, or Croat. And given the number of people who had left Selo, his assumption that she, too, went away is not far-fetched. And yet, his answer seemed to indicate that her fate no longer mattered to his present life in the RS. I wondered if he had ever considered that if she had been Muslim, she would not have "gone away" at all, but been forced out or even killed.

There seemed to be a disjuncture between the experiences of a young schoolboy living in Communist Yugoslavia and the musings of a recent university graduate living in the RS. The young man had no trouble recalling a favorite teacher who helped to take care of him when he was sick. He also did not seem to have any problem holding onto that memory as if it were a moment frozen in time, unconnected to the war or his postwar life in the RS. The young boy at the start of the war ended up having to flee with his family when the Dayton Agreement divided Bosnia into two different political entities where very different narratives of the war circulated. He grew up in an environment where local people heralded indicted war criminals as "heroes" and where challenges to nationalist accounts of the war were few (Steflja 2017). Even if people did not believe these versions, they knew better than to challenge them. In Republika Srpska, speaking about the unspeakable could bring violent retribution. In 1999, for example, Željko Kopanja, the editor of the biggest independent newspaper in the RS, published the names of all 228 victims of the Mount Vlasić massacre. In that incident, which occurred in August 1992, Bosnian Serb soldiers were transporting over one thousand non-Serbs to Bosnian government controlled territory. A paramilitary group stopped the convoy, separated out more than two hundred men, bussed them to a set of cliffs, and shot them dead as they knelt on the edge of the ravine. Kopanja's simple but courageous act brought swift response. A bomb exploded in his car and blew off both his legs (Wesselingh and Vaulerin 2005, 84, 200). Needless to say that most people were not like Kopanja; they were not willing to risk their lives by challenging the approved narrative in which Serbs were ever the victim of others' unjust actions. The young children who grew up in this atmosphere also learned what was important to remember and what was not. In this way, the nationalist narratives produced during the war continued to silence and quash alternative versions of the war and its aftermath.

Stuck in Time on the Eastern Shore

Not all silencing narratives are products of postwar politics, however. I discovered the same type of stories in the Eastern Shore of Maryland, located only two and a half hours by car from my home in Washington, DC. The events I was investigating had occurred over seventy years in the past when I began my research. I naïvely assumed that this was going to be "historical" research and that the events would no longer have any salience in the present. How wrong I was.

First Contact

On my first trip to the Lower Shore, comprised of Wicomico, Somerset, and Worcester counties, I felt like I had crossed an invisible line. Everything proclaimed me an "outsider," from my red compact car with DC license plates to my lack of local knowledge. My goal was to speak to anyone born before 1933, the year of the George Armwood lynching. My hope was that people of a certain age might remember the events or might have heard about them from adults around them as they were growing up. I had no idea how I would go about finding these people. I knew no one in the region and had no professional or personal contacts there.

In 2008, I took my first trip to Princess Anne, the site of the Armwood lynching. The downtown was quaint and compact. Graceful, large homes sat alongside churches, small shops, and a handful of government buildings. I parked my car and headed to the public library. The librarian who helped me locate materials was a thirty-something-year-old black woman. She was friendly and welcoming. I asked her to show me how to use the microfilm reader. I wanted to check out coverage of the lynching by the local newspaper that was in print at the time, the *Marylander and Herald*. She asked me what I was researching. I told her the Armwood lynching. She asked if I was family. I said I was not, but the question struck me. It seemed to imply that only family members would be interested in the Armwood case, as if outside researchers would not be. That was my interpretation at the time. Little did I know that nearly all history in the region is, in some way, family history.

As I began going through the microfilm, I encountered my first surprise. The lynching had taken place on a Wednesday (October 18, 1933). The *Marylander & Herald*, was a weekly that came out on Fridays. I located the October 20, 1933, issue and began scrolling. I was amazed by what I found. The first five pages of the edition were blank. I could not believe the very pages I needed were missing. Later, I made a trip to the Maryland State Archives in Annapolis. I was hoping that the state repository might have a different copy, but the same pages were missing. These empty, blanked out spaces seemed to be a metaphor for the lynching itself. As I learned later, the lynching did not figure in the history of the town or county that many local whites liked to tell. I was aware that communal silences can arise in many places for different reasons (Greene 2003). They are particularly common around violent events, where it might take decades or more for details to emerge (Carr 2006; Drakulić 2004, chap. 3; Phillips 2016; Schiff 2015; Tyson 2017). I was nevertheless surprised by this particular silence—in the very newspaper that was closest—socially and geographically—to the events.

As I moved beyond these missing pages, I began to understand what it meant to do history in the region. During my first official research trip a year later, I stopped at the Edward H. Nabb Research Center for Delmarva History and Culture (hereinafter the "Nabb Center"). (Delmarva is a combination of Delaware, Maryland, and Virginia, the three states that make up the Eastern Shore.) I noticed that most, if not all, visitors to the center were researching their family histories. For some families, their genealogies stretched back to the seventeenth century, when English settlers first arrived (Jones 2013).

For a few individuals, their interest in local history went beyond immediate family and even beyond the history of white residents to include that of black communities, businesses, landmarks, and individuals who had left their mark. This was the case with Linda Duyer, a local historian who had grown up in Salisbury.[1] I first met Linda after reading a flyer on the wall at the Nabb Center that advertised a series of talks on local, black history. At the bottom of the page was Linda's name and phone number. I promptly called and arranged to meet her later that day. As we talked, I was immediately struck by her deep knowledge and interest in all things local, from black cemeteries, churches, and schools to courthouses, neighborhoods, and small businesses. She was particularly interested in black history, which most local exhibits, walking tours, and books tended to relegate to a minimum of pages or overlook altogether.

Linda had written her own book on a black neighborhood in Salisbury called Georgetown, which was destroyed in stages in the 1940s and 1950s when the federal government built Route 13 and Highway 50, two major thoroughfares that literally ran through the neighborhood and, hence, destroyed it (Duyer 2007). The book was based on numerous oral histories Linda had conducted with former residents of Georgetown. Through these interviews, Linda developed close friendships with many of her participants and stayed in touch with them after the project ended.

Linda's relationships with older, black residents of Salisbury became a valuable asset to my own research, but I gained much more than contacts. She taught me to read both social and physical geographies. She took me on several driving tours of the region, which allowed me to see physical distances between towns, counties, houses, and neighborhoods. Through these tours, I became more familiar with the expanse of flat land, bordered by water to the east and west and crisscrossed by two-lane roads and narrow lanes that feature the family names of those who first populated the area. Daughertytown Road in Crisfield, for example, bears the family name of several men who worked in local law enforcement, including the Princess Anne Sheriff who was on duty the night a mob seized George Armwood from his jail cell [39Meth]. Other place names, such as "Queen Anne," "Kent," "Cecil," and "Somerset," evoke the first English settlers who arrived in the seventeenth century, while another set of names—"Wetipquin," "Nanticoke," "Tyaskin"—reference the Indian tribes that populated the region before the arrival of Europeans (Swain 1950; Wennersten 1992, 8).

Names also reflect the prominence of certain families, a legacy that endures to the present day (Ifill 2007). In every county, a handful of names pervades the social and physical landscape, from billboards advertising local businesses to membership rolls in historical societies, preservation groups, business associations, and school boards. In Wicomico County, for example, where the lynching of Matthew Williams took place, the names Pollitt, Handy, Dashield (also spelled Dashiell), and Outten are ubiquitous (Corddry 1981, 100). Matthew Williams was himself a Handy on his mother's side (Ifill 2007, 45). In Somerset County, the site of the George Armwood lynching, the names Dennis, Hayman, Pusey, and Cottman are everywhere. The winner of a high school essay contest who wrote about the Armwood lynching was a Pusey, for example. Many of these names are associated with black and white families, while a few are specific to white families only.

The people whom I interviewed were mostly in their eighties and nineties. I also talked to a few centenarians. All were mentally sharp when we met. Given their advanced age, my interviewees' lives constituted minihistories of their own. Some black interviewees were old enough to have had grandparents who were slaves or to have known former slaves when they were children (Smith 2008, 8). Most whites and blacks owned cars before they had electricity, indoor plumbing, or telephones. As children, they grew up picking strawberries and beans. As adults, they worked at gas stations, grocery stores, funeral homes, and restaurants. A few worked as watermen and farmers. Several had worked in sawmills. Some interviewees had only an elementary school education [Gold], while others had graduated from college, had obtained postgraduate degrees, and gone on to careers as educators and lawyers. All had grown up under Jim Crow, which structured childhood experiences for black and white alike at an early age (Ritterhouse 2006).

During interviews, many white participants used the terminology they had grown up with. One man, for example, talked about his father's boss who "jewed" him down. Others talked about poor white trash who had no morals, "Japs" during World War II, and "niggers" of all colors. I found people's use of such language, offensive as it was, oddly reassuring, for it indicated that they were not censuring how they talked to me. Indeed, one man seemed to revel in his use of derogatory language. He began our first conversation railing about "Japs" and how much he hated MacArthur, the famed World War II general.

It was my relationship with this particular interviewee that helped me to understand the contours of racism and race talk in this region. As historian Miles Barnes (2006, 19) points out, "Race relations in the South varied from state to state, county to county, doorstep to doorstep." Now I began to understand what he meant. Racism may have been a constant in the Eastern Shore (as in the rest of the country), but individuals, families, neighbors, and social circles could be racist in different ways. Baldly racist language and behavior, I suspected, lived alongside less racist attitudes and behavior—in the very same person. The same man who used "Jew" as a verb was also the only white interviewee who mentioned the kinds of indignities that Jim Crow forced onto black adults and children. The woman who referred to "Japs" also elected not to eat in the segregated cafeteria at her work place so she could have lunch with a black co-worker. I was not naïve about what these contradictions meant. They did not take away any of the privileges that whiteness bestowed on these men and women; nor did they inoculate black residents from the second-class treatment and limited opportunities imposed by Jim Crow. These contradictions did not erode the color line, but they pushed me to look more closely at the content of that line and the kinds of social forces that bent, buckled, and shaped it in various places.

Just as quickly as I learned about how race and racism operated on the Shore, I learned about another categorical distinction that seemed, in many ways, just as important, particularly to whites. People in the Eastern Shore make a clear distinction between people from the region and everyone else. The criteria that constitute a person as an "Eastern Shoreman" are quite strict. (The name is gender-neutral and applies to both men and women [Stewart 1990]). To be considered an Eastern Shoreman, one must be born on the Shore; otherwise, one is a "foreigner." The story that best illustrates this boundary rule is about a woman who happened to be born in Baltimore, because her parents had been passing through on their way home. A few days old, she arrived in the Eastern Shore and lived to be ninety-nine years old. When she died, her obituary read: "Baltimore woman dies in Princess Anne." Perhaps apocryphal, the story underscores the singular importance of birthright in determining who is and is not an Eastern Shoreman.

Eastern Shoremen are not only proud of their heritage; they can also be quite critical of those who move to the region from elsewhere. One term that expresses such displeasure is "come here." The term refers to those who "come here" (to the Eastern Shore) and want to change everything once they arrive. The term's very existence points to the importance of keeping things as they are and resisting efforts at change, particularly by outsiders. During fieldwork, discussions about whether a person was a "come here" sometimes sparked laughter. For example, Linda and I went to interview a white couple in their early nineties. We began by talking about Ed, the man who suggested we talk to them. Ed had lived in the area eight years and his grandparents were from Somerset county. The wife immediately commented that people like Ed "come here and want to change everything." Linda then asked if she would be considered a "come here" because she was not born on the Shore, although she had lived there since she was two years old. The husband chimed in, "Where were your grandparents buried? That's what determines if you're a 'come here' or not." Linda replied that one set was buried in Chestertown (Kent County, also on the Eastern Shore) and the other off the Shore. The husband quipped, "So you're half and half!"

Like most jokes, the underlying issue of who constitutes an Eastern Shoreman belied a very real suspicion of and disdain for outsiders that many white locals harbored. Part of that disdain may have come from a belief that "foreigners"—another term locals used to refer to people who had move to the region—did not have a stake in protecting the reputation of the town, county, or the Shore regardless of how long they had lived there. And because they had no stake in doing so, they had no reason to remain silent about topics that some believed should be kept under wraps. By contrast, many local whites were heavily invested in maintaining a narrative that omitted inconvenient truths and silenced other possible versions of past events.

Guarding the Past

Indeed, one of the first stories I heard was about Dr. Polly Stewart, a former professor at Salisbury State, a local university. By the time I began my research, she had already retired and had moved back to Utah. The story concerned an incident that occurred in the 1980s, when she received an invitation to give the keynote address at the annual meeting of the Wicomico Historical Society. Stewart had been a professor at Salisbury State for ten years at that point, so she was well aware of the honor the invitation bestowed. In addition, she considered many in the audience to be her friends. For her keynote, she chose to talk about a concept she was developing called "regional consciousness." She intended to use the concept to explain the lynching of George Armwood. Nothing prepared Stewart for what happened next, however.

> Everybody in the audience stopped listening as soon as I said "Princess Anne lynching"—about halfway through the talk—and spent the rest of the time getting ready for assault. Years afterward it is still hard to write about this. I was hurt and mystified at the vehemence of their reaction, horrified at the irrationality of their anger. These people were my friends, and they were turning on me. (Stewart 1990, 87)

Time did not heal any wounds. Stewart's longtime friends and colleagues neither forgave nor forgot. She summed up the painful encounter by pointing to her own misstep of overlooking the very norms she herself had been trying to analyze: "Had I not ignored two key points in the theory of regional consciousness—that it applies universally in a region by crossing all class and educational lines, and that it operates without reference to reason—I could have avoided so egregious a blunder. But I misjudged my audience and became, in their eyes, yet another

outsider telling local people what was what" (Stewart 1990, 87). Stewart had violated the most important rule on the Shore—so basic that locals never saw a need
to articulate it explicitly—that "foreigners" had no right to talk about the region's
past, especially events that might besmirch the county's reputation.

People's anger toward Stewart did not abate over time. More than ten years
later, in the early 2000s, law professor Sherrilyn Ifill (2007, 137–39) was researching her own book on racial violence on the Eastern Shore. During one research
trip, she was conversing with a man who was helping her locate photos. Ifill, a
black woman, made it a practice to bring up the lynchings whenever she met
whites of a certain age. She mentioned casually that she had heard there had
been a couple lynchings in the area. The man confirmed there had been two in
the early 1930s. He then went on, with no prompting from Ifill, to tell the story
of Stewart's talk. He himself was a member of the Wicomico Historical Society
and had been at the talk. He had considered Stewart a friend, yet painted a picture
of her committing an unforgivable act. According to his account, Stewart made
the mistake of not sticking to the "facts" and instead, blamed "all whites" for the
lynching. Ifill was struck by the "vehemence" with which the man relayed this
story; his anger was still palpable nearly twenty years later.

This practice of collective silencing arose in other public domains as well. In
1993, George W. Roache Jr., the only black columnist for the local newspaper in
Salisbury, wrote a series on the Matthew Williams lynching that had taken place
in that town on December 4, 1931. Roache wrote for the *Daily Times*, which in
the 1930s was called the *Salisbury Times*. In 1931, the paper refused to cover the
Williams lynching at all. Instead, the editor issued a "statement" that called the
lynching a "demonstration" and claimed that the facts were so "well known [that]
a repetition of them would be superfluous" ("A Statement" 1931).

Sixty-two years later, in 1993, Roache was revisiting these supposedly well-
known facts in a series of columns. He began by telling readers the many sources
he had consulted. Linda had provided him with copies from her extensive newspaper file. He did additional reading on his own. From his perusal of these materials, he paints a detailed and gruesome picture of the lynching. The mob, he
writes, did not just hang Williams but pulled his body up and down as it hung
from a tree in front of the courthouse. The mob then dragged the body to an
empty lot, filled up five-gallon cans with gasoline, and burned it. As a last act
of desecration, the mob tied Williams's body to the back of a truck and drove it
"back down Main Street" (1993a, b).

Judging by the response of some readers, Roache, like Polly Stewart, may have
broken a long-standing taboo against talking about such events in public. One
angry reader wrote a letter excoriating Roache. The letter writer, a local man
named Jerome W. Banks (1993), relies on his own memory of events "to correct

some of [Roache's] statements." Banks goes on to present the critical details he feels were missing from Roache's account. The first is the case of "Ewell [*sic*] Lee," who, Banks claims, murdered a white family of four but was defended in court by Communist outsiders, which made local people unhappy. "Now, another murder! People were incensed," he writes. He goes on to pin the blame for the lynching of Matthew Williams on outsiders from Delaware. He states as fact that Williams had murdered the elder Elliott and that the governor had made matters worse by sending National Guardsmen "to raid homes in the dead of night, to kidnap lynch suspects." Banks ends by insisting that Roache should not "delve into history" unless he is ready to proffer all the facts, including, he adds, a *rumor* that the Communist Party had paid Williams "$500 to commit the act [of murdering his employer]" and that other business leaders were "scheduled for like treatment."

What is remarkable about the letter is the free-flow of "facts," "counterfacts," and conspiracy theories that animate Banks's rejoinder to Roache's columns. Banks's notion of "facts" even includes unsubstantiated gossip about the lynching victim having consorted with the Community Party. Banks does not sound like he is writing in 1993, but in 1933. For Banks, the lynching of Williams is much less important than the larger political injustices that took place as a result of the event. The *real* wrong, according to his letter, is that outsiders had interfered in local matters. This was the outrage on which Roache should have focused.

The story would be notable if it ended there, but it does not. Seventeen years later, Linda Duyer had just published her book on the black neighborhood of Georgetown, that was adjacent to the area of the courthouse where the mob lynched Matthew Williams. A local reporter wrote a piece on the book and asked Linda about the rumor that it was Elliott's own son who shot him and not Williams. After the article came out, a descendant of the murdered Elliott called Linda and asked her to come to the family home. Linda agreed. The descendant politely acknowledged how horrible the lynching was, but quickly added that hearsay within the family had Williams committing a theft that day, the act that presumably motivated the killing of Elliott. The descendant then moved the conversation to his real concern, which was the lingering suspicion of the son's guilt in shooting Elliott. Linda insisted that the information she provided George Roache was based not only on her copious and careful reading of the newspaper coverage, but also from interviews she had conducted for her project on Georgetown as well as other accounts. The descendant pressed Linda for proof of her version and persisted in telling Linda how much the "incident" had adversely affected his family over generations.[2]

All these incidents reveal quite a bit about what many whites saw was at stake in telling the story one way and not another, even sixty years after the fact. This was not a contest between competing versions, but rather a way of talking about the lynching that made the brutal murder of an unarmed black man all but irrelevant to the story. I learned two important lessons from these stories. First, far from being "in the past," the lynchings in Salisbury and Princess Anne and the near lynching of Euel Lee in Worcester County were very much in the present. Second, all local history was highly personal and therefore, worth fighting to defend at all costs. For many whites on the Shore, history was a cherished relic that many held dear—not out of sentimentality, but out of pride. This sense of ownership of the past produced a stubborn determination to control its telling and retelling. Linda's experience of being "summoned" (my word, not hers) to the Elliott home and the letter excoriating columnist Roache for his "misuse" of history to the treatment of Polly Stewart by members of a local historical society were all evidence of this pattern. Many local whites claimed singular authority over who could tell stories about the past and what the content of those stories could be. Violating that unspoken "rule" invited swift censure, attack, and even ostracism.

I had my own experience with this policing of the past when I began interviews nearly thirty years after Polly Stewart gave her "controversial" talk. One of the first people whom I contacted was a woman whose great grandfather had been a local official in Somerset County in the 1930s. Though the woman no longer lived in Princess Anne, she maintained strong ties to the county and remained active in the local historical society. When I called to ask if she would agree to be interviewed, she rebuffed me with a stern lecture. "I don't know why anyone would want to write a book on that," she said authoritatively. She then added, "We are trying to build bridges with the African-American community." She overpronounced "African-American" as if she was trying to show me how racially sensitive she was, perhaps to fend off the idea that there was or still is racism in the county. "I don't know why anyone would want to write a book on violence," she continued. "No one is going to want to talk to you about that." I told her that my area of expertise was political violence so that was why I was researching the lynching. That quieted her for a moment. She pushed ahead: "I don't have any stories or family secrets." I told her that my aim was not to unearth secrets, but to learn about her family's history. I explained that by asking people about their families, I learned who was connected to whom (a strategy I developed during research for my first book, *Killing Neighbors*). I tried to reassure her that this was no witch hunt and that I was not out to tarnish her family's good name. Each time I tried to reassure her, she doubled down, insisting that she had nothing to tell. She loved Somerset County and did not want to talk ill of it.[3]

The vehemence of her refusal taught me how sensitive the lynchings remained for certain local whites, particularly those from prominent families who seemed to have the biggest stake in protecting their family name as well as the county as a whole, as if a stain on one was a blemish on the other. I also began to see that the passage of time did not provide distance or perspective, but instead had solidified an unspoken rule among local whites—that no one, especially outsiders, should talk badly about their community. Indeed, it was not for naught that Somerset County's motto was *Semper Eadem*, which means "never change" (Wennersten 1992). This protective stance never extended to the black community, however. The same whites who were so quick to defend the reputation of long dead family members did not hesitate to talk about the lynching victims (including Euel Lee) as guilty of the crimes they were accused of, as if the victims' alleged guilt exonerated the thousands of whites who participated in their brutal torture-murders. These narratives, in short, not only maintained a protective buffer around white culpability for past lynchings, they also preserved a view of lynching victims as responsible for their own murders.

Authoritarian Constraints in Rwanda

Not all silencing narratives are the product of communal norms around controlling narratives of the past. In Rwanda, the source of silencing is the government. The RPF, led by Paul Kagame, has been in power since the rebel army overthrew the genocidal regime and forced its leaders (and millions of ordinary Rwandans fearful of retribution) into exile. Since taking power in July 1994, the RPF has developed ever more sophisticated ways of silencing dissent, criticism, and any alternative way of viewing the regime, the country, or the country's complex political history that predates the RPF.

Technologies of Silencing

The main technique the government uses to police what people say and do is surveillance. The regime monitors its own population as well as foreigners, whether they are living in country or abroad. It goes after any individual or organization that challenges the story the regime likes to tell about itself (Pottier 2002). The "official" narrative is that the RPF, under Paul Kagame's leadership, single-handedly stopped the genocide as the international community dallied and dithered; it is also Kagame who brought prosperity and order to the country in the years since. In this official story, the RPF is the one and only hero and those who say otherwise—be they journalists, scholars, human rights groups, or diplomats—are the villains. In this the RPF operates like Serb nationalists in the RS except that the RPF's goal is not to promote nationalist ideas of Rwandanness, but rather to garner and coerce unmitigated support for Kagame as hero, savior, and leader of the new Rwanda.

The attacks on detractors and critics take multiple forms. In the case of scholars who dare to criticize the regime, regime stalwarts publicly defame the person and attack his or her credibility.[4] For example, after the publication of an edited volume entitled *Remaking Rwanda: State Building and Human Rights after Mass Violence*, regime proponents created a website that accused the book's editors, Scott Straus and Lars Waldorf, both highly respected and long-time experts on Rwanda, of fabrication and shoddy research. At conferences that feature any panel on Rwanda, Rwandans are always on hand to attack the scholars in person. Character assassination is the weapon of choice. At a conference on the History of Human Rights at the University of Chicago in 2015, for example, organizers included one panel on Rwanda. Just as the panel was starting, three Rwandans, who had not been attending the conference until that moment, entered the room and sat down. After the panelists had finished and the moderator opened up the floor to questions, all three raised their hands. The first accused Filip Reyntjens, one of the foremost experts on Rwanda, of working for the Habyarimana government (the regime in power when the genocide began). The second accused Reyntjens of helping to write the constitution that caused the genocide. The third hurled yet another, similarly outrageous charge. Reyntjens calmly replied that all the accusations were completely unfounded. He went on to say how predictable the attacks had become. "I knew what you were going to say before you said it," he remarked matter-of-factly. While Reyntjens was nonplussed by the aggressiveness of the three Rwandans, conference organizers were so alarmed they called campus security. Predictably, the three left after the panel was over, their mission of public denouncement accomplished.

Another tactic the regime uses to control what researchers say or write about the regime is to bar individuals from the country. Filip Reyntjens became persona non grata in 1995, when he published a brief "memo expressing concern" about the RPF governing style shortly after the rebel army took over power (Reyntjens 2015). In 1997, the government followed suit by banning Gérard Prunier. In 2008, the regime even prevented Alison Des Forges, the tireless human rights advocate who served as an expert witness at ICTR trials of the genocide's main architects, from entering the country on two separate occasions. The reason was most likely her continued insistence that the RPF be held accountable for the war crimes it committed during and after the war and her determination to expose continuing human rights abuses by all parties, including the regime.

In addition to foreign scholars, journalists have also been targets of the RPF smear campaigns or worse. Reyntjens (2015) and Sundaram (2016) both list a number of foreign journalists who have been expelled from the country. Shortly after barring Prunier in 1997, for example, the government "evicted" Reuters writer Christian Jennings, then a few months later, Stephen Smith, a writer for *Libération* (Reyntjens 2015, 125). The government later excoriated *Le Soir* for its "frenetic anti-Tutsi racism" and then went after Belgian journalist Colette Braeckman (Reyntjens 2015). In 2005, the government arrested and tried Father Guy Theunis, the editor of the Catholic newspaper, *Dialogue*. It also banned the Kinyarwanda version of BBC when it aired an interview with a Rwandan who claimed that many bodies found floating in Lake Victoria in 1994 were not victims of génocidaires but rather of the RPF (Reyntjens 2015, 126). Those whom the government expels from the country tend to be the most knowledgeable and hence, the most critical of the regime's flagrant use of violence to control the population's "sightlines" as well as those of the international community. Its pursuit of domestic newspapers and journalists is equally unrelenting. The regime has shut down small, local newspapers and jailed, tortured, and disappeared Rwandan journalists for saying the "wrong" things (Sundaram 2016).

The RPF's style of governing borders on the totalitarian, whereby the state seeks to dominate public as well as private space. As one convicted génocidaire explained to Sundaram: "In this kind of country, we don't know where the state ends and where we begin" (Sundaram 2016). The RPF's success at stamping out any and all independent thought has transformed the population into an extension of the state, whereby ordinary Rwandans serve as tentacles that extend the state's reach into the bodies and minds of every denizen.

Culture of Indirectness

Authoritarian surveillance is nothing new to Rwandans born before 1994. The population developed its own strategies for living under the watchful eye of the state long before the RPF took power. Under Habyarimana, the administrative hierarchy penetrated all the way down to the head of ten households, making the state a constant presence in people's daily lives. Local officials monitored people's comings and goings, communal work assignments, and moves to and from a given administrative unit.

In order to avoid or minimize the gaze of the state, Rwandans have relied on two main strategies. Both arose during casual conversations as well as formal interviews. The first is indirectness. Rather than saying what they think, Rwandans—especially those from the center of the country—talk in ambiguous language. Édouard Kabagema, an agriculturalist who worked in Butare before the genocide, commented on this trait in his memoir. A woman in Butare was trying to warn him to flee before the violence descended on the region, but her manner of doing so was so indirect as to be inscrutable: "When I arrived at her house, she started to talk to me in an offhanded fashion, dancing around the subject to make me figure out what she was really saying. I don't like this indirect way that Rwandans talked and I started to get ready to leave when she told me to stay a bit longer" (Kabagema 2001, 17–18). Kabagema was from Gitarama, a province in central Rwanda, where people had a reputation for talking in ambiguous ways, and yet, even he grew impatient with the woman's way of talking. Only through her insistence that he stay did he realize she had something important to tell him. She was trying to warn him to flee.

The second cultural trait is related to the first. Rwandans value keeping emotions inside, whether joy or sorrow, anger or regret, or any sentiment whatsoever. Whereas American culture considers outward expressions of emotion to be desirable and for the most part, healthy, Rwandans value just the opposite—emotive impenetrability. To show one's emotions on the outside is to act like a child or someone out of control. As Jennie Burnet (2012, 6) explains: "Rwandan culture admires people who master their emotions and who always show a calm exterior." Claudine Vidal (2005, 36) concurs: "One never gives in to one's emotions in public and never shows one's agitation."

Both traits—indirectness and lack of emotion—were noticeable during interviews I did in Ngali. One particular exchange typified both tendencies. I was interviewing a prisoner who had been sentenced to life for his participation during the genocide in 2011. At our first trip to the prison where he was held, we met him for the first time. He agreed to be interviewed. We talked in a corner of the central courtyard, out of earshot of other prisoners, visitors, staff, and guards. When I asked him if he had confessed, he said he had but offered little detail. (This was a question I asked all prisoners, not because I thought confessing indicated guilt, but to ascertain where in the release process they were. It was a cruel irony that prisoners who refused to confess because they maintained their innocence had no way to obtain release from prison; this led many who had not confessed in 2004 to confess later, even to acts they had not committed, just to obtain release.)

> *Did you ever confess?*
> I confessed.
>
> *What did you confess to having done?*
> To having participated in different *ibitero* [attack groups].
>
> *Is it true that you participated in different ibitero?*
> I can't lie because I promised you I'd tell you the truth. [Aug 2011]

The lack of detail was not unusual. Like many other prisoners I had interviewed, he began by saying he would tell us—my interpreter and me—the truth, but then talked in the vaguest of terms. This style of indirectness allowed him to say all the right things (e.g., "I promised to tell you the truth") but without telling us anything at all. Emotionally, he betrayed very little as well—not fear, remorse, anger, or any other emotion a man in his situation might feel. When we returned on subsequent occasions, he declined our request for another interview, each time through an intermediary who would inform us he was with his prayer group so he was unavailable to meet. This was his way of telling us the conversation was over.

Despite this culture of indirectness, I learned quite a bit more that I had not known in 2004, even after finishing *Killing Neighbors*. Two experiences were particularly informative. The first involved becoming acquainted with the social geography of Ngali. Most of the prisoners I had interviewed in prison in 2004 had been released by the time I returned to Rwanda in 2008 and 2009. I was now visiting former prisoners in their homes. Walking from one house to another let me see how close many were to one another. One could easily go from one house to the next in a few minutes. Some houses were even within shouting range of others. Given the clustered proximity of certain dwellings, it would have been fairly easy to mobilize many men at the same time. Physical closeness would have made it difficult for anyone reluctant to join the *ibitero* (attack groups) to opt out and stay at home. The groups needed only to knock on the door or yell as they passed by to pressure people to join. Indeed, such pressures could be exerted across several households at once through the group's sheer size and noise, which those inside could not have helped but hear and feel.

The other insight I gained was about new incentives that had emerged to tell stories one way and not another. In 2004, I tried to be mindful of consensus narratives among prisoners because they had been locked up together for so long. What I had not anticipated, however, was that being out of prison would create new incentives for revising old stories—that is, those prisoners had recounted in 2004. The reason was simple: former prisoners were trying to avoid rearrest. To win release, all had had to confess. Prisoners approached confessions strategically. Inside the prisons, many bought and sold their confessions; even those on the outside participated in this marketplace to avoid rearrest or going to prison at all (Tertsakian 2008). One prisoner claimed that patterns of imprisonment were a function of who was able to pay off judges and accusers. Those who had the money remained free, while those who did not remained in prison or vulnerable to rearrest and additional prison time.

The threat of being arrested and sent back to prison was very real. One prisoner whom I had interviewed in 2004 had been released in 2007 after thirteen years in prison. By 2009, he was back in prison, having been rearrested on new charges [interview, July 28, 2011]. He was still in prison when I made another trip to Rwanda in December 2011. A different prisoner whom I had also known since 2004 had been arrested three times. The first occurred in 1994. He was freed in 1999 but a year later, authorities rearrested him. He was released again in 2007. Two years later, authorities arrested him a third time and sentenced him to an additional ten years on top of the thirteen he had already served [interview, Aug. 8, 2011].

I did not doubt that money did play a role in who managed to stay out of prison. Money also seemed to shape who escaped new accusations. One interviewee (a genocide survivor) told me that there were no rape cases in his community because accusers and accused had made side deals, whereby the accused paid the accuser not to press charges.

Just as money could keep matters out of the public eye, personal grievances could also lead to certain ex-detainees being reimprisoned. One prisoner whom I interviewed in 2004, for example, was still in prison in 2008 when I returned to Rwanda, I asked him why he was still there when all the other prisoners from Ngali had been released the previous year. He said it was because of new charges leveled against him. A woman had accused him of having raped her during the genocide. I immediately thought of a neighbor whom he and his siblings had hid during the genocide. I asked if it was the same woman. He said yes. I probed some more, believing there must be a longer back story that might shed light on why this woman had accused him of raping her. (I did not know whether the rape charge was true or not, but I had my doubts.) The story came out in pieces. It turned out that he had multiple ties to this woman that predated the genocide. She was not just a "neighbor." She had had a child with the younger brother of a close friend. I could not ascertain what her actual motive was but I suspected it had more to do with the complicated ties the two had shared before the genocide than what had happened while he hid her.

This state of affairs shaped my research in a significant way. It meant that far from providing additional details to the stories they had told me in 2004, some former prisoners were now denying what they had said in those earlier interviews. In one case, for example, I asked a former prisoner about a story he related in 2004 about a man who had raped and killed a prominent woman in the community. In 2009, when I brought up the story again to find out what had happened to the rapist, the former prisoner protested vehemently: "I never said that. I never said that." His denials had the opposite effect he intended. They made me trust the original story more, not less. I tended to discount these later, revised versions because these former prisoners had too many reasons to maintain a narrative that ensured they stayed out of prison. In these cases, I also gave less credence to their stories because I assumed they were heavily modulated by political constraints. This experience also taught me that silencing narratives operated at all levels of society—not only among RPF stalwarts who policed for-eign journalists and scholars, but also among ordinary people, including prison-ers, ex-prisoners, and neighbors who also worked hard at *not* saying the "wrong" things because the consequences could be quite severe. At the very local level, silencing narratives took the form of ever changing stories colored and shaped by payoffs, side deals, fears of rearrest, and new accusations—not by the regime in Kigali, but by other neighbors.

Research about the past is always, at the same time, about the present. Under-standing the gravitational pull of silencing narratives and the source of their cen-tripetal force helps to deepen and expand our analytics. In all three research sites, I encountered silencing narratives. These were not simply consensus stories that people circulated long after the fact. These were stories that continually silenced other possible accounts. That is, they were political in their content and power-ful in their disciplining effects on people at all levels of society. They not only promoted a specific understanding of events; they also foreclosed other possible versions. In many cases, that was their raison d'être.

Silencing narratives are about narrowing observers' sightlines—blocking out what outsiders see and foregrounding a version of events that valorizes certain characters, highlights certain events, while rendering others irrelevant. In Bosnia, interviews in Republika Srpska revealed a nationalist outlook that still held sway in the region. The physical violence had ended but nationalist ways of talking endured, which valorized the "Serbs" and demonized all those critical of nation-alist politics. In Maryland, silencing narratives emerged from communal norms within a specific community—in this case local whites. These stories served to guard against alternative readings of the past by refocusing the outrage on the supposedly more outrageous "crime" of outsiders meddling in local affairs. In Rwanda, silencing narratives were part of the RPF's strategy to squelch any and all dissent and to promote its own heroic place in an imagined history. It was also about navigating local life in the hills, where keeping quiet was the best strategy for former prisoners to avoid rearrest.

In all three contexts, silencing narratives summarily removed all blame—and any responsibility—for acts of past violence. In Bosnia, nationalist narratives promoted "Serbs" as the victim and every act of violence committed in the name of Greater Serbia as a heroic attempt at "self-defense." In Maryland, narratives of past lynchings cast all blame on outsiders, thereby exonerating all local whites in extensive violence against unarmed black victims. In Rwanda, the RPF promotes stories of the war that paint the RPF as hero and any detractors as enemies and villains. In all three cases, the actual victims of atrocities, mass killings, lynch-ings, and desecration are nowhere to be found. Their place in the story has been removed from view, because their very existence challenges the very substance and focus of the silencing narratives. Challenging these stories means recognizing them for what they were: assertions of power that relate as much to present politics as they do to past events. What they reveal are the stakes of acknowledging and telling a version that implicates so-called "heroes" in unspeakable crimes and turns these so-called "victims" into perpetrators of the worst kind.

SIDESHOW

What is being carved in human flesh is an image of society.

—Mary Douglas, *Purity and Danger*

I tell myself that in the slogans of the genocide thinkers, there was no instruction booklet. The person who decided to make a barrier out of his naked mutilated body, he came up with that idea all on his own, he wasn't told to do so.

—José Kagabo, "Après le Génocide"

One of the most obvious contrasts between the Armwood lynching and the main attractions in Bosnia and Rwanda is the extent of extralethal violence. Extralethal violence refers to "physical acts committed face-to-face that transgress shared norms and beliefs about appropriate treatment of the living as well as the dead" (Fujii 2013, 411). Such violence often appears to be gratuitous or inexplicable, yet is anything but. In the previous chapter, only one of three main attractions (the Armwood lynching) featured high levels of extralethal violence, but such displays also took place during the Bosnian war and Rwanda genocide. Their audiences were smaller and more select but the violence was no less deadly and the effects no less transformative. Like the lynching of Armwood, these sideshows enabled willing participants to become part of something bigger than themselves; they also pulled all comers to the show, no matter their level of volition, reluctance, or revulsion.

To explain the sideshows of violence in Bosnia and Rwanda, I proffer two types of accounts, the first focuses on the particular and the second gestures toward the general. In Bosnia and Rwanda, the sideshows were less about larger projects of nationalist takeover or genocidal extermination, and more about personal relationships and individuals. In Rwanda, one particular display amplified the personal power of a local leader far beyond the bureaucratic authority bestowed by his position as bourgmestre. In Bosnia, extralethal displays, both banal and sensational, enabled actors to transform themselves. In one of the most notorious of all incidents, the lead actor used elaborate forms of sexual torture to destroy not just bodies, but bonds.

At a more general level, the logic driving these scenes of extralethal violence was aesthetic, not strategic. Like the main attractions analyzed in chapter 3, these displays were not a means to a larger goal; they were ends in themselves. Actors' primary concern was to attain a certain "look and feel" through staging the violence a particular way. Actors trained their sights on producing visual, aural, and emotional effects that shocked, titillated, and pleased those watching. In doing so, they continually generated opportunities for participants to insert themselves— vocally, emotionally, and bodily—into the action.

In the discussion below, I focus on sideshows that took place at the Omarska prison camp in Bosnia, drawing on testimonies from the trials of Dušan Tadić and Miroslav Kvočka, Milojica Kos, Mladjo Radić, and Zoran Žigić at the ICTY. I begin by contrasting these more extensive and regular displays to singular, one-time displays that a local bourgmestre in Rwanda staged. For purposes of brevity and scope, I do not examine all forms of extralethal violence that occurred during the wars and mass killings in Bosnia and Rwanda. For example, I do not analyze the mass gang rapes that took place in both countries; nor do I claim that what happened at Omarska or Ngali was representative of patterns across either country, though in some instances, I point to evidence that suggests what occurred at Omarska also took place elsewhere. My aim is to privilege depth over breadth—that is, to gain a deeper understanding of the meanings behind specific extralethal displays and the meaning-centered logics that drove them.

Show of Power in Rural Rwanda

In and around Ngali, sideshows were not the norm. Part of the reason was the general edict to kill quickly that genocide leaders promoted across the country. Participants heeded these orders and slaughtered at a shocking rate. One factor that contributed to the fast pace was that those fleeing often sought refuge in central locations, such as churches, schools, hospitals, and government buildings.[1] Organizers also lured Tutsi to such places because concentrating people in one spot made the task of mass killing easier. The results were deadly. In two parishes in Kibuye Province, for example, "the bulk of the killing around Bigihu and Kirinda was finished within a few days" (Longman 2011a, 291). At a church in Karama in Butare Province, killers managed to slaughter between seventeen thousand and forty thousand people at a single location (Des Forges 1999, 288–89).

A second factor that contributed to the rapid rate of killing was the removal of any official who tried to prevent violence. The préfet of Butare, for example, preached calm in the wake of the plane crash that killed the president. To jump start the killings, the interim government removed him on April 17, 1994, and installed a genocide-friendly replacement. Local authorities then made a point of showing their support for the genocide by killing quickly. In Cyahinda commune, for example, the bourgmestre pressed for massive killing "as if they had to hurry to catch up in order to meet the goals of the extermination campaign" (Des Forges 1999, 488).

The pace of the genocide did not necessarily obviate the use of extralethal violence. In the commune where Ngali is located, the bourgmestre, Joseph, seemed to have a penchant for extralethal violence [interviews, June 2004; December 2011].[2] He was an early and eager supporter of the genocide. He began dressing the part by sporting military attire, despite his status as a civilian [interview, December 2011]; he likely obtained a gun during this period as well [interview, June 2009]. In addition to organizing his commune for genocide; he also staged scenes of extralethal violence. These scenes were akin to one-man shows; they showcased Joseph as the undisputed (local) star of the genocide (Fujii 2013).

In one particularly brazen incident, he lured two young women to his house under the pretext of keeping them safe. (He had used the same ruse with other Tutsi, whom he turned over to some Interahamwe who killed them all.) Instead of protecting the women, he held them captive inside his home and allowed men to come to the house and rape them. Joseph likely took his turn raping the women as well. A few days later, he had the two killed and their nude, splayed bodies displayed in the town center, where everyone would be forced to see what no one should ever see (Fujii 2013).

This extralethal display had transformative effects. By positioning their bodies in a lurid, sexualized pose, he stripped the women not only of their dignity as persons but also their worth and standing as young, unmarried women. Through the display, the two became *objects* of horror and fascination, their bodies now available for public "consumption"—the viewing and gazing by one and all. Those who glanced or saw the bodies on display were instantly cast as spectators in Joseph's one-man show.

Joseph's penchant for extralethal violence emerged in other moments as well but the meanings were different. In one incident, Joseph was going around saying that "if anyone brings me the head of [a prominent, local businessman and personal enemy of Joseph], I will pay him." When he learned that someone else had already killed the man, Joseph went to see the body for himself. On seeing the corpse, he took out his gun and shot at it [fieldnotes and interview, June 2009]. He also ordered Jude, the genocide leader for Ngali, to cut off the heads of specific victims after killing them [interview, June 2009]. What was the reason for cutting off the heads of the dead, I asked one interviewee who knew both men. Why was it not enough to kill the victims? The answer came as a surprise. "It was not enough for him to kill them and leave them," he explained. "He [Joseph] thought they would come back to life. It's why he would cut off the heads of the dead bodies." Unlike the display of the dead girls' bodies, these decapitations seemed to have been less about transgressing shared norms and more about Joseph's determination to vanquish social and political rivals once and for all.

The extralethal violence that took place in Ngali seems to have been Joseph's own doing and not the result of orders from superiors. Many progenocide officials did not spend time putting violence on display. Jude, for example, saw killing as mere prelude to profit. His focus was on looting victims' property. Joseph, by contrast, saw the genocide as an opportunity to make himself into something more than he already was. By going beyond the pale, Joseph became more than just another génocidaire in a larger machinery of violence. By organizing the serial rape and display of the two women's nude, splayed bodies, he amplified his own personal power well beyond the political authority bestowed by his position as bourgmestre.

Repertoires of Brutality at Omarska (Bosnia)

In Bosnia, extralethal displays took a very different form than Joseph's one-man shows. A series of concentration camps, prisons, and detention centers provided a ready-made stage. These venues came equipped with a "captive" audience that included both prisoners and guards. The displays were much more systematic and pervasive than in Rwanda. Some occurred so regularly, they became ritualized. Others were more elaborate, with one incident standing out from all the rest.

In northwest Bosnia, known as "Krajina," takeover began on April 29–30, 1992 (Sivac-Bryant 2016, 3; Wesselingh and Vaulerin 2005, 21). At Hambarine, Kozarac, Kevljani, Biščani, Sanski Most, Ključ, and countless other small towns and villages outside Prijedor, Bosnian Serb forces used heavy weapons and terror tactics to establish full control. In a few places, local residents (including some Serbs) tried to mount a defense but the Bosnian Serb army quickly quashed these meager attempts at resistance. As part of the takeover, Serb paramilitaries, JNA soldiers, and local police separated all non-Serb men from the women and transported many of the male prisoners to three prison camps—Keraterm, Trnopolje, and Omarska—all located within close proximity to the town of Prijedor. The putative purpose of the camps was to detain non-Serb men of fighting age. Most of the prisoners were Muslim and Croat, but a small number of Serb men and non-Serb women were also among the detainees [Tad 3701, 3703, 3760–61].[3]

The conditions in the camps harkened back to another time and place. Food was scare, hygiene nonexistent, and medical care lacking. Beatings and torture, on the other hand, were abundant. Journalist Roy Gutman (1993) first broke the story of the camps in dispatches for the *Daily News*. A British television crew from ITN broadcast the first pictures of emaciated prisoners standing behind a barbed wire fence at Trnopolje. Not since the liberation of Nazi death camps in 1945 had images of the barely living so shocked the world. It was at these camps in Bosnia where guards, soldiers, commanders, and paramilitaries enacted both banal and exotic forms of extralethal violence—all out of range of prying eyes. The tortures were so extreme that when refugees crossed the border into Croatia, their stories sounded unbelievable to the journalists who interviewed them (Silber and Little 1997, 244).

The Usual and Habitual

Before the violent takeover of the region, Omarska had been a working mine. Despite its transformation into a wartime concentration camp, much of the work at Omarska remained routine. Guards worked twelve-hour shifts from 7:00 a.m. to 7:00 p.m. and 7:00 p.m. to 7:00 a.m., with a day off in between. Three shifts rotated throughout the week; each shift had its own leader. The prisoners quickly learned which shifts and guards were the most dangerous. All who testified at the ICTY agreed that the most brutal shift was number 3, that of Mladjo Radić, nicknamed Krkan [Kv 2818, 3141, 3576]. Krkan's group was so notorious that prisoners called it the "terror shift" (Hukanović 1996, 80).

A repertoire of violence also became routine. The sheer repetition of these daily displays ensured that every person working at the camp would be cast on a regular basis, whether they wanted to be or not. Beatings began as soon as prisoners arrived, for example. After the prisoners alighted from the vehicles, guards forced them to stand with three fingers above their heads while they searched and beat them. The three fingers (thumb, index, and middle finger) represented the Serb nationalist hand gesture. This ritual was the prisoners' introduction to camp life.

The beatings continued throughout the day. Guards beat prisoners as they ran to and from the canteen to receive their only meal of the day; to and from the toilet, and to and from "interrogation" (more below). Guards beat the prisoners with every possible object, from rubber truncheons to baseball bats and metal pipes. They also kicked and punched the captives with their hands and feet, often targeting the most vulnerable parts of the body, such as the head and kidneys. These daily acts of terrorizing prisoners were as much about performing for one another as they were about keeping the prisoners in their place. In this way, every space within the camp was a stage for *being seen* putting violence on display. And indeed, being seen was the point, for any guard not seen participating in the beatings was quickly removed from the camp and sent to the front.

The social intimacy between prisoners and guards did not act as a buffer, but added to the brutality. Many guards and prisoners knew each other from school, work, or the neighborhood where they grew up together (Pervanić 1999, 62–63). This intimacy operated as a source of terror, bringing out the worst in those guards intent on settling old scores, showing off for others, or both. Opportunities were rife. Even those who did not work at the camp could visit at any time and do as they chose. As Rezak Hukanović (1996, 68) recalls, Omarska was "open to all Serb volunteers who had one of 'their' people there—a prisoner on whom they wanted to vent their rage for one reason or another. Such prisoners were usually their next-door neighbors." If that person was not there for any reason, the perpetrator looked for a relative or acquaintance instead (Pervanić 1999, 65–66, 156–57). In other words, looking for a particular person became an occasion for putting violence on display, especially for those visitors who enjoyed showing off, such as Duško Tadić and his men (see below).

In a few instances, prior social ties did bring momentary respite from the violence, as when a former neighbor shared a cigarette or even refrained from killing his victim outright. In one incident, for example, a notorious guard named Nikica Janjić was beating a prisoner nearly to death when he suddenly stopped and exclaimed, "My mother has sworn me not to kill you and that is why I changed my mind." With that, Janjić stopped the beating, gave his former neighbor a few cigarettes (which served as valuable currency in the camp), and had the guard bring the man some water [Kv 1414].[4] These fleeting moments did not mitigate the terror, however; in a perverse way, they added to it because of their unpredictability and fleeting nature.

Rituals of Interrogation

In addition to the daily displays of mundane violence, certain practices in the camps became occasions for innovation. One such practice was "interrogation." All prisoners had to undergo this exercise, some on arrival; others, weeks later (Wesselingh and Vaulerin 2005, 24). Interrogators came from outside the camp. According to one former prisoner, they were inspectors from the Prijedor police station (Hukanović 1996, 28). These grand inquisitors followed the procedures of an actual police interrogation but the resemblance stopped there. Very quickly the interrogation simply became an occasion for a private display of violence.

Interrogators asked each prisoner a series of questions about any weapons the prisoner owned and his activities in the "resistance" or as an "extremist." It mattered little what the truth was—whether a given prisoner ever owned a weapon and if so, whether he used that weapon in an effort to resist the takeover of his town or village. In reality, most weapons prisoners had owned were legally registered hunting rifles. No matter the truthfulness of prisoners' responses, however, they generally suffered a beating. A few were subject to extra flourishes. At the end of his interrogation, for example, Edin Mrkalj, a federal-level policeman, had to undergo a mock trial. The "trial" was replete with a typist and "defense" attorney, whom Mrkalj described as "worse than the prosecution" [Kv 2905]. The interrogators even rendered a "verdict," though Mrkalj never learned what it was.

Interrogations usually ended with prisoners forced to sign a piece of paper. Prisoners had no idea what they were signing. When the prosecutor at Tadić's trial asked one former prisoner, Kasim Mešić, if he read the document before signing it, Mešić replied, "I did not dare read it. I only signed it" [Tad 3494–95]. The document that prisoners signed were "confessions" (Hukanović 1996, 28; Pervanić 1999, 127–28). Their content had little to do with any answers the prisoners had given. Indeed, some "confessions" verged on the absurd. A former judge in Prijedor who was "97% blind" nevertheless "confessed" to being a sniper (Hukanović 1996, 29; Pervanić 1999, 165). A doctor from Kozarac "confessed" to stealing medicine from the clinic where he worked and hiding it in his cellar. Only later did he realize what he had signed; his home had no cellar (Hukanović 1996, 28). Signing provided no protections. In some cases, interrogators simply used the signed confession as "evidence warranting the use of [further] force and torture" (Hukanović 1996, 28). Some who signed died from further beatings and torture, while others managed to survive (Pervanić 1999, 128). The ridiculousness of the charges against the prisoners points to a decided lack of strategic logic behind this ritual. Put differently, the interrogations were not about gathering information vital to the war effort. They were occasions for staging violence and becoming a star in a theater of the absurd.

Forced Singing and Beating

In addition to interrogation, other violent rituals pervaded camp life. These, too, seemed to be about enacting power and being seen going along with the "fun and games." One favorite pastime of the guards, for example, was to force prisoners to sing nationalist Četnik songs. The forced singing might start in the bus or van transporting the newly captured men to a location for detention or interrogation [Tad 3268, 3490]. The singing continued at the camps. At Omarska, guards forced prisoners to sing to obtain water [Tad 3596; Kv 2141] (Hukanović 1996, 30–32). The withholding of water was particularly tortuous in the hot summer weather, when temperatures could easily reach into the high thirty degrees Celsius (ninety degrees Fahrenheit). Because of the heat, prisoners were in constant need of water and hence, were constantly made to sing. As one former inmate explained: "Well, I remember still, and I tend to sing the song, 'Who Says, Who Lies.' That was one of the songs we would have to sing to get a bit of water. I got so used to singing it that sometimes even now I tend to slip into the song, the words of the song. It just happens of its own accord because it stuck in my memory" [Kv 2141]. Singing alone was not always sufficient to obtain water. The guards sometimes made a game of it, telling the prisoners "to sing louder and louder to get some water" [Kv 2142] or to "take it from the top!" (Hukanović 1996, 31–32). When the guards finally did give the prisoners water, they sometimes threw it through the window so that most of it fell on the ground [Kv 2142; Tad 3271].

Visits from outsiders were also occasions where guards forced prisoners to sing. When local dignitaries, such as Radoslav Brđanin, head of the SDS (Serb nationalist party) in Banja Luka, or Simo Drljaca, chief of police, came to the camp, the program often included forced singing by prisoners as if the guards wanted to show off their power to enact extralethal violence in "creative" ways [Tad 3334, 3665].

Forced singing seems to have been a common practice at other camps as well, with a few variations. Guards might force prisoners to learn new songs or new lyrics to familiar songs. As one former prisoner from Luka camp in Brčko (located in the northeast) recalled: "We did not know the text, the lyrics. They told us what were the lyrics and then we sing them in a chorus and trained." In addition to singing, the guards at Luka forced the prisoners to kiss a drawing of Draža Mihailović, the famous Četnik leader from World War II [Tad 650].

The forced singing also took place in camps in other regions. Two other prisoners received similar treatment as the prisoner in Brčko, but at a camp in Serbia. One was the former police chief of Bosanski Samac, Dragan Lukac, a Croat. Authorities transported Lukac and other prisoners from the same town to the JNA barracks at Batajnica, near Belgrade. At this facility, guards forced prisoners to learn new songs and at times, to line up and kiss a drawing of Mihailović that was hanging on the wall [Tad 650]. Military police also ordered the prisoners to learn how to cross themselves with three fingers, the way that Orthodox Serbs cross themselves in contradistinction to the two fingers that Catholics (Croats) use.

Another prisoner who spent time at Batajnica also recalled guards forcing the prisoners to kiss the picture of Mihailović: "In the morning when we got up, we had to come nearer and kiss him in his front and say: 'Good morning, General'" [Kv 681]. Guards singled out certain prisoners to perform songs that ridiculed particular organizations or persons. This prisoner had been chairman of the local SDA (Muslim nationalist party), so guards forced him and other prisoners to sing a song that mocked Alija Izetbegović, the national head of the SDA and Bosnian president. As the prisoners sang, the guards beat them while imploring them to sing "louder and louder" [Kv 682–83]. This prisoner eventually ended up at the Sremska Mitrovica prison in Vojvodina (also in Serbia) [Tad 687]. Here the guards were JNA soldiers who went even further in orchestrating and choreographing the forced singing. As this same prisoner explained: "They even made a choir out of us. Some of us that were more gifted musically and knew how to sing, we had to sing and lined up and the others were given cloths in order to wave with those cloths. Then they would single out somebody [to] beat, [sic] you and you had to continue singing and then they would bring you back to the choir and then you had to sing, continuing singing" [Tad 689]. If a prisoner refused to beat another prisoner, he himself would suffer blows from a guard or fellow prisoner.

At Omarska, forced beatings also occurred, but as a practice all its own. Mehmedalija Huskić, for example, described what occurred on his arrival at the camp.

> When we arrived at Omarska, they opened the door of the bus and there we got off, to the pista [open courtyard] there, and two guards took me and a friend of mine, Ferid Velic, and ordered us to box, the two of us. We hesitated a little, of course, and one of the guards, the one who was behind me, struck me with his rifle in the back and I realized I had to do it, and I began to hit Ferid here around the shoulders, but he was still hesitating. He was quite surprised, what do I know, but then he was hit in the genitals as another guard had kicked him, and then he also began dealing blows to me so that we exchanged several blows and stopped. Then one of the guards told us to go on. [Tad 3592–93]

The guards may or may not have known Huskić and the other man were friends. Guards regularly singled out friends and forced them to beat one another in order to add to the level of transgression.

These minidisplays of extralethal violence had many variations. In one case, former Kozarac policeman Edin Mrkalj (the man whose interrogation ended with a mock trial) regained consciousness after suffering a beating of his own and found a half-conscious, bloodied prisoner lying on the ground in the same room with him. His former friend, Duško Tadić, ordered Mrkalj to beat the semiconscious man. At each blow, the victim gave out a sound that Mrkalj could not find words to describe. As he tried to explain at Tadić's trial, "I do not know what it was" [Tad 3660]. When the prosecutor asked Mrkalj how Tadić looked throughout the ordeal, he replied: "At the first glance he looked as if [he was] perspiring, as if he had been doing something. There was sweat. I could see his cynicism. I could see his grin in his look, as if he was enjoying himself" [Tad 3663]. Indeed, Tadić would find many other ways to "enjoy" himself. He made a name for himself at the camp through the many extralethal displays he staged, all of which spotlighted him as the star.

Remaking Serb Prisoners

Serb prisoners were not spared any of the violent rituals. Though few in number, they, too, were subject to the same tortures and humiliations as non-Serb prisoners (Wesselingh and Vaulerin 2005, 51), their putative identity offering them no protection whatsoever. As one detainee recounted:

> Yes, yes there was one [Serb prisoner], Darko, a young man, twentyish, twenty-five perhaps. I saw him in front of the white house [one of two buildings used for torture sessions] begging the guards to spare him, to say, "I am a Serb, let me go," and they were forcing him to repeat his entreaty once again to try to prove that he was a Serb; he was trying to, they laughed. Then he said, "Let me go. I am urinating blood. I cannot stand it any longer. I cannot stand up." Throughout the time they were sprinkling him with water, with a powerful jet of water, which normally was—at normal times was used in the mines to wash tyres on those big trucks.[5] [Tad 1279]

The treatment of this particular prisoner went far beyond name-calling or taunts. The de-Serbianization of this man occurred through torture, as if tearing back the skin would reveal the man's "true" identity underneath (Appadurai 1998). The visible marks that these acts inscribed on the man's body rendered visible his social (and political) recategorization. These marks were proof that the man no longer qualified as a "real" Serb and, as such, was another enemy of the new Bosnian Serb Republic.

The torture of this "former" Serb was not a unique incident. Hukanović (1996, 78) also recalls three Serbs—two men and one woman—who were prisoners at Omarska. Their crime was helping "those others." Authorities released the female prisoner who was the wife of one of the two men after two months. Her husband, however, did not fare as well. Guards subjected him to days of torture before finally killing him. As with the other man tortured to death, this prisoner, too, was no longer a Serb. The torture he endured was "proof" enough of his guilt.

Omarska was not the only prison camp that housed Serb prisoners. When soldiers captured Armin Kenjar, a Muslim from Kamičani, and detained him in Bosanska Dubica, guards placed a Serb prisoner in the cell with him, then ordered Kenjar to beat the man. When Kenjar only slapped the Serb prisoner lightly, the guard struck Kenjar hard, telling him "That's how you should beat him." After forcing Kenjar to beat the Serb prisoner with greater force, guards moved the

Serb prisoner to another cell, which held another Muslim prisoner. Guards then forced the Serb captive to beat that prisoner [Tad 3888–89]. Like the torture of Serb prisoners at Omarska, the forced beatings of this Serb detainee at Bosanska Dubica showed everyone what happens to Serbs whom the new authorities no longer considered to be "real" Serbs.

Camp personnel could also be subject to accusations of not being real Serbs. The most important criterion was how a guard acted toward the prisoners. Guards who were "good" and "honest" were transferred out of the camps after a few days and sent to the front. The one or two who managed to remain working at the camp continued to help prisoners whenever they could, by passing them extra food, for example. They were well aware of the risks they were taking (Hukanović 1996, 77). Indeed, the pressure on all camp personnel not just to go along with the violent norms of the camp, but also *being seen* doing so was constant. As Pervanić (1999, 64) notes: "There were stories that every guard member was required to kill somebody in the camp. It was said that those refusing to participate in these orgies of violence would be forced by others to take an active part, so that later they could not say they had not been involved in killings." While some may have been concerned with future liabilities, for others, the reward was experiencing a new basis for collective power, which put a premium on brutalizing former friends, neighbors, and schoolmates.

Even highly placed commanders at Omarska did not escape suspicion about the kind of Serbs they were *at heart*. Shift leader Miroslav Kvočka also fell under suspicion because of his personal ties to the Muslim community. Kvočka was married to a Muslim woman from a prominent Prijedor family [Kv 710]. His two sisters were also married to Muslims [Kv 679, 681]. Kvočka testified at his own trial that he managed to protect his brothers-in-law (his wife's brothers), so that the men only spent a few days at Omarska and not the two to three months that most prisoners had to endure. To ensure his brothers'-in-law safety and to return them to their homes, Kvočka went to Simo Drljaca, the chief of police, to ask for a pass. This meeting led Drljaca to accuse Kvočka of not being a "real" Serb. As Kvočka himself testified:

> After my first introductory statements and my requests, he [Drljaca] jumped out of his chair, and said, "What's wrong with you, Kvocka? The Muslims seem to have got your brain." He said, "Well, perhaps you're not a Serb actually at all. Take your pants off so I can see. Perhaps you're a Muslim yourself. I could deal with you very easily were it not for some other people here in SUP, in the police station." [Kv 952–53]

The remark about "taking your pants off" refers to the practice among Muslims to circumcise male children. Drljaca may have been joking when he made the comment, but the meaning behind it was clear. He was questioning Kvočka's loyalties because of the latter's ties to a prominent Muslim family and his attempts to use his position to protect his Muslim in-laws. Such efforts were reason enough for Drljaca to accuse Kvočka of not being a real Serb, despite the fact that Kvočka worked at the most notorious camp in the region.

As these varied examples indicate, being a real Serb was predicated on behavior, not self-identification. When self-identified Serbs were not willing to cut off prior relations with non-Serbs or to toe the nationalist line, they were subject to the same tortures and violence as non-Serbs. Their refusal to act like "real" Serbs in the nationalist sense meant that they could no longer be Serb in any practical sense. "Real" Serbs did not maintain ties to former non-Serb friends, neighbors, and family. "Real" Serbs cut those ties and made sure others saw them do so.

In addition to decertifying men and women who once identified as Serbs, the inverse also occurred. Guards allowed a few prisoners to become "one of them." Both Pervanić and Hukanović remark on how a handful of prisoners were able to recast themselves as one of the "guards." Pervanić refers to one such group of prisoners as "traders." These were men who bought and sold food and cigarettes. Pervanić (1999, 84) details the process of transformation of one fellow prisoner.

> As a former employee of the mine, he knew some of the guards well. He had spent a lot of time in their company sharing their rations and making deals. While the rest of us wasted away, he was gaining weight. Not even the fact that his mother was held amongst the women inside the administration building—or that his father was recovering from a wound inflicted by a Chetnik bullet—could prevent him from exploiting the situation. He became one of them.

The very possibility of "becoming one of them" points to the transformative effects of putting violence on display. The constant and frequent displays created constant and frequent opportunities to cast oneself and others. That possibility of grabbing a role even existed for certain prisoners. In addition to the "traders," Pervanić (1999, 222) describes a man who worked as a "kapo" for the guards. He, too, became more and more like the guards, adopting their "methods" of ferociously beating fellow prisoners and spending more and more time with guards rather than with the prisoners. These examples, though few in number, point to the ways in which belonging was predicated on behavior and such behavior, in some instances, trumped prewar categorizations. Participating in the violent displays allowed non-Serbs to become "real" Serbs within the confines of the camp, just as refusing to participate turned former Serbs into non-Serbs.

In all these displays of extralethal violence, acting the part was key to status, belonging, and proximity to power. Belonging was predicated on behavior; being seen participating in the displays was crucial, but being seen taking pleasure in the pain and humiliation inflicted on the prisoners was even better. Such pleasure added to the extralethality of the displays. By yelling "louder," for example, guards could promptly hear the increased volume of the prisoners' voices and the extra effort the prisoners had to exert. By ordering the prisoners to "take it from the top," they could instantly hear the prisoners "rewind" the song to the beginning. The effect of their commands was immediate. By forcing a badly beaten prisoner to beat another, a perpetrator like Tadić could instantaneously see the effect on both Mrkalj, the beater, and the half-conscious prisoner whom Mrkalj was forced to beat. Tadić could hear and see the indescribable sounds emanating from the half-dead prisoner with each blow and perhaps could see the reluctance, shame, or humiliation on Mrkalj's face as he did what he was told. These noticeable effects were vital parts of the show; they added to the aesthetics or look and feel of the scene. The capacity to create such effects demonstrated not only the unchecked power that perpetrators wielded in the camp, but also their willingness to use that power to violate the most fundamental social norms that prisoner and perpetrator shared before the war. These daily extralethal displays cast participants as "one of them" or, more accurately, as "one of us." It enabled participants to show unequivocally that they had severed all ties with their prewar friends, colleagues, and neighbors, and had indeed become new men.

Violence Extraordinaire

Indeed, the most spectacular extralethal display that occurred at Omarska was all about becoming someone new. Even by the violent standards of the camp, this one incident stood out—not for the numbers killed or the number of men taking part, but for the type of extralethal violence meted out on the victims. This incident also showcased a single man. His name was Duško Tadić.

Tadić came from Kozarac, a mostly Muslim hamlet just outside the town of Prijedor. Before the start of the war in Croatia in 1991, being Serb or Muslim mattered little to residents. Neighbors were neighbors. People quarreled and held grudges, but they also drank coffee together; cheered and played on the same football teams; attended the same schools; served together in the army; married into each other's families; served as *kum*, or best man, at each other's weddings; and became godparents to each other's children.

Tadić was one of the few Serbs who lived there. His house was located in the heart of town, surrounded by the homes of his Muslim neighbors [Tad 3193]. He and his family were well-known and "prominent," according to one resident [Tad 2934]. Tadić's father had been a decorated veteran of World War II and had also fought for Tito's Partizans [Tad 25, 44, 3191]. Tadić, too, was well-known. He was an expert in karate, the Japanese martial art popularized in action movies from the 1970s and 1980s. Many local boys (and, no doubt, girls, too) idolized the local sports hero for his karate prowess and expertise (Vulliamy 2012, 61).[6] Tadić also stood out physically. He was sturdily built and had a distinctive gait. One former resident said he walked like a bear [Tad 3863]; another described his walk as someone who was "full of himself" [Tad 4233]. Yet another former acquaintance, Edin Mrkalj, the prisoner forced to the beat another half-conscious prisoner, said that Tadić "walked like an athlete, mostly to be seen, to be, you know, to stand out" [Tad 3655].

By most accounts, Tadić was well liked. As one former neighbor testified, Tadić "was on good terms with almost everyone" [Tad 2574]. When he built his house and put a coffee shop on the ground floor, his Muslim neighbors pitched in to help, as is custom in Bosnia (Bringa 1995, ch. 3). One neighbor, Eno Alić, brought Tadić some lumber [Tad 2574, 2608]. Another lent him money [Tad 3342]. Not surprisingly perhaps, his closest friends were Muslims. His best friend was Emir Karabašić, a local policeman who also came from Kozarac. The two shared an interest in karate and spent a lot of time together [Tad 2657, 3002].

With the takeover of Prijedor and surrounding hamlets in late April 1992, Tadić began acting in new ways. Violence quickly became his calling card. He was present when a group of fifteen or so paramilitaries arrested his friend, Emir, along with five other Muslim policemen. The soldiers forced the captured men to put their hands behind their necks and stand in a line. A man standing across the street saw what happened next. Tadić pulled one of the captives out of the line and slit his throat, then stabbed him. Blood gushed from the victim's neck [Tad 2698]. Tadić did the same to a second man: pulled him out of the line, then stabbed him and slit his throat. A volley of gunfire followed. As all this was taking place, the soldiers with Tadić were waving their weapons at passers-by, motioning them not to stop or to look at what was happening [Tad 2665–69, 2697]. Eventually, soldiers also arrested the man who witnessed the scene from across the street, Nihad Seferović. They beat Seferović and took him to Omarska. In the crowded room where he was assigned, Seferović saw Emir Karabašić, erstwhile best friend of Tadić. Emir shared some bread and a cigarette with Seferović.

The next day, June 18, 1992, was one that no prisoner at Omarska would ever forget [Tad 2754, 2790, 3906]. In the late afternoon, around 5:00 p.m., guards called out Emir's name. This was not unusual. Summoning prisoners occurred day and night. Some men came back badly beaten; many never came back at all. Emir was in the upper-level room and was recovering from a recent beating when he heard his name [Tad 3924, 3981]. When the guard opened the door, a prisoner sitting near the door could see Tadić and another man standing behind the guard.

Tadić was wearing a camouflage uniform and carried a pistol in his belt and a rifle in his hand [Tad 2754]. Like Joseph, he, too, was dressing the part.

Shortly after guards called out Emir, a soldier wearing a blue shirt, police pants, and a white belt (the uniform of military police) came to fetch Jasko Hrnić, who was staying in the ground floor room, directly below that of Emir. The guard kept mistakenly calling for "Asko" Hrnić so Jasko Hrnić chose not to respond [Tad 4026]. After several calls for "Asko Hrnić," Tadić himself appeared at the door and yelled, "Jasko, get out. I know you are in there. I will kill you all." At this, the other prisoners in the room beseeched Hrnić to go [Tad 4088]. Hrnić finally began to make his way to the door and left with Tadić [Tad 4079–80].

After Hrnić was taken out, a guard came for Eno Alić, who was in the same upstairs room as Emir [Tad 3928]. Before the war, Eno was one of the people who had helped Tadić build his new house. At first, Eno refused to go. A guard went to fetch Eno's father, Meho, who was in a different room in the camp, and brought him back to coax Eno to go. Meho found his son shivering with terror [Tad 3955]. His son did not want to go. His father gently pleaded with him. Eno finally relented. A prisoner put a leather jacket on Eno, to protect him from the blows that were surely coming. Eno's father led the way down the stairs [Tad 3982–83]. Almost immediately, guards took hold of Eno and ordered Meho to leave. As Meho left, he could hear his son pleading with Tadić. "Dule, brother, how have I wronged you? Why do you beat me?" [Tad 3956].

After guards had removed all three men, the prisoners could hear the threats and screams coming from the ground floor hangar. They could hear soldiers and guards yelling: "Pull, pull harder!" "Squeeze tighter!" [Tad 2756] "Bite the balls!" "Give it a blow!" [Tad 3904]. "Where is your karate now?" [Tad 4082]. Music was playing in the background. The screams and moans of the victims were like nothing the other prisoners had heard before. These were not the wails that came from being beaten; they were something else entirely. As one prisoner explained: "Your blood froze in your veins when you heard those screams" [Tad 2957]. The screams seemed to last an eternity.

One prisoner in the upstairs room had a vantage point where he could also see what was happening. Halid Mujkanović, a man from Kozarusa, a village near Prijedor, was crouching in a corner and stole several glances. After the initial round of beatings and atrocities, Mujkanović saw soldiers (not regular camp guards) come back to the rooms that held the prisoners and ask for two "volunteers." The soldiers threatened to kill someone if no one "volunteered" [Tad 3985]. Two prisoners left with the men. From his spot, Mujkanović forced himself to look. The first time he glanced up, he could see one of the "volunteers" holding what looked like the body of Emir, while one of the perpetrators ordered the other "volunteer" to bite off Emir's genitals. The next time Mujkanović looked up, he saw one of the soldiers bring a pigeon to a victim lying on the ground and then order the victim to eat it [Tad 3986–87] (Another prisoner heard this story as well [Tad 4028].) Mujkanović then saw a soldier strike Jasko Hrnić. Hrnić fell but showed no signs of life [Tad 3987]. When an ICTY prosecutor asked Mujkanović how the soldiers looked while this violence was going on, he replied: "Well, they looked as if they were attending a sports match, as if they were supporting a team" [Tad 3987]. Tadić and his men seemed to be having the greatest time.

One of the two "volunteers" (referred to as Witness "H" at Tadić's trial to conceal his identity) testified about what the soldiers forced him and the other "volunteer" to do. His testimony fills in and corrects details of Mujkanović's account. Witness H testified that after the first screams had died down, a young and scared-looking guard, whom Witness H had seen regularly at the camp, came and asked for two prisoners to help carry out some men [Tad 4028]. The guard led Witnesses H and G to the hangar. The first body Witness H saw was that of Emir [Tad 4030]. A soldier then led Witness H toward the "canals," which were below-ground grease traps that collected oil and other fluids from the mining equipment during servicing and maintenance [Tad 3818].[7] Here, Witness H saw the bodies of Eno Alić and Jasko Hrnić [Tad 4031].

One of the perpetrators then ordered Witness H to pick up Eno Alić's body, but as he began to do so, Alić began to move—he was still alive [Tad 4031–32]. The order then came for Witnesses H and G to pick up and remove Jasko Hrnić's body [Tad 4032–33]. The two prisoners dragged Hrnić's body by the feet toward the hangar door; once they arrived, soldiers ordered them to drag Hrnić's body back to where they had first picked him up. The two had to repeat the scene several times [Tad 4033].

Next, soldiers ordered Witnesses H and G to put Jasko Hrnić's body down and start to do push-ups [Tad 4033–34]. Next, they ordered Witness H to jump into the canal, lie down, and crawl through the muck [Tad 4036]. When Witness H reached the end, soldiers ordered him to turn around and repeat, then to drink the oil mixture in which he was "swimming" [Tad 4037]. At that point, another prisoner, Fikret Harambašić, a policeman who had worked in the Omarska police station before the war, jumped into the canal. He was naked and so badly beaten that Witness H, who knew Harambašić before the war, did not recognize him. Someone then ordered Witness H to "lick his [Harambašić's] ass" and Witness G to suck on Harambašić's penis [Tad 4037–38].

Next, the order came to hold Harambašić's mouth closed. Witness H obliged, lying on his back. One of the soldiers put a knife to Witness H's head and threatened to gouge out his eyes if Witness H did not keep Harambašić from uttering a sound. As the soldier was making these threats, another began trampling on Witness H and putting a foot on his neck [Tad 4039]. Meanwhile, soldiers ordered

Witness G to bite off Harambašić's testicles, which he proceeded to do, as soldiers made fun of all three victims [Tad 4040]. Witness H recalls comments such as, "Look what they are doing to each other. Can you imagine what they would do to us?" [Tad 4058] All the perpetrators seemed to find the ordeal highly amusing [Tad 4058].

This same incident made its way into several other sources. Two different US State Department reports mention this episode. Each cites a different witness, who gives slightly different versions of events (US State Department 1992, 1993). Another version comes from journalist Roy Gutman (1993, 98–99), who quotes a witness who had been in the same, upper-level room with Emir. According to Gutman's source, the guard who called out Emir had had a grudge against him and another guard held a grudge against the father of Jasko Hrnić. Gutman's source then provides a slightly different version of the violence, but confirms that the prisoner forced to carry out the "castration" (presumably Witness G) returned alive to his room and "could not speak for 24 hours" (Gutman 1993, 99).

The same incident also features in the memoirs of two former inmates of Omarska, Kemal Pervanić and Rezak Hukanović. Hukanović (1996, 75–76) places this incident in a long list of "horrors" that prisoners had not "been lucky enough to survive." He adds little detail. Pervanić says much more. He refers to Witness G as "E.J., a young boy from the northern part of my village" (Pervanić 1999, 82). He, too, mentions that it was "outside" visitors who conducted the torture-killing of the men, which is consistent with testimonies cited by the State Department and those made at the ICTY. Nearly all the prisoners saw Tadić that day and all knew that he did not work at the camp as a commander or guard. He came and went as he pleased and the men with him were also not from among the camp personnel.

The discrepancies in accounts are likely due to vantage point and the vagaries of memory. Most prisoners could hear, but not see, what was happening. The one exception was Halid Mujkanović who had a partial view, but Mujkanović could not bear to watch the whole episode, so he only looked up at intervals. What is consistent across all the accounts are the types of extralethal acts that soldiers forced the prisoners to do, from drinking motor oil to carrying out sexual mutilations on fellow prisoners; all accounts also mention the screams coming from the victims, the excited yelling by the perpetrators, and the music that played in the background. Where they differ is who was doing what to whom. Witness "H" recalls Fikret Harambašić as the victim of the forced genital mutilation, not Emir Karabašić, who may have already been dead by the time the two volunteers entered the scene. If that was the case, then Harambašić became the final victim because the three others—Emir, Eno, and Jasko—were already dead or too near death to respond to any more acts of violence. It seems clear that the two "volunteers" were nothing more than walk-ons or stagehands—called on to enact yet new and novel forms of extralethal violence.

What is also clear from the various testimonies is that Tadić did not choose his victims randomly. He chose the four men precisely because of his prior relationship to them. Tadić knew Jasko Hrnić, Eno Alić, and Emir Karabašić quite well [Tad 3974–75, 4104]. Before the war, all four had similar life experiences and trajectories. Tadić had been a karate coach and ran a coffee bar; Eno Alić had been a truck driver, Emir had been a policeman, and Jasko Hrnić owned a shipping business. Jasko Hrnić also drove motorcycles and owned trucks, which made him popular and well-known in the same way that Tadić's karate made him popular [Tad 3899, 4104, 4141]. Given patterns of relations before the war, it is unremarkable that the four knew one another and socialized regularly. It is also unremarkable that Tadić, a Serb, and Emir, a Muslim, were best friends. This prewar intimacy, however, became a source of torture in its own right, for this prior relationship amplified the transgressions. It is one thing to enact extralethal violence on a stranger's body, as was the case in the lynchings of Matthew Williams and George Armwood; it is quite another to enact the same kind of violence on those who, a month earlier, were close friends.

Why would Tadić target former close acquaintances and his best friend, Emir? Why not stage the violence on prisoners who were strangers or men he knew less well?

One answer comes from testimonies of former camp inmates. Perpetrators like Tadić were generally intent on eliminating anyone who had witnessed a particular incident and could identify the perpetrators later. As former prisoner Husein Hodžić explained, "That is what we felt, because if someone saw an act, a monstrous act, which had taken place, shortly after that he would also disappear, but not all, fortunately not all, not all of us" [Tad 4151]. And because prisoners and personnel came from the same hamlets, towns, and villages, the chances that prisoners might recognize the perpetrators were quite good.

If Tadić's goal was simply to eliminate witnesses, then why not just shoot his former friends or order his men to do so? And why ask for two additional "volunteers" to join in the violence and let them live to tell what happened? Indeed, one of the volunteers, Witness H, testified in horrific detail about the episode at Tadić's trial at the ICTY. If Tadić was out to eliminate witnesses, Witnesses G and H should have been killed along with the other victims. There must have been more than strategic logic at work.

One possible answer is that Tadić sought the kind of singular power and notoriety that comes from staging extralethal acts. Going beyond the standards of brutality at Omarska would have constituted Tadić as uniquely and personally powerful, not unlike the ways that extralethal displays elevated Joseph to a perch of power that eclipsed his administrative position as bourgmestre (Fujii 2013). This answer, however, does not explain why Tadić singled out former friends and acquaintances for such treatment. If all Tadić sought was greater *personal* power, he could have chosen his victims at random. He would have had no reason to single out his former friends and best friend for such treatment. Unlike Joseph who singled out rivals, Tadić had singled out friends and even his best friend, Emir, people he should have had reason to protect rather than persecute.

I argue that this particular incident was not just about enhancing personal power. It was about transforming who he was. Tadić's power was already considerable. He could do whatever he wanted, to anyone, at any time. There was not much more he could gain in terms of personal power through yet another violent display. The significance of this incident lay elsewhere. It was about shedding his old skin to become someone new. It was about destroying who he was before by desecrating the very ties that made him who he was before the war. In Bosnia, as elsewhere, a person's identity is a matter of social location—the family, friends, schoolmates, and neighbors that embed the person in a particular community and social networks. It is these ties that make him who he is. For Tadić, these relations included many Muslims, the very people now deemed to be enemies of the new Bosnian Serb state. What better way to sever such long-standing ties than by desecrating them through an elaborately staged extralethal display that specifically targeted the social bonds that tied Tadić to his former self. What more graphic way to declare oneself a new man than by enacting extralethal violence on the backs, fronts, heads, and genitals of erstwhile friends—including, and especially, on the body of his best friend, Emir? There could be no more powerful show of Tadić's transformation into a *real* Serb than to stage an orgy of extralethal acts on the bodies of the very friends who made him who was before the war. This extralethal display remade Tadić. By putting on a spectacle, Tadić showed everyone what a "real" Serb looked like.

Comparing Extralethal Violence across Settings

These sideshows were not atypical, either in Bosnia or Rwanda, even if their prevalence varied from context to context, site to site, perpetrator to perpetrator. While extralethal displays may not have been the norm during the Rwandan genocide, they did occur. Joseph created his own opportunities to put violence on display and the effects of those displays redounded to him. They made him a star and provided him a form of power that went beyond the bureaucratic authority bestowed by his position as bourgmestre. In Bosnia, extralethal displays were a daily occurrence at places like Omarska. These semiprivate settings provided ample opportunities for men like Tadić to go to beyond the norm—whatever that norm was—and to stage a spectacle that no one would ever forget. These displays also ensured maximal participation from all the guards, including those reluctant to mistreat the prisoners. The sheer range of activities guaranteed participation. Certain displays could induce participation from the most reluctant actors. Telling prisoners to "sing louder," for example, is something anyone can do, much like eating stolen meat in Rwanda.

If we take a step further back and compare these sideshows to the main attractions explored in chapter 3, we find common elements that run through all the displays, no matter their form, scale, or content. First, none of the displays were free-for-alls or chaotic. No one tried to pile on or wrest control of the scene from others. Rather, all those who participated willingly worked together toward a common goal—to stage violence for full effect, whether staging a mock trial or forcing prisoners to sing for water. In addition, participants' attention did not stray, wander, or sag. No one became distracted by other goings-on or grew disinterested over time. On the contrary, participants' attention remained rapt during mundane as well as large-scale displays. It did not matter that many had no choice but to see or hear the goings-on. What mattered is the power of these displays to command attention, thereby inducing ever more participation.

Second, perpetrators in Bosnia and the Eastern Shore created and sustained an atmosphere of fun, frivolity, and sport by interacting with one another through violence. Participants responded directly to the visual, aural, and *sensational* effects produced by the violence as well as their own cheering, clapping, yelling, laughing, mocking, and jeering. It did not matter if or when a victim had died. In most cases, perpetrators could not have known the moment of death. What they were responding to was the violence—the array of extralethal acts taking place in front of them, staged in a way to amplify the transgressions to persons, bodies, and in some cases, prior social ties. These responses were not ancillary the display; they helped to constitute it as such—a veritable spectacle staged for "popular" consumption and audience effect.

Third, what helped to sustain the atmosphere was a trajectory of violence that was crowd pleasing. In Bosnia and Rwanda, specific displays became increasingly shocking over the course of a single episode and reached a "high point" before coming to an end. In the torture-killings at Omarska, for example, the violence did not stop with the near killing of the original four prisoners. It continued with the addition of the two "volunteers," whose very presence created new possibilities for innovation and escalation. It was only when the two joined the scene that additional sexual tortures and mutilations could and did take place. In Rwanda, the display did not end with the murder of the two young women. Their murder was prelude to a much more transgressive act according to cultural norms—the display of their nude bodies, posed in splayed—that is, hypersexualized—fashion in a public place.

Fourth and finally, an aesthetic logic permeated every scene of violence. Actors took care with how they staged the action. They demonstrated an implicit awareness of stagecraft by making sure that the "look" of the violence would command spectators' attention, even if the number of spectators at the scene was limited. In Rwanda, Joseph had the dead women's bodies displayed in the center of town, ensuring maximum "exposure" to witting and unwitting passersby. In the extralethal displays at Omarska, the staging was more dynamic. Routine displays of brutality—forced beatings of fellow prisoners and forced singing—took place on a daily basis and out in the open. More elaborate displays took place in more private spaces, such as the so-called White House where "interrogations" were held and the hangar where Tadić staged the killing and sexual torture of four friends. In these more intimate spaces, the atmosphere was not sedate. In fact, by most accounts, it resembled a sporting match.

Casting Process

What is also apparent is that the casting process works similarly no matter the scale or nature of the display. The only apparent difference is the foreshortening of the casting process when those in power are able to grab lead roles knowing that everyone else will (have to) go along. Joseph and Tadić, for example, had no rivals or superiors to check or challenge their status as "stars." Both men enjoyed a ready-made supporting cast that would instantly affirm them in that role. The ease with which each man cast himself as the star stands in stark contrast to the contingent process by which individuals emerged to lead the mob in the Armwood lynching.

The supporting cast in the sideshows may have also been smaller in number as compared to the supporting casts in the Armwood lynching, the parade in Bosnia, and even the killings of the Roland's children in Ngali. But the smaller size of the supporting cast did not lessen the brutality of the violence. The men with Tadić in the hangar, for example, were a select group, numbering around twenty or so [Tad 4061]. They were Tadić's men—all "outside visitors" who had no official position in the camp. According to Pervanić (1999, 81–82), these outside visitors were often soldiers on leave from the "front line." Prisoners referred to them as "the colored ones" because of the camouflage uniforms they wore. Even the guards were afraid of these men [Tad 4079].

Tadić's men, like the crowd at the Armwood and Williams lynchings, seemed to revel in their role, playing music and drinking alcohol—both of which made the men even more "aggressive" than usual [Kv 1933]. They cheered and jeered with abandon. It was their collective actions that generated an atmosphere of frivolity, one that Tadić working alone or with only "young and scared-looking" guards would have had a hard time creating by himself. Tadić's supporting cast, in short, was key to creating and sustaining a certain look and feel during the entirety of the display.

The casting process also ensured that across the divergent settings, people were unwittingly pulled into the show by virtue of their physical proximity to it. For the guards at Omarska, this might have been an opportunity they relished— to play spectator to Tadić's violent fun and games. For the rest of the prisoner population, the opposite was the case. Much like black residents who could not avoid seeing or hearing the lynchings of Matthew Williams or George Armwood, the prison population at Omarska was cast as spectators, forced to hear and even see an episode of horror that none would ever forget.

Transformative Effects

All the violence displays, from main attractions to the sideshows, also transformed all those involved. The violence recategorized victims. Joseph's desecration of the bodies of the two women he lured to his home, for example, transformed the victims from virtuous to vile. At Omarska, the forced acts of sexual violence recast former friends and associates as "sexual deviants"—that is, morally depraved, repugnant subjects deserving of abusive and lethal treatment. As such, they were men with whom no true Serb would ever associate.

At the same time, the violence turned participants into new men and women. Joseph became someone much more powerful than a simple bourgmestre, someone who not only determined who would live and die, but also *how* a person would die. The torture-killings of Tadić's former friends recast the perpetrators from social equals with their victims to their superiors. Only the perpetrators had the power to determine the content and direction of the display. Despite forcing the victims to debase themselves, their debasement confirmed the social and moral superiority of their tormentors and torturers. Like minstrel shows that featured corked-up white actors performing a white fantasy of blackness, Tadić and his men were performing their own fantasies of Serb and Muslim identity, constructing the two categories in highly exaggerated and oppositional ways— "Serbs" as morally upstanding and all powerful and non-Serbs as "naturally" deviant and powerless. All these shifts in self-understanding occurred through the process of putting extralethal violence on display.

The crowds of onlookers and spectators were also transformed. The process of transformation occurred through the smallest of acts. As Amy Louise Wood (2009, 143) points out, "The act of clapping connects the individual to the larger group while subsuming any individual reaction." The same can be said of cheering, hooting, hollering, taunting, jeering, and laughing. Like clapping, these activities also link the individual to the larger collective while subsuming any individual reactions that might deviate from or challenge the atmosphere the spectators helped to create. In this way, spectating transformed the spectator. It consecrated those taking part as extraordinary, for only the most special could cross the line between normative and transgressive with such abandon and glee. The power of communal transgression is in the doing, after all. As Joseph, Tadić, and mob members in Princess Anne knew, anyone can kill. It takes men and women with a keen sense of stagecraft to tap into the power of putting extralethal violence on display.

ENCORE

Justice pursues the body beyond all possible pain.

—Michel Foucault, *Discipline and Punish*

When taking power, the RPF inherited a country it hardly knew.

—Filip Reyntjens, *Political Governance in Post-Genocide Rwanda*

One hoped that the dead would stop being existential hostages of the living.

—Danielle de Lame, "Deuil, Commémoration, Justice dans les Contextes Rwandais et Belge"

I had never been to the church in Kibuye.[1] After three days of rest and relaxation at the bucolic lakeside town, my friends and I headed back to Kigali. On our way out of town, we passed the main Catholic church, which sits perched on the side of a hill. I asked if we could stop and take pictures. My research site was hours away in a different préfecture, but many people from Kibuye had fled eastward when the violence began there in 1994. Several communes in Gitarama had absorbed these refugees, and in some cases, tried to protect them (Kabagema 2001, 37).

Two years after the end of the genocide, in 1996, the church in Kibuye became the first mass grave exhumed by a group of forensics experts sent by the UN (Koff 2005). Their job was to unearth the remains of those buried alongside the building to determine the victims' identities and cause of death. The goal of the forensics team was essentially the inverse of that of Team Genocide. In 1994, killers had lured victims to the church promising safety, but instead set them up for high efficiency mass murder.

During the genocide, those targeted for extermination included anyone with a Tutsi identity card or who "looked" Tutsi, and those commonly referred to as "Hutu moderates" who were known to have opposed the extremists in power. What forensic analysis reminds us is that delineators such as "Tutsi," "people who look Tutsi," or "Hutu moderates" are fleeting and impermanent. In death, the human body does not retain the social markings that would link the living to a political party or ethnic group. In the hands of forensic experts, the bodies reveal the nature of the crimes committed, not the social categories to which the living once belonged. These social facts are not visible in the remains. They can only be identified through the artifacts or material objects found on or with the remains, such as identity cards or a piece of clothing. Even then, it is not the card itself or the torn *chemise* that ties a particular set of bones to the person who once was, but rather, some living person who is able to make the link between that object and a former family member, friend, or neighbor. In other words, it is through reading physical artifacts—the desiderata of everyday life—that the living can make *social* identifications. Absent those readings, the bodies could belong to *any* category.

Ironically, then, what the forensics team found in the mass grave beside the church in Kibuye were not the remains of Hutu or Tutsi, but those of men, women, and children whose violent deaths had left lasting evidence in and on their bones. Some of the adults had had their Achilles tendons cut, for example, as if the killers wanted to prevent them from running away (despite there being no place to run *to*). Very few bodies showed any defensive wounds as if the victims had not had the time or strength to ward off the blows. Viewed forensically, the bodies constituted graphic evidence that a horrendous crime had taken place both inside and outside the main Catholic church in the town. What they did not find were the physical markers of a social category since such traits do not remain affixed to the body in death. The dead eschew such transient labels. Their bones have enough to do, settling into the soft, muddy earth, waiting to be disinterred and reconnected to the person who once was.

Not every site of mass murder becomes the site of a forensic dig, however. Not every dead body is disinterred to prove a crime. Some dead bodies go on long parades, traveling thousands of miles in order to be reburied elsewhere, as some famous corpses did in the former Yugoslavia and Romania (Verdery 1999). Some are laid to rest in newly established "national" cemeteries because their sheer numbers eclipse the capacity of their families to bury them, as occurred with the hundreds of thousands killed in the American Civil War (Faust 2008). Others are put on permanent display in museums and memorials as the RPF has done in Rwanda. Yet others are dumped and left out in plain view, as occurred with the body of George Armwood. What explains this variation in treatment of the dead? And what does treatment of remains in the present have to do with violent displays long past?

In this chapter, I make three arguments. First, beneath the surface differences in the treatment of George Armwood's body in Princess Anne and the thousands of dead in Rwanda lie common threads. In both cases, actors incorporate the dead into a singular story about the past. In these retellings, the dead serve as vital props signifying everything and nothing at the same time, an entire category of persons and no one in particular, a mass of bones too numerous to count or a body lost to obscurity. Turning dead persons into mere objects in a larger story not only helps to drown out competing accounts; it also helps to silence the living. Second and more generally, treatment of the dead—through *political* displays of actual remains or public commemorations of past events—can extend *violent* displays from the past into the present, and in doing so, generate new audiences. Third, through these political displays, actors are able to recategorize the dead, turning perpetrators into victims and victims into perpetrators as in Rwanda or insiders into outsiders as in the Eastern Shore.

All of these pathways are made possible by the body's capacity to stand in for social bodies and bodies politic, as well as the ambiguity that inheres in all physical bodies, dead or alive. There is nothing inherently black or white, Hutu or Tutsi, about any person or her remains. This is precisely why the living can fit them into whatever category they choose through rituals of alchemy that transform *who* the dead were in life and how they came to be dead in the first place.

Bodies on Display in Rwanda

The genocide and mass killings that took place in 1994 generated two masses of dead bodies. The first was comprised of hundreds of thousands of victims of the genocide. These included mostly Tutsi but also some Hutu, all victims of various génocidaires, from militia, soldiers, National Police, and Presidential Guard to ordinary farmers mobilized to carry out genocide (Des Forges 1999; Fujii 2009; Mironko 2004; Straus 2006). The other mass was comprised of tens of thousands of victims—mostly Hutu but also some Tutsi civilians—all massacred by RPF units during the course of the war and following the rebel group's seizure of power in July 1994 (Reyntjens 2015; Ruzibiza 2005).

The different political contexts for these killings led to different treatment of the dead. During the genocide, the disposal of corpses was often an afterthought. Burying the dead became secondary to the more lucrative practice of looting victims' homes and fields. Killers often left the bodies of victims where they lay in order to rush to the victims' homes to carry away anything of value, from cooking pots to roof tiles, doors, windows, crops, and livestock. Looting took such precedence that in some places, local officials had to pay people to help with the task. At the church of Kansi in Nyraruhengeri commune, Butare, "local people were too occupied with searching for survivors [presumably to finish off] and plundering to dispose of the bodies. Dogs came to eat some of them. After the six days, the burgomaster sent men to help with the burial. The church paid for the labor" (Des Forges 1999, 454).

The situation was similar at the parish in Simbi. After the massacre of three to five thousand people who took refuge in the church and health center, the bourgmestre "rewarded" those who helped to bury the bodies with a kilogram of rice, taken from the stock of rice the church intended to distribute to the poor (Des Forges 1999, 452). In some cases, the line between burying and killing blurred. Karemano (2003, 73) recalls a scene on April 22, 1994, shortly after the genocide had begun in Butare. Local authorities were calling on all men and women to assist with burying the bodies. In one instance, the pile of dead included a woman, still alive, clutching her baby. A local pastor took the woman by the arm and told her to "take her place" among the dead. He shoved her infant in her arms, then ordered everyone to bury the woman and infant along with the dead bodies surrounding her.

In and around Ngali, local leaders, including Jude, also prioritized looting over burying the dead. So intent were local leaders on accumulating loot that conflicts broke out among them (interviews, 15 and 27 Dec 2011). Burying the victims was necessary to staunch the odor of decay and to keep stray dogs from eating the corpses. Expedience was the driving principle. Bodies were generally buried where they lay—in open fields, courtyards of homes, and existing cavities in the ground, most often pit latrines.[2] For local leaders like Jude, the dead were a nuisance. They were "matter out of place," to use Mary Douglas's (2003) felicitous phrase. As such, they needed to be put in their place so that Jude and his men could attend to more profitable activities. Jude accorded the bodies no extra significance, for the real earthly prize was the loot the dead left behind (Vidal 2004, 2).

After the genocide was over, bodies littered the landscape, some buried hastily in mass graves, others rotting on roads and footpaths, and yet others lying in open fields. Not all the bodies were victims of génocidaires, however. Many were (or would soon become) victims of the RPF. In most places, residents were well aware of which mass graves held which bodies and indeed, which graves held both types of victims.

Once the RPF took power, the war and violence came to an end. Only then could local officials and communities turn their attention to *acknowledging* all the people who had lost their lives. At first, dealing with the dead was a local affair, as had been the case historically. Before the spread of Catholicism and other forms of Christianity in the early twentieth century, burial and funereal practices were family matters. Rituals and practices varied such that no single model existed. People adapted their practices to the specific context in which the person died (e.g., after a long illness or abruptly at a young age) (Spijker 1990). As Anna-Maria Brandstetter (2010, 10) explains:

Neither graves nor graveyards existed in pre-colonial times. The dead were laid to rest either in a remote marsh or forest, or placed somewhere close by: on fields in or near the compound (often in the banana grove), or laid out in the house of the deceased, which was then deserted, or the body was left in a part of the house, to which access was then prohibited. Only close relatives and neighbors assisted the family in the burial and the ritual of mourning. No vigil by the body was held, and generally the burial was carried out rather quickly and formally.

With the spread of Catholicism came the spread of Christianized burial practices. Traditional practices nevertheless persisted. As Brandstetter (2010, 11) further explains, Rwandans did not suddenly become attached to the notion of cemeteries and grave markers. "Remembering the dead in Rwandan culture was, and still is, not based on a 'cult of the corpse,' rather the dead are remembered in ancestral worship, in family stories and historical narratives." It was the memories of a person, and not the body of the deceased, that the living embraced. Survivors maintained that person's memory through family lineages and oral histories, not through rites focused on the physical remains.

The aftermath of the genocide, however, presented an unprecedented situation because of the sheer number of corpses. In some locales, local officials and religious leaders took it on themselves to disinter and rebury the dead according to religious practice. In Butare, Catholic church leaders published an appeal suggesting that each (Christian) community draw up lists of dead parishioners, to create a monument to mark their death, and to decide on a date for collective commemoration. The call made no distinction among the dead but referred to Hutu and Tutsi victims of the genocide as well as victims of the "war." These exhumation and reburial ceremonies, however, became occasions for individuals to make public accusations against the living (Buckley-Zistel 2006; Vidal 2004, 576–77). The denouncements made the ceremonies less about the dead and more about the living. But even these individuals were no match for the RPF, which quickly took control of how the population would remember the dead and just as importantly, what it would forget and never speak of again. In the hands of the RPF, the dead quickly became a prop in the story the regime wished to tell.

Techniques for Recategorizing the Dead

The parading of dead bodies, as Katherine Verdery (1999) teaches us, takes place in the service of nation building. Dead bodies are the perfect raw material for rewriting narratives of the past. No political actor in Rwanda knew this better than the RPF. Its techniques for recategorizing dead bodies proved much more powerful than forensic science. Where forensic specialists disinterred the bodies in and outside the church in Kibuye for purposes of identifying the victims and collecting evidence showing crimes against humanity had occurred, the new postgenocide regime was intent on a very different goal—using these same bodies to erase any evidence of its own crimes and to silence any mention that they had occurred at all.

The problem the regime faced, however, was that multiple sources had documented RPF war crimes that occurred during and after the war. A former officer in the RPA (the military wing of the RPF), Abdul Joshua Ruzibiza, wrote a book that chronicled his own and others' experiences "fighting" for the RPA.[3] He includes activities in which he himself was involved as well as those of other participants, whose narratives he reproduces as faithfully as possible. According to Ruzabiza, the RPF had a clear policy of killing civilians when it served its ends. Special units were assigned to slaughter entire communities, then incinerate the victims' bodies and/or bury them in mass graves (Reyntjens 2015, 101; Ruzibiza 2005). These killings were based on the RPF's version of what Nick Turse (2013) calls the "mere gook rule." During the Vietnam War, the "mere gook rule" referred to the practice of including all Vietnamese dead, regardless of age, background, or circumstances of death, in the day's "body count" in order to please commanders. The RPF applied its own version of this rule. Everyone whom the RPF killed was "made" guilty by the very fact they had been killed by the RPF. The logic was conveniently circular: whoever died at the hands of the RPF must have been guilty of committing genocide, fighting for the Rwandan government, or a similar crime; otherwise, they would not have been killed.

The RPF killed tens of thousands of civilians (Reyntjens 2015, 99–100, 102). The targets varied by location. In Kigali, its victims included political allies such as civil society leaders and politicians who were known to oppose Habyarimana and the genocidal regime (Des Forges 1999, 713; Reyntjens 2015, 99 101). In Byumba, RPF units were under orders to kill as many Hutu civilians as possible (Ruzibiza 2005, 259). After the downing of President Habyarimana's plane (an attack that Ruzibiza claims in great detail was the work of the RPF), soldiers killed twenty-five hundred people in the main stadium (Ruzibiza 2005, 274–75). In Gitarama, RPF soldiers "decided" that everyone they encountered in a single secteur had participated in the genocide, even Tutsi; they proceeded to kill everyone they came across (Des Forges 1999, 716). In Nyarubuye in Kibungo, the 157th Mobile unit killed the entire population. The officer in charge declared that there were no more "Tutsi" in the area, and indeed, by virtue of killing everyone, the RPF transformed all the dead into Hutu, making the officer's lie appear to be "true" (Ruzibiza 2005, 264).[4]

The RPF's indiscriminate killing even targeted Hutu who helped save Tutsi during the genocide. In his memoir, Édouard Kabagema (2001, 114), who lived in Murama commune in Gitarama, relates several incidents where the RPF killed families who saved Tutsi, such as a local pastor and his wife who had saved more than one hundred people. Des Forges (1999, 710) tells a similar story of a PSD member in Murama commune. When RPF soldiers arrived, they found the man, a wealthy businessman who lived in Kigali, sheltering fifty people in his home. After a few days, soldiers took all the Tutsi away and then killed the man and all those left in the house. Even in Giti, a commune in Byumba, famous for not having succumbed to any violence, the RPF slaughtered thousands indiscriminately (Des Forges 1999, 705).

After the war, various organizations began sounding the alarm of RPF war crimes. By late 1994, UN representatives were pointing to the "systematic and sustained killing and persecution of civilian Hutu populations by the RPA" (Reyntjens 2015, 4). Many within the regime protested and denounced the "extremists" within the RPF, who saw even Tutsi survivors as Interahamwe who needed to be eradicated (Reyntjens 2015, 11). Critics from within and without the regime quickly came under threat. Many began fleeing the country in the first years after the RPF takeover. Those who fled included genocide survivors, such as the former speaker of the National Assembly, Joseph Sebarenzi, and presidential advisor Assiel Kabera. The latter was assassinated on March 6, 2000 (Reyntjens 2015, 16). That same year, Kabera's brother, the vice president of Ibuka, an association of genocide survivors, went into exile along with the organization's founder and its general secretary (Reyntjens 2015, 58). Once the original leadership of the organization had fled the country or been killed, the RPF replaced them with regime stalwarts. Ibuka was now under the control of the regime (Reyntjens 2015, 58). The RPF then used the organizations under its control to destroy the rest of independent civil society. It took particular aim at human rights groups like LIPRODHOR, whose leaders fled in July 2004 (Longman 2011b; Reyntjens 2015, 60). In addition, the regime began muzzling the press barely a year after taking power (Reyntjens 2015, 63). Over time, its threats against journalists who were not toeing the line grew ever more draconian (Sundaram 2016). The regime achieved its stranglehold over every possible source of dissent through domestic and international intelligence services that operated with military precision. As Reyntjens (2015, 71) aptly sums up, "Rwanda is an army with a state rather than a state with an army, and it is effectively run by a military regime."

During and after these killings, the RPF not only took control of the living, they also took hold of the dead. Karemano (2003, 104) notes that "according to RPF strategy, every dead body had to be recovered. Every person who had been killed, either on purpose or by accident, had to be taken away and buried some-where that only the FPR [RPF] would know." The RPF took "ownership" of the dead in part because they were producing more and more of them. In some cases, soldiers dumped the bodies of its victims into the same mass grave as Tutsi victims of the genocide. In other instances, they burned the bodies so no remains would be recoverable. In yet others, they threw the bodies into the river so they would float away and never be seen again (Ruzibiza 2005, 290).

Bare Bones as Props

After the RPF took power, it also took control of all commemorations. On Octo-ber 1, 1994, only four months after the end of the genocide, the RPF declared a national holiday and organized festivities marking the anniversary of its invasion in 1990 (Newbury and Newbury 1999). The new regime was intent on celebrat-ing its victory, not on remembering the hundreds of thousands of dead killed during the genocide. As Newbury and Newbury (1999, 293) note, "This celebra-tion was designed to commemorate the culmination of a long power struggle, not the closure of the more immediate genocide." At the same time the RPF was focused on celebrations, Alphonse-Marie Nkubito, newly named justice minister and former procureur général under Habyarimana, was organizing a mass to honor all the dead. It was Nkubito who had defied the Habyarimana government and ordered the release of thousands of Tutsi arrested shortly after the October 1990 invasion. By organizing the mass, Nkubito was simply continuing his work of the recent past. He wanted to honor the dead, not celebrate the victory of a rebel army, many of whose members had never stepped foot on Rwandan soil before the invasion. Attendance was sparse but the gesture was significant (New-bury and Newbury 1999).

By 1996, the second anniversary of the genocide, the annual commemora-tion had become an entirely state-led affair. The regime stripped the ceremony of any and all religious content, which radically reconfigured what it meant to "honor" the dead. As Vidal (2004, para 24) explains: "In the African context, to honor the dead without religion is unthinkable. The decision to desacralize the funeral ceremony, which the Rwandan authorities took in 1996, constituted a mental rupture. This was equally true when it came to exhibiting the dead bod-ies." The state-led commemorations replaced religious content with officially sanctioned narratives about *whose* bodies the government was disinterring and reburying and at *whose* hands those "victims" had died. The state's mode of com-memorating the genocide quickly became the model for the rest of the country. Through highly scripted ceremonies, the state was able to silence and intimidate anyone inclined to deviate from the official story. As Jennie Burnet (2012, 103) writes: "Given the prominence of the national ceremonies and the tendency to model local-level ceremonies after them, Rwandan citizens had little public space left to mourn in the fashion that best suited their needs." Reyntjens (2015, 174) situates these state-led commemorations in the larger state project of social "engineering"—a part of the larger effort to create new Rwandans for the new Rwanda: "There even is an effect of modernization on the dead, as the way in which the regime organizes the memorialization of the genocide is contrary to burial rites in Rwandan culture." That deviation was by design. For left to their own devices, Rwandans might stick to their own stories of what happened and to whom. The state tried to ensure that would never happen. Rwandans learned the lesson quickly. If people disagreed with the official narrative of the genocide, they knew better than to voice their dissent out loud (Brandstetter 2010, 6).

The lead-up to these carefully choreographed "ceremonies" has been the exhumation of bodies. Burnet's interviewees expressed their belief that many of the exhumed bodies had been victims of RPF and not the genocide (Burnet 2012, 94–95). She describes one conversation she had with a local woman:

> On a visit in 2000 to a rural community in rural Kigali prefecture (now North province), I passed a monument. I asked my Rwandan companion who was from the community whether it was a genocide memorial. She laughed and said, "Well, we buried bodies there this past April [as part of the national mourning], but everyone around here knows that there were no Tutsi here before the genocide, so who knows whom we buried there." (Burnet 2012, 108)

These testimonies were not isolated. Others knew that among those being buried and officially "mourned" as genocide victims were genocide perpetrators and victims of RPF killings (Brandstetter 2010, 13).

In other cases, local people were denied the opportunity to identify the dead because the state literally seized all the bones. As one of Susanne Buckley-Zistel's (2006, 138) interviewees explained: "We cannot identify the people they put into the memorial sites. They took all bones." Claiming all the bones was useful to the RPF. The regime had forbidden any mention of RPF war crimes, which, as Burnet (2012, 117) notes, "far outnumbered the carefully managed official descriptions of individual revenge seeking or 'excessive use of force.'" Taking control of disinterring, reburying, and declaring all remains as "victims of genocide" supported this effort further. It transformed all RPF victims into victims of the genocide; and it showed the public to whom all bones now belonged—the state. Additionally, the government did not permit relatives of those killed by the RPF to mourn or even mention family members they had lost, for doing so would point to crimes that the state has decreed *never took place*. To ensure their silence and that of the rest of the population, the regime also passed a law prohibiting *divisionisme*, or promoting genocidal ideology. It made sure to write the law broadly enough so that it could cover any and all challenges to the official narrative of the war and genocide. The mere mention of any RPF atrocities by any Rwandan continues to be sufficient grounds for arrest, imprisonment, or even murder (Longman 2011b). The regime has also tried to muzzle foreigners. At a conference in Kigali in 2008, the regime accused human rights advocate Alison Des Forges of promoting genocidal ideology (Waldorf 2011, 48).

In addition to helping to transform RPF victims and genocide perpetrators into genocide victims, state commemorations also became public platforms for promoting a narrow and highly politicized definition of "genocide victim." As early as 1995, at the ceremony in Kibeho, the site of a refugee camp where the RPF massacred tens of thousands (see Reyntjens 2010, 105–106), Kagame made clear that there was no such thing as Hutu victims of the genocide. He assigned collective blame to all Hutu using a contorted but politically effective logic: since the genocide was committed in the "name" of all Hutu, then all Hutu should ask for forgiveness (Vidal 2004, para 30). The regime defined the term *victim (rescapé)* such that only Tutsi could qualify. Hutu women married to Tutsi men or Hutu children with Tutsi mothers were henceforth not to be considered rescapés. As Karemano (2003, 126) puts it, "The practice and discourse at the annual commemorations or the reburial ceremonies only recognize Tutsi as victims. The guilty are the Hutu." By restricting the category of "genocide victim" to Tutsi only and by constructing all Hutu as guilty—including those who risked their lives to help save Tutsi—the state was able to make itself the *sole* savior of the country. This move effectively nullified what experts like Des Forges (1999) had pointed out in the first pages of her magisterial account of the genocide—that for every Tutsi who survived, it was because of a Hutu friend, neighbor, family member, or stranger.

Every state commemoration became henceforth an occasion for reinforcing this highly revisionist binary of Tutsi as victim and Hutu as perpetrator. And because the state had decreed genocide victims to be Tutsi tout court, the reburial of *any* body, including those of known génocidaires and victims of the RPF, "officially" became the bodies of "Tutsi" by virtue of undergoing official reburial. That was, in fact, the point of the exercise. State-run commemorations and reburials became platforms for the RPF to show (off) its power to dictate *what* the population would remember about the war and genocide and how they would talk about those events, both now and in the future.

Vidal (2004) argues that dictating how all Rwandans can remember and mourn is itself a form of symbolic violence. She calls these state commemorations instances of "forced memory" (borrowing from Paul Ricoeur). Jens Meierenreich (2011) uses the similar term of "underprivileged memory" to refer to that which the regime leaves out, overlooks, or bars people from acknowledging. The effect of both types of memory—forced and underprivileged—is the same: since all Hutu are guilty, no Hutu can mourn their *proches* [loved ones] who died at the hands of génocidaires or the RPF (Buckley-Zistel 2006). Forced and underprivileged memory work in tandem. The former disciplines thought and action to match that which the RPF decrees is the "truth" while the latter keeps other realities out of sight and out of mind.

In addition to disinterring and reburying the dead as a way to promote a singular "truth" about the past, the RPF also showcases human bones. Like the annual commemorations, these, too, are shows of power. The displays vary in form but are consistent in their presentation of bones as such. Some memorials feature stacks of bones in glass-enclosed crypts or glass wall panels. At the state-sanctioned memorial at Nyamata church, for example, the bones are displayed in windowed crypts, piled by type—skulls, femurs, tibias. Displayed in anatomically sorted piles, the bones become an undifferentiated mass. As such, they are infused with political signification while at the same time stripped of their association to specific individuals. As Brandstetter (2010, 8) explains: "The intention behind this spectacle of exposed mortal remains and bone chambers is to fortify the struggle against 'negation' and 'revisionism.' The naked bones seem to be naked, hard facts, something no one can deny. The bones and mummified bodies, with their visible traces of violence, testify silently but unmistakably that the genocide really took place." But the supposed hard "fact" of bones on display turns out to be more malleable than at first glance. Bones do not speak for themselves. They are made to "speak," as forensic scientists like Clea Koff (2005) make clear through their physical analysis.

Political actors can also make them speak, not by analyzing the bones as evidence, but by incorporating them as graphic props in a particular story. To tell the "official" story of the genocide, the RPF must first strip the bones of their original providence, turning them into a tabula rasa on which it can inscribe its own account of who killed and who died. By stripping the bones of their identities—their ties to the actual persons who once lived—the RPF effectively renders the actual genocide victims all but irrelevant to the story, not unlike the way that generations of white Eastern Shoremen have rendered lynching victims irrelevant to accounts of lynchings in the region. In the case of the RPF, writing the actual victims out of the story is crucial for a different reason—not because the tellers insist that it is outsiders who are to blame, but because the story the RPF tells does not jibe with accounts of those who actually lived through the violence. In the hands of the RPF, these relics are no longer "hard" proof that mass killings took place; they are actively transformed into hard proof *that only genocide—and no other crime—took place.*

Genocide survivors—or those allowed to mourn as rescapés—find little solace in the graphic displays of bone, precisely because they have become government property. As such, they are no longer the remains of specific families or individuals who died. Instead, their meaning has become transformed (Brandstetter 2010, 11; Meierhenrich 2011). As Sara Guyer (2009, 163) points out, the way the regime displays the bones transforms them into a mass of unknowns and unknowables. "*Any*body can make bones" (emphasis added), she notes (Guyer 2009, 159). But in the Rwandan context, only one actor is allowed to talk about how living persons became a pile of bones. Only the regime is vested with the power to interpret these artifacts. In the hands of the regime, the bones "serve as an instrument of repression" (Guyer 2009, 160), not only by leaving onlookers "speechless," but also by rendering unthinkable any other story about how the pile of bones came to be. To turn bones and remains into political displays requires forcing people to see and not see at the same time. In this way, the RPF is engaging in what Diana Taylor (1997) calls "percepticide." Percepticide makes alternatives ways of seeing and noticing *verboten* and punishable by arrest, torture, and death.

Percepticide is at also work at the memorial at Murambi, a former technical school located in Gikongoro, where it is not piles of bones on display but whole skeletons. Laid out on tables in classroom after classroom are lime-covered corpses. Viewers can see how old or young, big or small the person was. In some cases, tufts of hair still cling to the skull. Hand, arm, leg, and finger positions are frozen in time, curled or bent as if warding off a blow. And yet, even here, as Guyer (2009, 173) argues, the bones are not meant to remind visitors of the people who once lived; they are meant to render the dead as "a single anonymous form." This anonymizing of skeletons helps to foreclose pertinent questions about who the victims were, how they died, and who killed them. These are questions that an investigator would ask if viewing the bones as evidence of a crime. But remarkably, the regime has never been interested in the bones as evidence. As former justice minister Alberto Basomingera told researcher Susan Cook in 2000, the dead bodies are not necessary for determining who did what to whom; since everyone knows what happened, oral histories would suffice (Cook 2006, 291). Rather than examining the bones for their evidentiary value, the regime harnesses them for their power to make people see what it wants people to see and to make them *not* see what should not be seen. The very claim that oral histories would suffice since everyone knows what happened echoes the *Salisbury Times'* refusal to cover the lynching of Matthew Williams. As the editors claimed, such coverage was unnecessary since everyone already knows what happened. These silences by the RPF and the newspapers editors are not benign oversights. They, too, are part of the story each set of actors is trying to tell. The holes in the story—the silences and "missing" evidence—say as much as the rest.

Another advantage of displaying bare bones is that such graphic representations drown out any reflection on the present political situation, and more particularly, the extreme authoritarianism that has marked the RPF rule since July 1994 when the rebel group took power. As Meierhenrich (2011, 289) argues, "By remembering the past in a very particular, macabre manner, these memorials facilitate a forgetting of the present." I would go even further. The display of bare bones, whether in full body form or anatomically sorted piles, forces all to see the génocidaires—and by extension, all Hutu—as the only *possible* perpetrator of all violence and therefore, as the one and only perpetrator of violence. And the more murderous the génocidaires, the more innocent the RPF of any war crimes. Once evidence of the latter (RPF war crimes) is alchemically transformed into "hard" evidence of the former (genocide), the trick is done. By speaking louder than words, the bones help to mute any memories, knowledge, or stories of RPF crimes. In doing so, the bones function solely to serve the RPF's larger political project of achieving total impunity by controlling what people say about the past by controlling what they see.

Days after the Lynching in the Eastern Shore

At first glance, there might seem to be no basis for comparing the dead in Rwanda and the dead in the Eastern Shore. In the former case, killers slaughtered hundreds of thousands in less than one hundred days. In the latter, thousands participated in the killing of two men and tried to lynch a third in the span of two years. Yet, surface differences belie a common political thread. As in Rwanda, the treatment of the dead in the Eastern Shore helps to perpetuate a particular narrative of what happened and why. As in Rwanda, the bodies of Matthew Williams and George Armwood lose all signification of specific persons who once lived; instead, they become props in the story that some whites continue to tell to the present day. In the following section, I focus on the immediate aftermath of the Armwood lynching to show how Armwood's body is transformed through a larger narrative that nullifies his very humanity.

Stories and Artifacts

The "fun and games" did not end with the physical murder of George Armwood. Its immediate aftermath was filled with activity. After the crowd dispersed, Armwood's body remained in place for hours (Player 1933b). As the *Baltimore Sun* reported: "Deputy Sheriff Dryden said about 11 o'clock that he had received a call from Sheriff Daugherty at Crisfield, wanting to know what the situation was.

The situation, so far as Deputy Dryden was concerned, was quiet—though the body of the Negro still was in the heart of the town" (Player 1933b). Eventually a state policeman finally removed the body but "would not divulge its where-abouts for fear of further mutilation by souvenir hunters." (In fact, according to Clarence Mitchell, a town official had called a local black undertaker and asked him to remove the body, but the undertaker refused.) As the body lay on the street in the middle of downtown, "many women ventured to the ringside to view the charred remains of the alleged assailant of Mrs. Mary Denston" (Player 1933b). Even in death, Armwood's body elicited onlookers and spectators.

Additional activity followed the next day. Gawkers descended on the town in search of souvenirs and stories of the night before. Young boys earned money pointing out "various spots of interest" while locals gave white visitors detailed accounts of what had occurred the previous night. The same questions posed by curious blacks, however, were met with "scowls" ("Town Flooded" 1933). This narrativizing had two functions. Each retelling extended the spectacle over time; and by only including other whites in these conversations, the talk itself helped to enforce the newly inscribed boundaries between "white" and "black" that the lynching had inscribed.

Those wishing for more than a story also tried to locate artifacts. As the *Afro* reported: "Many of the white visitors searched for pieces of rope with which the youth was hanged. Others chipped pieces from the tree near the courthouse from which he was taken and his body burned beyond recognition" ("Town Flooded" 1933). Curiously, the rush for souvenirs did not include stripping Armwood's body of flesh and bone, as occurred in many other spectacle lynchings (Downey and Hyser 1991; Dray 2003; SoRelle 1983). Armwood's body was no longer the main attraction it had been just hours before.

One of the first reporters on the scene was Clarence Mitchell. At the time, Mitchell was a twenty-two-year-old recent college graduate. The *Afro* gig was supposed to be short-term as he was planning to head north to medical school (the University of Maryland refusing to accept any black students at the time) (Mitchell 1986, 1). What Mitchell found in Princess Anne, however, changed his life. He located the body in a lumberyard. Most likely, it was a policeman who had dumped it there the night before, after the town's most prominent black under-taker refused to remove it, insisting it was the city's responsibility to do so. The next morning, the owner of the lumberyard, a white woman, lodged a vehement protest against use of her property as the final dumping ground for the victim's body (Mitchell 1933b).

Proof of the tortures were visible on Armwood's body. All his clothes had been ripped, burnt, or torn off. The body also bore signs of mutilation. His skin was blackened from the burning; blisters were visible in the photo that the *Afro* ran on the front page of its October 28, 1933 edition. The caption beneath the photo explains the white spots on Armwood's leg and shoulder as "blisters raised by the fire" ("Mad" 1933). Mitchell (1933b) also noted in his own piece that Armwood's "tongue, between his clenched teeth, gave evidence of his great agony before death."

A different photo taken the same morning also shows signs of the "great agony" that Armwood endured. In this photo, Armwood's body is lying on the grass of the lumberyard, next to several discarded boards. Debris is visible around his feet. Someone—Mitchell himself perhaps—has covered the body with burlap sacks so that only his head and feet remain uncovered. His head strains upward in an unnatural position, as if the rope from the two hangings left it permanently askew. The skin on his head also appears blackened and molted from the burning. His feet are splayed and his left knee pokes out from under one of the burlap sacks. This was no resting position but a posture exhibiting horrific pain. Like so many skeletons at the Murambi memorial in Rwanda, this body evinced clear signs of the agony the living had suffered before death.

Armwood's body lay in the lumberyard until noon the next day. This provided local people, both black and white, ample opportunity to view the remains. According to the *Afro*, "Women and children, modest under normal circumstances, pressed to gaze at a naked, tortured body" ("Mad" 1933). Black residents also saw the body as they passed by on their way to work, though their gaze was solemn, not celebratory. Black children, too, caught a glimpse as they walked to school (Ifill 2007, 42). One local black woman, who was a teenager at the time, recalled decades later: "On our way to school the following morning, my brother and I went to the lumber yard. We saw the parched, seared, black and red body of the Negro whose ears, nose and genitals had been cut off" (Hayman 1980).

White schoolchildren, by contrast, avoided seeing the body because they rode the bus to school, rather than walked, and because the bus deviated from its usual route the morning after the lynching to avoid passing by the lumberyard (interview, 19 May 2010). Going home from school was another matter. The lynching had emboldened white students, who, even under normal circumstances, could hurl verbal invectives from the safety of the bus to their black counterparts walking home. One black woman, who was fifteen at the time, recalled with vivid clarity walking home from school the day after the lynching. As the bus passed by her, one of the white students yelled out, "We lynched a nigger last night and we're going to come back and get you!" [interview, 18 June 2010].

Eventually, local officials located someone who was willing to remove the body and bury it. William James, a black man sixty years old and weighing "not more than 90 pounds," took on the task with the help of his twenty-year-old nephew (Hayman 1980; Stump n.d.). James nailed together a pine box and then lifted Armwood's body "none too tenderly" into the casket and transported his remains to Potter's Field, about eight miles away (Matthews 1933). Over time, the graveyard for the indigent would fall into complete disrepair to the point of becoming unlocatable. Armwood's body became a piece of forgotten trash, no longer relevant to the story of the lynching that would endure long after his death.

The disposal of Armwood's body stands in stark contrast to that of Matthew Williams and Euel Lee. *Afro* journalist Ralph Matthews had been present in the aftermath of the Matthew Williams lynching and noted the contrast. While Armwood was buried in a hastily constructed pine box and placed in an unmarked grave, Williams was laid to rest in a "velvety coffin of steel grey, with silver handles" in the funeral home of a well-known black undertaker in Salisbury. A local pastor "committed his soul to peace" as Williams's family members wept. By contrast, no family member was present when William James took Armwood's body away (Matthews 1933). Even if Armwood's family had been willing to come forward to claim the body, the cost of a funeral, like that which Matthew Williams's family provided him, would have likely been beyond their means.[5]

The treatment of Armwood's body also contrasts with that of Euel Lee, whom the State of Maryland executed on Friday, October 27, 1933, nine days after Armwood was lynched. Maryland officials pronounced Lee dead just after midnight ("Euel Lee Hangs" 1933). Outside the penitentiary, the scene was celebratory. As Clarence Mitchell described, "The crowd outside made merry, even to the extent of eating peanuts and cracking many jokes." Mitchell also overheard people talking about the Armwood lynching that had taken place several days earlier (Mitchell 1933a), indicating that Eastern Shore whites *were* making a clear connection between Lee's case and the mob execution of Armwood. In spite of the macabre scene just outside the execution site, the prison superintendent told the *Sun* that Lee would be laid to rest in the "colored" cemetery, per Maryland state law, and that the prison chaplain would conduct the funeral ("Euel Lee Hangs" 1933). This meant that Euel Lee, convicted of a quadruple murder, and Matthew Williams, accused of killing his white employer, both had "proper burials" whereas Armwood did not. These ceremonies acknowledged and honored the humanity of Matthew Williams and Euel Lee; the disposal of Armwood's body, by contrast, turned his into a piece of trash that needed to be collected, rather than the remains of a human being who died a horrific death.

Crafting Narratives from Dead Bodies

With Armwood's death came the crafting of an official narrative through ritualized public acts. These did similar work to the carefully scripted commemorations organized by the RPF. They were meant to tell people how they should talk about what happened and by extension, how they should remember it.

The day after the lynching, Sheriff Daugherty "handpicked" the men who would serve on the coroner's jury from a group of whites who had been standing around and talking in front the courthouse (one of whom would be arrested later as an alleged mob leader). He escorted the jurors to the lumberyard "where they viewed the charred remains of Armwood." From there, they went to the office of the magistrate, Edgar Jones, who also served as coroner ("Coroner Probed" 1933). The coroner surmised dryly: "I expect it will be found that the man died from hanging" (Player 1933c).

Meanwhile, the state's attorney for Somerset County, John B. Robins, remained at his home in Crisfield, some twenty miles from Princess Anne. He refused to talk to anyone and even took his phone off the hook to staunch the deluge of calls he had been receiving all day (Player 1933c). Six days after the lynching, on October 24, 1933, Robins participated in the formal Inquest. He began the proceedings with an accounting of what had happened.

> We believe in justice being promptly administered and that is what the County authorities were trying to do. The Sheriff went to Baltimore and on Wednesday morning about three o'clock George Armwood was safely lodged in the Somerset County jail in a cell inside the jail where those charged with felonious crimes are incarcerated. Everything in Somerset County was quiet and peaceful during Wednesday, but sometime that night crowds began to congregate, mostly from foreign soil, and about nine o'clock this crowd broke into the jail; assaulted George Armwood, took him from the custody of the jailer and Sheriff and dragged him on the road and hung him on the limb of a tree, burned him with gasoline and threw his body on a vacant lot. (Robins 1933, 11; Testimony . . . Inquest 1933, 4)

Robins's opening statement places the blame on those from "foreign" soil, a reference to counties outside Somerset. So began the process of ensuring impunity for all those from Somerset County who participated in the lynching. Through the Coroner's Inquest, Robins was rebranding known participants as unidentifiable "outsiders." County officials were not as murderous as the RPF, but they were following a similar path toward exonerating themselves and all whites of Somerset County from any involvement in or responsibility for Armwood's killing. Like the RPF, they did so despite overwhelming evidence and widespread knowledge as to who had, in fact, participated in the torture-murder.

After making his opening statement, Robins called twenty-one witnesses, including Sheriff Daugherty, the deputy sheriffs on duty that night, the sixteen other prisoners in jail with Armwood, and the doctor who took a cursory look at Armwood's body the morning after the lynching. In his testimony at the Inquest, Sheriff Daugherty stated that no one in the mob was wearing a mask or trying to hide his identity; he nevertheless claimed he recognized no one. His main concern, he testified, was to protect John Richardson, the white man whom police suspected had driven Armwood to his brother's home, where police arrested Armwood ("Epithets" 1933; "Rush" 1933).

The parade of witnesses continued with Deputy Sheriff Maddox. Maddox, too, denied recognizing anyone in the crowd, except for a man named Rusty Heath and three others who were in the crowd but who did "not" participate in what he referred to as the "crime" (*Testimony . . . Inquest* 1933, 15). Deputy Sheriff Norm Dryden testified that two men had expressed their regret to him about the lynching (17); yet, he, too, denied recognizing anyone in the mob (18). When Robins asked about a newspaper story that claimed that Dryden knew one of the perpetrators, Dryden replied, "That was wrong. I straightened that out over the 'phone'" (18). Another Deputy Sheriff testified that he saw no one because when the crowd broke through the jail door, he went to a "rear room" (21). Sixteen prisoners also testified, eleven black and five white. The majority of prisoners said they did not see or hear anything. None of the prisoners identified a single individual in the crowd.

The final witness was Dr. Harry Lankford who testified that he did a "superficial external examination" when he viewed Armwood's body in "Mr. Hayman's lumber yard" (31). When Robins asked his opinion of the cause of death, Lankford replied in clinical language that belied the extensive tortures that were visible all over Armwood's body: "One of several things might have caused his death. Might have died from head injuries, strangulation, or bled to death. I am a little inclined to believe he bled to death because the blood was all over his shirt and a dead body doesn't bleed very profusely. I came to the conclusion he died from the loss of blood rather than the other things" (31). When Robins asked him about Armwood's head injuries, Lankford noted that Armwood's head was "battered up from the stone road" and had contusions all over it. As his penultimate question, Robins asked, "Would you say he died from a natural death or from some wounds?" Lankford responded with characteristic understatement: "I would think he died a violent death, not from natural causes" (32). This was the only reference to the evidentiary value of Armwood's charred, mutilated, and battered body. After the final witness, Robins adjourned the Inquest indefinitely, pending instructions from Maryland State attorney general Preston Lane.

The Inquest was a legal ritual concerning an extralegal act—the torture-murder of an unarmed black man by a large white mob. Like the annual commemorations staged by the RPF, this officially sanctioned activity recast the mob as "outsiders" from "foreign" soil. Robins's narrative also exonerated all local state actors, from the lowliest deputy sheriff to Robins himself while recasting all white Somerset countians as upstanding, law-abiding citizens. Through his questioning of various witnesses, Robins establishes the crowd as a nameless, faceless, unidentifiable "mass" and yet one that is "clearly" identifiable as coming from outside the county. The preferred "origin" story is that most mob members came from Virginia. A *Sun* reporter quoted Daugherty saying as much shortly after the lynching: "I did not see a single man from Somerset county in the bunch." Daugherty added that he believed most of the mob had come from Virginia or other Maryland counties—everywhere, it seems, but Somerset (Player 1933c). The supposed unidentifiable mass is the Eastern Shore version of the masses of anonymous bones in Rwanda. Missing or erased identities are the basis for the preferred narrative.

Other public rituals followed. Some of these deviated from Robins's script, indicating that not every actor at the time bought the story that he and other local officials were promoting. In December 1933, two months after the lynching, Daugherty and Robins were called to testify at a habeas corpus hearing on behalf of John Richardson, Armwood's former white employer and the man suspected of driving Armwood twenty miles from the alleged crime scene to his brother's house. Richardson's wife had sought his release from the Baltimore jail where he had been held since Daugherty had smuggled him out of Princess Anne the night after Armwood's lynching. The setting was a Baltimore Circuit Court and the judge in the case was Eugene O'Dunne. O'Dunne had an unusual professional résumé for his day. In 1919 he had vigorously defended a young black man named Isaiah Fountain against accusations that he had raped a fourteen-year old white girl, a highly unusual move for a white lawyer at the time (Ifill 2007, 11–15). In his courtroom, O'Dunne was no less the maverick. Daugherty claimed it was "too dark" to recognize any of the mob members, a deviation from his account at the Coroner's Inquest. The judge pressed Daugherty about the level of protection that he and his men had actually provided Armwood. The *Afro* printed the exchange.

> "Why didn't you lock them [the mob members] in?" asked Judge O'Dunne.
> The sheriff admitted that he never thought of that.
> "How did they get out; did you give them passes," asked the judge.
> Sheriff Daugherty again squirmed in his seat. ("Witness Stand" 1933)

O'Dunne's questioning of the sheriff prompted Robins to rise from his seat to object. Robins protested, "We are handling that investigation ourselves" ("Epithets" 1933). O'Dunne overruled Robins's objection and continued his questioning of

Daugherty. Both Daugherty and Robins continued to argue that John Richardson should remain in jail and not be released because of his involvement in protecting Armwood and for his possible involvement in the assault on Mary Denston, the white woman whom Armwood allegedly assaulted.[6] O'Dunne was unmoved by their protests. He asked Daugherty if Richardson would be safe to return to his home in Somerset County. Daugherty replied that he would "do all in his power to protect him" at which point, O'Dunne pointedly asked "if the protection would be like that given in the past." Daugherty was silent ("Epithets" 1933). What stands out about this exchange is that a white judge refuses to go along with the story that the local sheriff and state's attorney are trying to tell, a story that conveniently exonerates both men for their *in*action the night of the lynching, hence their complicity in the crime. Robins's only defense is to assert that the lynching is a local matter that would be handled locally.

Robins would have the final say in the matter. At the behest of Attorney General Lane, Robins would bring the case to court but with an outcome that was predetermined. When the local judge asked Robins if he had any evidence to present, Robins said, "No." The judge then dismissed all charges and declared the case closed, despite the sworn depositions by state police that identify several leaders and active members of the mob.

Soon afterward, another public forum for discussing the Armwood lynching arose. On February 20–21, 1934, the U.S. Congress held hearings on the Costigan-Wagner Act, a bill that would make lynching a federal crime. Because the Armwood lynching had occurred so recently, a range of people testified, including reporters and some Somerset County whites who may have even participated in the lynching. *Afro* reporter Clarence Mitchell testified at length.

> Directly after the victim had been lynched[,] John M. Dennis, a local undertaker, was called by a civil officer and asked to remove the body. The officer declared that he would promise the undertaker protection, but the latter refused, and the naked body was tossed into a lumberyard where it remained until near noon the next day.
>
> Evidence of severe and brutal treatment was not wanting. The face had been battered beyond recognition, and severe heat, as is usually associated with the burning of highly volatile substance, had caused the outer layer of his skin to be charred and broken in many places.
>
> No extra precautions were taken to prevent the curious persons from looking at the body and from sunrise until the time of its impromptu burial the corpse of George Armwood was the object of the entire town's attention.
>
> The main street of the town was crowded all day following the lynching, and many versions of it were openly discussed by spectators. Some

described how the leaders of the mob helped to drag the body through the streets. Others forcefully insisted that Armwood had gotten what he deserved. ("Punishment" 1934, 168)

Mitchell went on to say that a month after the lynching, when John Richardson, the white man who had tried to protect Armwood, asked if he could return to Princess Anne, state's attorney Robins denied the request, saying that (in Mitchell's words) "he felt the community was not a safe place to have Richardson return to" ("Punishment" 1934, 168). According to Mitchell's testimony, both Robins and Sheriff Daugherty believed that "the feeling was still running high" about the lynching and more specifically, the crime local whites had pinned on Armwood ("Punishment" 1934, 169). According to Mitchell, despite the passage of time *and* the state execution of Euel Lee at the Baltimore penitentiary on October 27, local officials were asserting that they could still not ensure the safety of John Richardson, a white man with a personal connection to Armwood.

The hearing involved countless witnesses, including a few men whom state police had identified as leaders of the mob. One of those was William H. Thompson, who ran a drugstore in Princess Anne. Thompson claimed he had not even been in Princess Anne at the time of the lynching and that he had only arrived "after it was over" around 9:45 p.m. ("Punishment" 1934, 203–4). Thompson went on to deplore the lynching while claiming he knew nothing about it. He had even served on the coroner's jury that decided the cause of death ("Punishment" 1934, 211). Thompson gave all the right answers to the senators questioning him. When Senator McCarran asked him point blank whether he would support a lynching in "extreme cases," that is, where a "colored man is charged with criminal assault upon a white woman," Thompson did not take the bait. Instead he replied: "I believe in the law taking its course. I believe in law and order; yes, sir" ("Punishment" 1934, 214). Thompson's wife backed up her husband's story that the two had gone to Salisbury that evening to see a movie and returned to Princess Anne close to 10:00 p.m., when the lynching was already over. When Senator McCarran asked her what movie she and her husband had gone to see, she could not remember ("Punishment" 1934, 229). It is unclear whether the senators did or did not believe Thompson, Thompson's wife, or Clarence Mitchell. Regardless, the bill never made it to a floor vote and Thompson's version of events, consistent with that told by Somerset County officials, continued to go unchallenged.

Counternarratives and Rebuke

Despite local officials' efforts to pin the blame on outsiders, people from outside the Eastern Shore condemned the lynching in the strongest terms. The most searing came from H. L. Mencken of the *Baltimore Sun*. Mencken excoriated all

Eastern Shoremen through colorful language and name calling. The rejoinders were swift. In local newspapers, responses to Mencken took up as much space as coverage of the lynching. Local white elites quickly circled the wagons. James E. Byrd, the editor of the *Marylander and Herald*, the white newspaper based in Princess Anne, spent an entire column disparaging the reporter from the *Baltimore Sun* who covered the lynching. Byrd claims the reporter (whom he does not name but may have been William O. Player, whose byline is featured in all the articles on the lynching) was drunk the whole time he was in Princess Anne and never ventured beyond the lobby of his hotel to gather information. Byrd pins the blame for the lynching not on the mob, but on the decision of state police to take Armwood to Baltimore: "We honestly believe that had Armwood been lodged in the Somerset County jail that night, without State, or local protection, there would have been no lynching. The taking of this man to Baltimore too vividly recalled to the citizens of this section the Euel Lee case; and many other cases where the man charged with such crimes had been carried away" (Byrd 1933). Byrd sums up by saying, "Had there been built around Somerset County that night a fence that would have excluded all outsiders, there would have been no lynching" (Byrd 1933). Byrd's story is identical to that maintained by Robins and Daugherty. He pins all the blame on interference by outsiders. He makes no reference to the savage violence, the carnivalesque atmosphere, the souvenir-taking, or the dumping of Armwood's mutilated body in a local lumberyard. Blaming outsiders is both an explanation of the lynching and a defense of it. For Byrd, the real "crime" is interference by outside forces, including commentators such as Mencken.

Over the next decades, the narrative that "outsiders did it" and "we are being unfairly attacked" would continue to circulate. What helped to bolster it is the assumption that all three men—Euel Lee, Matthew Williams, and George Armwood—were guilty of the crimes they had been accused of committing. This assumed guilt continuously moved the question of "why" away from the lynch mob (as in why would so many "upstanding" citizens participate in such a horrific act) and toward factors that were beyond the control of Somerset countians. For example, in 1961, a high school student named David Pusey won an essay contest with a paper he wrote on "the whys, hows, and results of the lynching in Princess Anne" (Pusey 1961). The young author provides a detailed account of the lynching, starting with the Euel Lee case. He takes for granted that everything printed in the white newspapers is true, to wit: Euel Lee murdered a white family of four because of a dispute over unpaid wages. Matthew Williams shot and killed his white employer over an argument over wages. George Armwood assaulted—that is, "raped"—a white woman. The arc of this narrative ends not with an analysis of those who took part, but rather the tug-of-war between state and county officials. The former include Governor Ritchie and Attorney General Lane, both of whom insisted on prosecuting the ringleaders. The latter include state's attorney Robins, Sheriff Daugherty, and the coroner—all those in positions of authority within the county who sought to absolve everyone from Somerset County. Thirty years after the fact, the high schooler maintains a story that focuses on the violations committed by outsiders, rather than the violence perpetrated by insiders against George Armwood and Matthew Williams, repeated attempts by locals to lynch Euel Lee, and assaults by locals in Worcester County on black residents going about their business, and assaults on Bernard Ades and the two women traveling with him.

There is additional evidence this version continued to go unchallenged over the next decades. In the 1970s, for example, a professor at the local university assigned his students the task of conducting an oral history with a family member or friend. Judging from the collection, I presume he also gave them the theme for these interviews: racial violence on the Shore. Most students interviewed parents, grandparents, or some other family member. While the "oral histories" are quite brief, usually no more than a page, they all provide the age, race, name, and residence of both the interviewer and interviewee. And although I located only thirty-two in the archives, even with this small number it is possible to pick up on differences between the ways white and black respondents talk about the Armwood and Williams lynchings. Like other whites, white respondents simply assume the guilt of both lynching victims. For example, a seventy-two-year-old white lawyer from Salisbury (who would have been in his thirties at the time of the two lynchings) related the story this way: "There was an Armwood lynching in Princess Anne a few years ago. They hung a man in front of the judge's house cause he had assaulted a woman. I'm not so god damn sure it wasn't right and I was states attorney about that time. He certainly got the kink out of his neck anyhow."[7] Recalling the event forty years after the fact, this man's tone is perfunctory as well as taunting. For this respondent, the passage of time has not changed how he views or talks about the lynching.

Black respondents, by contrast, talk about the same events using very different language that bears little resemblance to the way whites talk about them. For example, a fifty-five-year-old woman who identified herself as a domestic worker cites details in the Armwood lynching that none of the white respondents mention. She also frames details about what Armwood did as "alleged" acts, not facts.

> It involved a white lady and a negro who had been working for her. It is believed that a white man in the neighborhood raped her and the blame was placed on the negro.

> The Governor called and asked Judge Duer if he had enough protection and the Judge said yes. They put him in jail and that night some of the town people (white) broke into the jail and took him out.

> They drug him down main street and stopped in front of Judge Duer's. When he would not let them hang him in his yard, they drug him past Elizabeth Richard's and went back up Beckford Avenue. They carried him a block from the jail and set him on fire. They left him there and that morning all the school children went by to look at him.

In this retelling, the details focus on the violence done to the victim. Nowhere is there any assumption of his guilt. In fact, in this version, the man who actually raped the "white lady" is a "white man." The interviewee may have been referring to John Richardson, the white man jailed for helping Armwood flee the scene of the alleged crime by driving him to his brother's house. The details also suggest that the woman knew about the lynching firsthand. She would have been a teenager at the time so she may well have had her own firsthand memories of that night since she lived through it.

Several black interviewees also remark on what happened to members of the mob, a point that no white interviewee includes. This same woman, for example, ended her story by noting that "all the people involved did some terrible suffering" and mentioned one man who had died in a "terrible accident" after losing both his legs. Where the official version erases the violence and torture that the victims suffered, the version that black respondents tell focuses on the allegations that led to the violence and the suffering that mob members underwent in the years following the lynching. In these retellings, violence to the lynching victims remains front and center.

White officials, however, continued their efforts at erasing the lynching from the county's history. In 1975, the president of the Somerset County Bicentennial Commission hired John Wennersten, a historian at the local university, to write a history of the county for the bicentennial celebration (Wennersten nd, iv). When Wennersten produced the manuscript, the official refused to publish it because it included a chapter on the Armwood lynching. Despite the commissioner's refusal to publish, Wennersten continued to circulate the manuscript so that other scholars (including me) could read and cite it.

The capacity of the lynching to provoke controversy did not wane. In 2010, a local black leader in Princess Anne organized the first ever commemoration of the George Armwood lynching. He brought in scholars who had published books on Princess Anne to speak. He opened the event to the public. He invited audience members to ask questions or share their personal stories. Around the time of the commemoration, I heard a startling story from another Princess Anne resident. He said that two men had recently walked into the hardware store ask-ing where they could buy tickets to the "re-enactment." Astonished, I went to the store myself. I asked the woman who worked there if the story was true. She con-firmed it was. I asked if the men meant it as a joke. She seemed to think not. She herself had not waited on the two men, but the young man who did had told her about the exchange right away. Nearly eighty years after the fact, the story of the "last" lynching in Princess Anne is not a story about George Armwood, a black man from a poor family who suffered an endless stream of extralethal acts. For some, the lynching continues to be a source of fun and amusement.

What to make of these stories that never end? I argue these retellings help to extend the original violent displays over time and space. They bring the dis-play continuously into the present. They do so in different ways. In Rwanda, the RPF uses displays of bare bones to decouple the link between a particular set of remains and the person who once lived, thereby rendering the masses of bones "anonymous." Then, through annual ceremonies of exhumation and reburial, the RPF recategorizes those anonymized remains as "genocide victims," despite local knowledge that many of the dead were victims of RPF massacres or per-petrators, rather than victims, of the genocide. These political displays help to promote and enforce a narrative that constructs all Hutu as guilty and the RPF as innocent and heroic. They recast the living and dead in the service of the RPF's ultimate goal of maintaining complete and unfettered control over how people—Rwandans and foreigners alike—see the past and how they talk about it.

In the Eastern Shore, the retelling also brings the original violent displays—the lynchings of Matthew Williams and George Armwood—into the present. The "official" version has remained largely intact over many decades through state rituals, like the Coroner's Inquest as well as the hearing for the Costigan-Wagner Act. This narrative has also circulated as "fact" for generations of whites. Accord-ing to this narrative, there is no doubt that the lynching victims and would-be victim Euel Lee were guilty of heinous crimes, just as there is no doubt the "real" offenders were "outsiders" who interfered in local matters. These outsiders included unidentified "Virginians" as well as specific individuals, such as Bernard Ades, the communist lawyer who defended Euel Lee, and Governor Ritchie and an attorney general who were intent on punishing local mob leaders.

What links these retellings in Rwanda and the Eastern Shore is the centrality of the body as a potent signifier. In neither context do the bodies matter in terms of the people they once were. Instead, they operate as graphic props in the narra-tives these actors like to tell; as props, they represent entire categories of persons, to wit: "black beasts" in the Eastern Shore and "Tutsi victims of the genocide." The bodily remains are fitted into these categories even though the actual people who once lived may have had nothing to do with either category. The bodies and remains, however, are fungible—they can be made to fit any category by the living. It is the ambiguity inherent in the remains that makes that possible. It is also the symbolic power of the human body to stand in for larger social bodies that makes human remains so valuable as props in the larger story that actors wish to tell. In the Eastern Shore, the bodies of Euel Lee, Matthew Williams, and George Armwood, once the focal point of the mob's excitement, become stand-ins for the anonymous "black beast" from which local whites must protect themselves at all costs. In Rwanda the masses of all the dead, which include victims of RPF massacres as well as génocidaires—are reamassed into the category of "Tutsi genocide victims" whom the RPF purports to "honor" through the very practices (exhumation, reburial, memorializing) that recategorize the dead. In both settings, the bones of the dead are indeed made to speak. But what they are made to say is rooted in the present, not the past. Their bones figure in stories that the living are trying to tell. They are normative signifiers of how the living should view the dead and how they should—and *should not*—talk about how and why the dead came to be so in the first place.

FICTIONS

The Making and Unmaking of Boundaries

> **Me and Branko, we were one soul, we were so close,
> and that's how it was in my village.**
>
> —Feriz Dervišević, author interview

During the Vietnam War, US soldiers engaged in practices that harkened back to medieval modes of violent display. Examples include beheading corpses and dragging bodies behind vehicles through local villages (Turse 2013, 163). Lynchers in the United States engaged in similar activities. After murdering their victims through slow fire or hanging, lynchers sometimes drove the victim's body through black parts of town or hung them from a tree or lamppost in a black neighborhood (Raper 1933, 7; SoRelle 1983). A group of Bosnian Serb soldiers also partook of this same practice during the Bosnian war. Just outside Prijedor, soldiers tied a man to the back of a tank and dragged him through the mostly Muslim town of Kozarac (Maass 1996, 39). In all three contexts, the act of desecration was not a meaningless prank, but a graphic form of meaning-filled communication. But why send a message through the display of a dead body?

The answer lies in the semiotic or meaning-making power of the human body. It is the capacity of the human body to stand in for entire social categories—to give substance to and proof of imagined social bodies that endows violent displays with such power. Violent displays inscribe new meanings onto abstracted social bodies not only through the violence inflicted on victims' bodies, but also through the violence expressed through participants' bodies—as they kick, drag, pull, punch, slice, cut, laugh, and cheer. It is they who are transformed through the process. It is they who experience a new and novel basis for belonging.

And yet, these newly inscribed meanings do not necessarily stick or endure. Neither do they signify uniformity across time and place. Despite the best efforts of extremists, nationalists, and supremacists, some people will not go along with the categorization of bodies established by and through violent displays. Some Serbs will still help, rather than hurt, their non-Serb neighbors; some Hutu will protect, not denounce, their Tutsi friends; some white sheriffs will keep a black suspect from the lynch mob rather than turn him over. And by doing so, they not only violate the meanings that violent displays construct, they also reveal how flimsy, fleeting, or variable those meanings are. In spite of perpetrators' best efforts, large and small gestures of aid are also a fact of war, genocide, and mob violence; and regardless of the success rate, the very impulse to help, rather than hurt, or the simple act of refusing to go along constitutes a breach in the line. It is a reminder that even violence cannot keep everyone on the "correct" side, however one defines those sides. In this chapter, I show that violent category making—whether through violent displays or other forms—is a highly contingent process and its effects are uneven and at times, unexpected.

Confounding Patterns of Racial Violence in the Eastern Shore

In Maryland, as elsewhere, lynchings were semirare events. White mobs lynched roughly thirty-five hundred black people across the country between Reconstruction and the 1930s.[1] Aggregate numbers, however, belie the extent of variation that characterize this form of violence. Rates varied by state, even within the South (Tolnay and Beck 1995, 36–38); within the same state, they varied further—by county (Stovel 2001) and region (Brundage 1993). Even in high lynching states, patterns were confounding. Counties with high numbers of lynchings might sit next to counties with none (Stovel 2001, 848). Rates also varied over time. While scholars refer to the period of 1882 to 1930 as the "lynching era" or "lynching epidemic" (Hagen, Makovi, and Bearman 2013, 763), rates in Southern states, where the vast majority of lynchings occurred, varied considerably from year to year (Tolnay and Beck 1995, 29).

Part of this variation is due to differing notions of white supremacy. As Fitzhugh Brundage (1993, 105) explains, what constituted a threat to white supremacy varied considerably from place to place such that "behavior that might spark white retribution in one region went unnoticed in another." In the coastal region of Georgia, for example, "where whites seemingly should have felt a constant need to keep blacks in their places," the area is notable for the *infrequency* of lynchings that occurred there (Brundage 1993, 133).

Historians largely agree that by the 1930s, lynchings were on the decline and were becoming a "rarity" (Brundage 1993, 36–37). One reason is the "impressive rise in the number of prevented lynchings" noted by Tolnay and Beck (1995, 203). By the 1930s, they estimate that 84 percent of possible lynchings were prevented, oftentimes by law enforcement, which offered the best protection of black arrestees. Other scholars concur, though their estimates are more modest. They estimate that about one-third of lynching attempts were prevented, usually by law enforcement (Griffin, Clark, and Sandberg 1997, 26; Hagen, Makovi, and Bearman 2013, 758). Averted lynchings were not restricted to less serious allegations. According to Hagen et al.'s (2013, 768) inventory, 90 percent of averted lynchings in North Carolina (a border state like Maryland and less dependent on cotton than Deep South states) were cases where lynching inciters had accused the would-be victim of murder or rape of a white person, the most serious charges that could be leveled at a potential lynching victim.

Even on the Eastern Shore, law enforcement officials could and did successfully prevent lynchings, which highlights the complicity of law enforcement at the Williams and Armwood lynchings. Indeed, one of the most striking cases in light of the Matthew Williams lynching of 1931 and the George Armwood lynching of 1933 is that of a young, black man named William Lee. In 1906, at the height of the "lynching epidemic," Lee went on a spree of robbery and rape in Somerset County. As an outsider with no known roots in the community, Lee was even more vulnerable to rough justice (Pfeifer 2004) than someone from the area; hence, it is all the more puzzling that he escaped the mob.

Lee arrived in Somerset County by steamer on Sunday, June 10, 1906 (Barnes 2006, 2).[2] Shortly after alighting the ship, Lee met a white man named Mr. Townsend who was on his way to church. While the family attended Sunday services, Lee broke into their home and stole money, jewelry, and a family photo (2–3). Later the same day, he encountered a young white woman who was out walking with her baby and teenage cousin. The trio had just come from a five o'clock service at the local Episcopal church (3–4). Lee proceeded to rape the young mother and attempted to rape her cousin as well, but the teenager fought him off. Lee fled to another part of the county. By evening, he had reached the town of Rehobeth where he stole a carriage and drove to Pocomoke City (6). After hiding overnight in a boxcar, he caught a train to Cape Charles City in the Virginia part of the Eastern Shore (8). As soon as Lee set foot on Virginia soil, the town sergeant of Cape Charles City arrested him (8).

The sergeant waited until nightfall, then he and the local sheriff, Samuel A. Jarvis, took Lee to the small town of Eastville in Northampton County, Virginia (10). Once he had locked up Lee, Jarvis quickly summoned volunteers—not to lynch Lee but to keep him from being lynched. That afternoon a mob from

Maryland descended on the small town, bent on taking Lee back to Somerset County, the site of his alleged crime spree. Sheriff Jarvis and his volunteer posse, which included a county judge and the mayor of the town (13–14), kept the mob of Marylanders at bay. The mob retreated but did not go home (18).

At 4:00 p.m., the Marylanders "pressed to within a few yards of the jail" (19). Some in the mob tried to strike a deal with Sheriff Jarvis, promising that if he gave up Lee, they would not lynch the young man on Virginia soil. Jarvis refused. By six-thirty that evening, Virginia militiamen, whom Virginia governor Swanson had called up earlier in the day to reinforce Sheriff Jarvis, arrived and secured the jail. Virginia authorities eventually returned Lee to Maryland where, following a trial and conviction, county authorities executed the prisoner on a deserted stretch of marshland that was within Somerset county lines.

What is remarkable about the Lee case is not that he was executed for his crimes, but rather the lengths to which a small-town sheriff from the Virginia Eastern Shore went to keep Lee safe from a Maryland mob that was intent on lynching the young man for his alleged crimes in Somerset County. Miles Barnes, the chronicler of William Lee's story, argues that it was not a lack of commitment to white supremacy that made the Eastern Shore Virginians determined to keep Lee safe, but rather an abhorrence for the practice of lynching. From the governor's mansion to the small town of Eastville, Virginians had rejected lynching as a form of punishment or technique of social control. Sheriff Jarvis and his men were confronting not just a group of outsiders, but a mob that had crossed state lines to engage in a practice that Virginians had rejected. As Barnes (2006, 17) explains, "The idea of a Maryland mob defying the laws of Virginia filled [Virginia governor] Swanson with indignation." Unlike Governor Ritchie of Maryland some thirty years later, Governor Swanson of Virginia did not hesitate to call out the Norfolk militia regiment to secure the jail and keep the prisoner safe from the Maryland mob, despite accusations that Lee had raped a young, white woman and attempted to rape another.

The Lee case underscores the dramatic difference in how two neighboring communities in the Eastern Shore responded to allegations that a young, black man had robbed and raped several local whites. Virginians were not more "liberal" than Marylanders when it came to issues of race; nor were Virginia Eastern Shoremen more tolerant than their Maryland counterparts when it came to infractions of the racial code. What distinguished the two groups was the remedies each saw as appropriate to the situation. For Marylanders, only lynching would do; for Virginians, only law and order. As Barnes (2006, 20) explains, "Unlike other places in the South, Northampton had eschewed riot and political terrorism. Nor, even in instances of black-on-white murder and rape, had they lynched."

The William Lee case was not unique. A similar case was taking place at exactly the same time in Worcester County, Maryland, which twenty-five years later would become the site of the murder of the Green Davis family and the near lynching of Euel Lee for that crime. Police had charged John Henry, son of a prominent black resident, with assaulting a white woman. Authorities later upgraded the charge to rape. The police arrested Henry in the town of Berlin, and when a crowd formed to lynch him, they took Henry to the more secure jail in Snow Hill, about fifteen miles away. The day after William Lee's execution in Somerset County, officials in Worcester County executed John Henry. Despite both men being charged with the rape of white women, neither was lynched; instead, both were executed by the state. The distinction is not semantic; both men were executed to be sure but neither man suffered the extended and extensive tortures of mob justice. These cases also demonstrate the capacity of local officials and law enforcement to protect a prisoner from a lynch mob when they were determined to do so. This is precisely the task that local sheriffs and officials would fail to do thirty years later in the cases of Matthew Williams and George Armwood.

The passage of Jim Crow laws across the South and in border states like Maryland, while enforcing racial hierarchy, did not succeed in infusing "black" and "white" with universal understandings of the proper response to violations of the color line. The same black-on-white crime that called for lynching in one community did not in another. This variation suggests that racialized systems designed to maintain a vividly etched color line failed to take into account that the symbolic material used to maintain the line would vary from place to place, community to community, and as Barnes (2006, 19) argues, from "doorstep to doorstep." This is not to say that race was more or less important in some places than others; neither is it to argue that the courts actually guaranteed black defendants equal protection under the law or a presumption of innocence. Countless cases on the Shore prove otherwise (Ifill 2007). What I argue instead is that what it meant to be "white" did not produce uniform practices or the same outcome every time local whites accused a black man of raping a white woman or killing a white person. The lynch mob did not always get its way. Put differently, the institution and ideology of white supremacy did not depend on the practice of lynching.

Microviolations of the Nationalist Line in Bosnia

Just as understandings of whiteness and white supremacy varied by county and community within the Eastern Shore, so, too, did notions of "Serbness" vary within Bosnia. Nationalists in Bosnia sought to enforce their own brand through violent attacks that targeted not just territories but also relations between Serbs and non-Serbs, the very existence of which violated the nationalist cause. The war in Bosnia was a contest over what it meant to be Bosnian and whether one could be Bosnian and "Serb" at the same time. Competing nationalists, Franjo Tuđman of Croatia and Slobodan Milošević of Serbia, shared a common vision of Bosnia's future. Both made claims about the Croat and Serb communities that lived in their respective republics, arguing that each belonged with their fellow Croats in Croatia and Serbs in Serbia. The "solution" both envisioned was not the migration of Bosnian Croats into Croatia or Bosnian Serbs into Serbia, but rather the removal of any and all communities from Bosnia that did not accord with the two leaders' shared vision. Carving up communities, however, required undoing long-standing relationships that regularly crossed the lines of perceived ethnicity and religion. Indeed, because these relations were so long-standing and intertwined, nationalists had to use violence to destroy them (Gagnon 2004). Even with violence, however, vestiges of the "old" way of doing things still remained.

In the spring of 1992, Bosnian Serb forces led by Radovan Karadžić began the systematic and forcible takeover of large swathes of Bosnian soil. The goal was ethnic unity through forced purification. In Sarajevo, however, there were many who shared a very different vision of Bosnia's future and what it meant to be Bosnian. On February 29, 1992, the government held a referendum that asked voters whether Bosnia should declare itself an independent country of "citizens." The word *citizen* was important, because it avoided references to regional or nationalist claims on Bosnian territory (Burg and Shoup 2000, 107). An overwhelming yes vote would also mean the further dismantling of Yugoslavia, which had just "lost" the republics of Slovenia and Croatia one year before, when both declared themselves independent countries. Support for the referendum would lead Bosnia down the same path; it would also leave the rump Yugoslav state with only three of its original six republics: Serbia, Montenegro, and Macedonia.

To render the vote meaningless, Karadžić called for Bosnian Serbs to boycott the referendum. He ordered road blocks to go up in Serb-controlled neighborhoods of Sarajevo to prevent the delivery of ballot boxes. Despite these moves, the vote went ahead and the vast majority of the population, including Serbs who were not supporters of Karadžić or the SDS (the Serb nationalist party), voted overwhelmingly "for a sovereign and independent Bosnia-Herzegovina of equal citizens" (Burg and Shoup 2000, 117; Malcolm 1996, 231). The same pattern held outside Sarajevo. In Ključ, for example, one resident recalled that two-thirds of the votes were in favor of independence [Konz].

On April 6, 1992, the European Community formally recognized Bosnia-Herzegovina as an independent, sovereign state. Karadžić, whom urbane Sarajevans had once dismissed for his peasant ways, was no longer someone others could ignore.[3] He had become head of the SDS, then backed by Milošević, and was now making threats. He warned that if Bosnia should gain international recognition, it would mean war. He promptly declared the establishment of the "Serbian Republic of Bosnia and Herzegovina" (later renamed Republika Srpska). Killing began in Sarajevo the same day (Malcolm 1996, 234; Silber and Little 1997, 224, 228). Across the country, Bosnians were demonstrating their support for the referendum (Gagnon 2004, 111). In Sarajevo, as fifty thousand people of all backgrounds marched through the city to express their support for a multicultural Bosnia and their opposition to the nationalists, snipers began firing from the Holiday Inn, the unofficial headquarters of Karadžić's SDS party (Maass 1996, 21). With these first shots, violence became the new basis for determining who was who.

The first to die were two young female protesters. One was a twenty-one-year old medical student from Dubrovnik who was Muslim (Silber and Little 1997, 227), and the other a mother of two and a Serb (Bringa 2002, 221n15). Little about the victims' origins or identity would have mattered to the snipers, however. They were not shooting at the protesters because of their putative national identities. They were shooting at people who, by virtue of their protest activity, were challengers to, hence enemies of, the nationalist project. It would have made little difference if some identified as Serb because these men and women, by dint of their protest activity, no longer be counted as "real" Serbs according to the nationalist cause. According to this logic, one could not be Serb and a supporter of a multicultural, independent Bosnia at the same time. Indeed, nationalists found it so difficult to fathom the idea that there were Serbs who self-identified as Bosnians first that they "simply declared them nonexistent" (Gjelten 1995, 11).

This contest over the fate of Bosnia and what it meant to be Bosnian was taking place in nearly every community located in territories that RS authorities were wresting from Bosnian government control. From the very beginning, the new authorities were targeting relationships—those that violated the nationalist meanings of what it meant to be a "true" Serb. They were creating a new basis for alliance and association—a new "us" in opposition to the new "them." To become one of "us" required wielding violence against former friends and neighbors or, at the very least, not preventing others from doing so. The violence placed lifelong friends and neighbors on opposite sides. This was the whole point of targeting the most integrated regions of the country, for only violence could undo years and generations of close friendships and deeply interrelated communities (Gagnon 2004).

Vinko and Omer

In Ključ, many friends and acquaintances fell victim to this strategy. One in particular stood out. The friendship between Vinko, a Serb, and Omer, a Muslim is a typical Bosnian story. The two had grown up together. They knew each other from school, served together in the army reserve, and became close friends through Omer's older brother. Both became highly respected members of the community: Vinko as chief of police and Omer as a teacher. So close was Vinko to Omer's family that Omer's father treated Vinko like a third son. He even sold Vinko a prized plot of land that had been in the family for generations "for a very small amount" in recognition of the friendship. The sale brought the two families closer together [Konz]. It also promised to bring the families geographically closer since the plot sat next to the other Filipović (Omer's surname) family homes. Vinko was in the process of building his new home when the war started [interviews].

When nationalist politics was on the rise in the late 1980s, the two men joined different parties. Omer initially joined the SDA, the Muslim party headed by Alija Izetbegović, but then switched to the more moderate MBO (Muslimanska bošnjačka organizacija, or Bosnian Muslim Organization).[4] Vinko joined the SDS, the Serb nationalist party. Joining two different parties did not necessarily mean the two were becoming more nationalistic. In the lead-up to the 1990 elections, all political parties were presenting themselves as moderate, promoting a nonnationalist platform, and emphasizing cooperation among the different parties in order to win votes (Gagnon 2004, 49). Joining different parties did not change their relationship. The two men continued to work together and to talk on a regular basis. They remained friends until June 1991, when political turmoil roiled neighboring Croatia and Serbia. From that point on, according to one man who knew both Omer and Vinko, the two began going their separate ways [Konz].

When mass firings of all non-Serbs began during the start of the war in Bosnia, Omer lost his job as head of the national guard unit for Ključ (known locally as the TO, or Teritorijalna odbrana). He may have sensed what else was coming. His twentieth high school reunion was planned for May 5, 1992, but Omer did not want to go. He was afraid someone might try to kill him. His wife laughed, saying, "Who would kill you?" [8Fil]

On May 29, 1992, authorities searched the houses of Omer and his brother, ostensibly looking for weapons [Coll; Bra]. At the time, Omer was at a nearby village where he was trying to calm tensions after a shooting had occurred. Rather than flee the area with others, he called Vinko and told him to come and pick him up [Konz; 8Fil]. According to a close family member, Omer had realized that the situation had already gone beyond his ability to keep the peace; the war was on. Before authorities took him away, they allowed Omer one phone call to his family. His last words to them were of reassurance, not alarm. "I'm going to a concentration camp and my father was at the concentration camp at Auschwitz and he came home alive and I hope to do the same, too" [8Fil].

Authorities first took Omer to the police station in Ključ, then to an old jail in Stara Gradiška, a Serb-controlled town in Croatia about two to three hours away [Konz]. On June 15, 1992, authorities transferred him along with his brother, a friend named Esad Bender, and other prisoners from the area to Manjača concentration camp. Manjača was a former military farm and training facility [14Col; Brdj 2216; Tad 1812–13]. Prisoners were kept in barns with no running water or toilets [Brdj 2226]. The majority of captive men, who were mostly Muslims but also a small number of Croats, came from nearby towns, such as Sanski Most, Prijedor, Ključ, and smaller villages.

The day before Omer's arrest, authorities had arrested his brother, Muhamed. Police had found Muhamed in his garden. A Serb friend came to escort him to the police station. Muhamed credited the man's actions with saving his life. Without an escort, he explained, the snipers would have simply shot and killed him. At the police station, Muhamed was subject to hours of beatings. He did not recognize his tormentors; they were not local Serbs but came from outside the region. As chief of police, Vinko was presumably in charge of these operations, but Muhamed did not see him that day. It was Vinko's deputy (and one of his own neighbors) who finally came into the room and ordered the men to stop [Coll].

When prisoners arrived at Manjača, their induction into camp life was violent. Camp personnel "registered" the prisoners, a cruel euphemism for the beatings each prisoner had to undergo as soon as they stepped foot on the grounds [Brdj 2229]. As New York Times reporter Chuck Sudetic (1992) described: "Most prisoners were forced to run a gauntlet of guards swinging bats and cable, and drunken guards would take men out of their stalls between 10 and 11 at night and beat them." The guards came from all over the region. A few were from Ključ. They were free to do whatever they wanted. They starved the prisoners and beat them regularly with wooden clubs [toljage] and metal cables [Coll; Hum] The beatings were sometimes targeted at specific people and other times at those randomly selected from the prison population [Brdj 2229]. When I asked one former prisoner if some guards were worse than others, he replied, "It's difficult to say. They were all the same. Even if [a guard] wanted to act better, he couldn't" [Coll]. Like other Serb-run camps, Manjača was a space for guards and soldiers to show they were "real Serbs" by acting the part. But some performances were more "felicitous" than others, suggesting that even in the midst of violence, some guards did their best to resist pressures to join in the violence.[5]

Omer was one of the prisoners the guards particularly targeted because of his status as a local Muslim leader. Even in prison, Omer continued to lead by example. When a delegation from the humanitarian organization Merhamet visited the camp on June 18, 1992, Omer spoke openly about the conditions in front of the guards. He told the Merhamet representatives how guards were starving and abusing the prisoners [Brdj 2229]. Among the prisoner delegation, Omer was the only one to speak frankly. When the Merhament representative, Adil Medić, testified years later at the ICTY, he would confirm what Omer had told the delegation. Most of the prisoners Medić saw on that first visit were wearing civilian clothing and were "barefoot" and "half-naked" [Brdj 2220, 2223].

Omer and his brother stayed together in the same barracks. At first, Omer received "proper treatment." That changed, however, when he refused to appear in a propaganda film declaring on camera that the war in Ključ was started by the "Green Berets," a group of supposedly radical Muslim fighters. After he refused to be in the film, the beatings began. The guards would take Omer to solitary confinement for these pummeling sessions. As another prisoner explained, "They couldn't kill him there (in front of us). So they took him. They were beating him to death" [Coll]. Though beaten daily, Omer managed to keep his spirit up for the sake of his fellow inmates. As another prisoner noted, "Every day when they called his name, he literally jumps up and goes out. He wanted to show other prisoners, 'Look at me, there is no reason to be afraid'" [Konz].

On July 28, 1992, Omer's body finally gave out.[6] On his last day, guards had beat him with hammers [Coll; Konz]. The next morning, a soldier called out his brother, Muhamed, to view the body. Muhamed asked his cousin to go with him. The two followed the soldier to the building where they found Omer lying on the ground naked. Guards had "cleansed" him the old-fashioned way; they had beaten him to death. His brother said a prayer for him. The soldier put his arm around Muhamed in a gesture of comfort and respect [Konz; Coll]. However small, such a gesture was out of place in the context of the prison camp, where camp personnel were under constant pressure to go along with the violence and to never, ever show even the smallest kindness to the prisoners.

News of Omer's death traveled serendipitously. The authorities had sent his and his friend's (Esad Bender's) bodies to a cemetery in Banja Luka. By coincidence, the same Merhamet worker, Adil Medić, who had visited Manjača in June, was in the cemetery because of another Muslim who had died in Banja Luka. While there, Medić overheard someone referring to two bodies from Manjača. He knew instantly they had to be those of inmates. He went to see them and recognized the body of Omer. Medić made a formal request to the RS authorities, asking to take possession of Omer's body [Brdj 2230]. He then learned that Omer's close friend, Esad, had died along with him. Guards had also beaten Esad to death, though not as severely as they had Omer [Brdj 2230–31; Coll].

Medić phoned Omer's wife. She was stunned. He gave her the details of the burial which was to take place in Banja Luka in the next day or two. He assured her that he would take care of everything. All she needed to do was to get herself to Banja Luka, about two and a half hours away through Serb-controlled territory. She called Vinko, her husband's former best friend. Vinko was shocked by the news and said it could not be true. He made a phone call to confirm what he had heard. He then called back Omer's wife, saying the cause was "a heart attack," as if Omer had died of illness rather than been murdered [8Fil].

Omer's wife beseeched Vinko in the name of friendship. Vinko had not been the one to order the arrest of Omer, his transfer to Manjača, or his subsequent beating and murder; he was, however, in a position to help his friend's wife attend the funeral. Vinko arranged a police car with a policeman and soldier as escorts to take Omer's wife, sister-in-law, and young daughter to Banja Luka [Coll; 8Fil]. One of the escorts, a former student of Omer's, asked the women as they got into the car, "When did professor die?" as if Omer had died of natural causes [8Fil]. The journey was surreal. The car had to pass through several checkpoints. When those manning the checkpoints asked the driver who the women were, the driver would respond simply, "Family" [8Fil] and with that, the car was allowed to pass. Omer's wife made it to the funeral and afterward, her escorts returned the family safely back to Ključ.

Instances of Succor

The story of Omer Filipović, like so many other non-Serbs killed during the war, is ultimately one of murder. But the target was not just a local Muslim leader who refused to kowtow to the new nationalist order. It was also the kinds of relationships between Serbs and non-Serbs that nationalists wanted to eliminate. Some were long-standing friendships like that of Omer and Vinko; others were less intimate. Even these less intimate friendships could provoke Serbs to act in ways that violated the new nationalist order. In Manjača, all guards were under intense pressure to behave a certain way; and yet, a soldier allowed Omer's brother and cousin to view the body. Why? The guards knew whose body it was. They did not need Omer's family members to identify it. When I asked Muhamed if they took him to see the body as an act of cruelty, he said no. The gesture was spontaneous, as was the guard's impulse to put his arm around him when he laid eyes on the battered and lifeless body of his brother. There is no question that an atmosphere of brutality reigned at the camp. And yet, amidst this brutality, small moments that harkened back to prewar norms still emerged. These tended to happen when no one was looking—that is, when violence was not on display.

Such gestures also occurred in the town of Ključ and the nearby village of Selo. Interviewees tended to recall anyone who acted decently, no matter how big or small the gesture. Viewed one way, the salience of these memories points to how rare such gestures were. Viewed differently, however, that they occurred at all points to how difficult it was for nationalists, even with overwhelming force, to keep people on their "own" side of the nationalist line. Lives and relationships were simply too intertwined.

Other examples abound. A man from Ključ was held in the town of Sitnica before being transferred to Manjača. While at Sitnica, prisoners received no food, only water, for five days. Many suffered beatings, especially the prisoners from Ključ. One day a guard called the man outside. A Serb friend was waiting for him. He had brought him "a big sandwich, homemade bread with meat." Years after the war, the two men met up again. While catching up, the former prisoner learned new details about his captivity in Sitnica. His friend told him that during the men's detention, a special unit arrived, comprised of local Serb recruits; apparently, there were plans afoot to kill all the prisoners but the women of the town protested, saying that they would not allow what happened during World War II to happen there again. If the recruits wanted to shoot and kill people, they would have to do it somewhere else [Konz]. Both stories—the sandwich brought by a Serb friend and the thwarted killings—suggest that not all local Serbs responded the same way to the takeover. Certainly many saw it as an opportunity to claim power, but others continued to follow prewar norms of neighborliness and friendship, regardless of which side of the nationalist line a particular person fell.

In town, the situation was similar. Several interviewees recalled Serb neighbors who brought food to Muslim neighbors who did not flee, but remained in Ključ for the entirety of the war [interviews]. One woman recalled the simple kindness of a nod as convoys began taking away non-Serbs who were fleeing. As others were laughing and making fun of those leaving, one man and his wife showed respect for their former neighbors and warned those taunting them that they might be next [17Comp]. Another interviewee told the story of two Serb women who shared their food with her and allowed the woman to sleep at their house for safety. This same woman recalled another neighbor helping her one night, when a man with mental illness wandered into her house. When the neighbor heard noises, he came over and chased the man out [Soe].

In Selo, interviewees also talked of similar acts of succor or simple decency. One such man was the local police chief who helped people in various ways, despite taking part in the arrest, detention, and killing of local men. One woman recalled him giving her three hundred German deutsche marks just before she left on a convoy so that she would have something to turn over to the soldiers who regularly robbed the passengers just before the buses arrived in Bosnian government held territory [Tab]. Other interviewees recalled the local police chief protecting them by checking in on them or whisking away captive men before they could be killed [5Bou; Fle; Chap]. Besides the police chief, other neighbors, too, extended small courtesies that were consistent with the norms of prewar relations. One interviewee, for example, said a local Serb warned the soldiers and military police not to hurt him; the man would also regularly drop by the interviewee's house to make sure no one was harassing or harming him [Chap]. Another story I heard was about a woman who brought a basket of bread to the men held captive in the school; the woman boldly, and without asking permission, walked right past the soldiers and into the school [fieldnotes].

The new authorities were not simply intent on taking over territory; they were also determined to destroy prewar relations. Violence, and more specifically, displays of violence, made it impossible for people to reclaim what they had before. It ensured that former friends were no longer "of" a community where a prominent Muslim man could treat his son's Serb friend like a third son. Violent displays helped to destroy these old meanings and put in place mutually exclusive categories maintained by force and terror. The threat of violence also ensured that Serbs who wanted to continue to act neighborly toward their non-Serb friends and neighbors would fall in line. As one interviewee said of Vinko: "He had to act a certain way in front of his Serb friends; to be a good Serb he would have to do that" [8Fil]. The same pressures to act a certain way were in place at Manjača and other detention centers. Some guards relished their newfound power. And yet, amidst the pressure to act a certain way, some former neighbors, friends, police, and soldiers did, at times, defy "orders" and acted decently. These small acts constituted cracks in the nationalist lines. And cracks in that line meant that competing notions of what it meant to be Serb continued to shape people's actions. Different understandings led some people to continue to act decently toward their non-Serb neighbors and in some instances, to help them. These actions, in turn, helped to sustain prewar meanings about what it meant to be Serb or Muslim. Like lynch mobs, nationalists did not always get their way.

Ambiguity during the Rwandan Genocide

In Rwanda, violence was also a mechanism for enforcing specific meanings of belonging and for categorizing bodies according to those meanings. However, this effort required removing ambiguity about who was who, an ambiguity that was much more marked in the Rwandan context than in Bosnia or the United States. The technique for removing this ambiguity was genocide. There were two targets of annihilation. The first was "Tutsi" as a whole; this included anyone with an identity card that read "Tutsi," anyone who "looked" Tutsi, or anyone suspected of being Tutsi. The second target was any Hutu who did not support the extremists in power and their campaign of genocide. By destroying both groups, the genocide would create not only "ethnic," but more importantly, *political* uniformity, neither of which had ever existed before. The project of annihilating ambiguity, however, only put existing contradictions into starker relief than before. Even in the context of extreme insecurity and mass killing that marked the period of 1990 to 1994, the lines of ethnicity and political affiliation continued to be blurred at the edges and the line itself was often in flux or in motion depending on the context.

One of the most incendiary tactics used in the period just before the genocide was assassination of major political figures. On February 20, 1994, assassins tried to murder Faustin Twagiramungu, the prime minister-designate and head of the MDR, the largest opposition party in the country. The assassins failed but they did manage to kill one of Twagiramungu's bodyguards (Des Forges 1999, 163). The next day, assassins killed Félicien Gatabazi, a government minister and secrétaire général of the PSD (Parti social démocrate), a small opposition party based in the south. They killed him just as he was leaving a meeting of opposition party leaders that included the RPF (Des Forges 1999, 125). His assassination dealt quite a blow to moderates from all parties. According to Charles Karemano (2003), a highly placed member of the PSD, Gatabazi was the true driver not only of the party, but also of the opposition movement more generally. Karemano (2003, 52) describes Gatabazi as "neither ethnically nor regionally focused as some have others believe." He was also not an opportunist, like so many politicos at the time who were more than willing to align themselves with whatever party would ensure their rapid rise. Indeed, his principled stand made him truly unique in the political landscape. The government did little to investigate the murder. Those linked to the crime came from Habyarimana's inner circle (Des Forges 1999, 125), causing a fury among PSD supporters who were based in the south.

The day after Gatabazi's killing, a crowd of angry PSD supporters in Butare, a university town in the south, recognized Martin Bucyana, the president of the CDR (Coalition pour la défense de la république), a radical wing of the president's MRND party. Bucyana was on his way back to Kigali from his home in the southwest préfecture of Cyangugu. The crowd in Butare, led by PSD youth group members, encircled Bucyana's car as it drove through the town. Two people in the car fled, but the crowd pursued them to a communal office where they tried to kill them on the spot. One of the first victims was Bucyana's son. When the crowd discovered that Bucyana was not among those killed, it began going door to door, locating Bucyana hiding in someone's home. The angry mob proceeded not only to kill Bucyana, but also to "torture" his dead body, as if murdering him was not enough to avenge the killing of their own party's leader the day before (Kabagema 2001, 11–12).

The two assassinations would be notable on their own terms, for both incidents helped to make assassinations part of a shared repertoire of party politics. What confounds simple analysis, however, is the credible claim by a former RPF officer that the assassins behind the murders were RPF agents who had infiltrated both political parties and their affiliated youth groups. According to the carefully detailed account by Ruzibiza (2005, 224–25), the RPF kept a list of highly placed politicians to be assassinated; the rebel group's larger goal was to "sow chaos" throughout the country, thereby paving the way for their own eventual victory. In order to kill Gatabazi, RPF agents had infiltrated the Interahamwe and hid themselves in a taxi. After killing Gatabazi, they killed the taxi driver to ensure her silence. The next day, RPF agents were also among the crowd of PSD supporters that murdered Bucyana in Butare. The very fact that the RPF was able to infiltrate *all* political parties and youth groups is testament to the ambiguity surrounding "who" was really "who"—even during wartime. The RPF simply harnessed that ambiguity for its own ends. In killing the leader of the PSD, the rebel group had knowingly and deliberately eliminated one of its few political allies. To achieve its larger goal of sowing chaos and creating instability, however, the rebels were more than willing to sacrifice political allies.

When the president's plane crashed on April 6, 1994, the pattern of eliminating rivals continued in full force by all parties. One of the first figures whom extremists targeted was the moderate (Hutu) prime minister, Agathe Uwilingiyimana, who had planned on addressing the country over the radio to preach calm in the wake of the president's death. UN peacekeeping commander Roméo Dallaire had sent fifteen UNAMIR troops to protect Uwilingiyimana, but Rwandan government soldiers came in force, disarmed the ten Belgian blue helmets, and took them to a nearby military camp where they killed all ten and piled their bodies in the corner of a shed. The soldiers then tracked down Uwilingiyimana in her hiding place and killed her before she could get to the radio station. They left her body with her underclothes lifted over her head and a beer bottle shoved into her vagina (Des Forges 1999, 150). By killing her, the extremists decapitated the entire "body" of moderates. By putting her defiled body on display, they were also defiling the very notion that one could be "Hutu" and politically moderate at the same time. They were broadcasting their contempt for the category "Hutu moderate" and declaring it a violation of the political unity they sought to achieve—a unity of support behind the extremist program, not moderate politicians.

The assassination of the prime minister and display of her sexually mutilated body drew the line for everyone, Hutu and Tutsi alike. Henceforth, "Hutu" would be a political category enforced through violence. Belonging would be based on *political* positions and a willingness to commit violence, not self-identification. The process of violently redefining what it meant to be Hutu unfolded swiftly in the capital. In the next three days, the genocidal regime would target all political rivals, sending soldiers, police, and militia door-to-door with lists in hand and with orders to kill everyone they found at the home. The majority of these targets were "Hutu" but their politics made them among the first to be killed because of their *political* opposition to the extremists in power.

The mass killing of Hutu moderates reverberated outside the capital as the violence spread to other parts of the country. Outside Kigali, the vast majority of Rwandans were subsistence farmers for whom the political goings-on in the capital were distant events. And because the killings that occurred right after the plane crash targeted mainly Hutu political figures, some rural denizens interpreted the violence as an extreme form of *kubohoza*, or the forcible recruitment of people into a particular political party. As Des Forges (1999, 156) explains: "Because some of the first victims had been highly visible Hutu and because assailants continued to target Hutu adversaries of the MRND and the CDR, many Hutu also feared for their lives. They saw the killings as broader than a genocide and as constituting also an extreme form of kubohoza with victims chosen on partisan, regional or economic grounds." This may help to explain why everyone did not immediately understand that the genocide was targeted at Tutsi for *ethnic* reasons, even after months of virulent propaganda in newspapers and on the radio accusing Tutsi of supporting the RPF (Chretien 1995; Straus 2007). Ignored were multiple organized massacres of Tutsi in the north and eastern parts of the country that began as early as January 1991; military attacks staged by the government to foment fear of the RPF; real attacks carried out by the RPF; and assassinations of party leaders. Despite years of violent politics, many in the countryside had still not received the message that Tutsi and moderate Hutu were the mortal enemy to those in power. Some local officials even chose to join the side of moderates and work against the extremists, rather than with them. The bourgmestre of the commune Giti in the north, for example, and the préfets of Butare and Gitarama all responded to the extremism by preaching calm and maintaining peace (Des Forges 1999, 270; Straus 2006). It was not until the interim government removed these men, replaced them with progenocide appointees, and bussed in outsiders that the killings would begin in these communities.

The political nature of the genocide helps to explain one of its most confounding features: the fact that more than a few high-level genocide leaders were themselves Tutsi or had Tutsi spouses and family. For example, none other than the president of the national committee of the Interahamwe, Jerry Robert Kajuga, was born of a Tutsi father and Hutu mother, making him Tutsi by Rwandan category rules (Des Forges 1999, 227). In other words, the head of the militia that was specifically recruited, armed, and trained to kill Tutsi was himself a Tutsi. The other notable example is that of Paulina Nyiramasuhuko, who, at the time of the genocide held the role of minister of family welfare and women's affairs. In her home préfecture of Butare, she personally incited the militia (which included her own twenty-four-year-old son) to rape Tutsi women before killing them. After Nyiramasuhuko's indictment at the ICTR, a *New York Times* reporter interviewed her mother. From talking to her, he learned that "Pauline," as everyone called her, had a Tutsi great-grandfather, who, on losing his wealth, became Hutu.[7] In other words, according to the extremists' definition of who counted as Tutsi, Pauline herself fit the category (Landesman 2002).

In addition to highly placed national leaders of the genocide, many other leaders had Tutsi wives, girlfriends, and family members whom they made sure to protect. The sous-préfet of the region where Ngali is located protected Tutsi women and girls. In Ngali, Jude, too, accepted money and other offerings (e.g., beer) in exchange for ensuring the protection of certain Tutsi, men as well as women.

It is also the case that in regions where there were no more Tutsi left to kill, killers sometimes began going after Hutu. In Nyakizu commune in Butare préfecture, for example, an ambitious and avaricious man named Ntaganzwa who claimed the position of bourgmestre by forcing out his predecessor (as Jude had done), targeted many Hutu. He even went after some of his own supporters in a single-minded quest to accumulate money and looted property. He had Hutu arrested at roadblocks under the pretext that their papers were "out of order." He ordered the killing of three Interahamwe from a neighboring commune because he coveted their Jeep (Des Forges 1999, 25). Ntaganzwa's actions, in turn, gave others in the commune permission to follow suit. Other residents began stealing looted property *from those who had originally stolen the goods* from Tutsi victims. Young men manning roadblocks began "attack[ing] anyone if he looked like he had money" (Des Forges 1999, 426–27). The case of Ntaganzwa points to another key driver of the violence that had nothing to do with ethnicity—a quest for power.

In Rwanda, ambiguity was a card that all actors could play, from genocide leaders to the RPF. Even before the genocide began, a person's "ethnic" category was becoming increasingly a function of a person's *political* leanings. And political loyalties, like ethnic categorizations, could change swiftly depending on the context. The RPF exploited this ethnic and political ambiguity to sow chaos and make conditions ripe for renewing the civil war, which it was sure it would win. For some Tutsi, ambiguity provided an opportunity to "become one of them" as in the case of Interahamwe leader Robert Kajuga and former Minister Pauline Nyiramasuhuko. For others, the political basis for the genocide made them target some Tutsi while protecting others. Ambiguity, in short, meant the ethnicity line was often in motion and just as often blurred at the edges.

In all three contexts, violence became the mechanism to inscribe new meanings for old labels and to categorize people according to these new meanings. But the process was uneven and contingent precisely because these meanings defied uniformity and fixity. In Bosnia, nationalists targeted not just individuals, but also relationships, particularly those between Serbs and non-Serbs. The arrest and murder of Omer Filipović was not only an attempt to decapitate the local Muslim community by killing its leader, it also made it impossible for *any* Muslim to be best friends with *any* Serb, in the way that Omer and Vinko once were. The targeting of relationships was an effort to destroy one set of meanings and replace them with another. Through this process, Omer had to be destroyed but so, too, did Vinko's prior self. Vinko had to become a new kind of Serb or suffer the same fate as his friend.

In destroying Vinko and Omer literally and figuratively, RS authorities were also destroying the social body the two men symbolized and represented. This body was constituted by many similar kinds of friendships between Serbs and non-Serbs. Vinko and Omer were more visible than most because of their status in the community. To be sure, their friendship did not protect Omer or keep him from being killed. On the contrary, their highly visible friendship had to be destroyed for its very existence was a violation of and challenge to the nationalists. When Vinko arranged transport for Omer's family to attend his funeral, he did not become a hero. But the very fact that he went ahead and did it—in the name of friendship—is important. This gesture, like that of the guard who put his arm around Omer's brother when he saw his brother's dead body or the Serb friend who came to the detention center in Sitnica to bring his Muslim friend a sandwich—all these acts constituted chinks in the nationalist line. They could neither prevent nor overcome the violence, but they were evidence that the line nationalists were trying to erect between "real Serbs" and everyone else sagged in many places and was tenuous in others—despite sustained and unrelenting violence and terror on the part of the Bosnian Serbs and the militia that acted in their name. This is the very reason that nationalists had to go to such great lengths to create and shore up the new nationalist line they were trying to create—because that demarcation, like all other social boundaries, was insufficient to keep people on the "right" side all the time.

In Maryland and Rwanda, differences in meaning were, in many ways, most visible within a given category rather than across them. So-called "whites" in the Eastern Shore and "Hutu" in Rwanda had never been unified or homogenous groups. Marylanders and Virginians, for example, each drew the color line through different sets of practices and divergent notions of what constituted law and order. In Virginia, maintenance of the boundary between black and white did not depend on mob executions; indeed local understandings proscribed such actions. In Maryland, the opposite was the case. The obvious response to William Lee's alleged rape of a white woman was to lynch Lee on the spot; anything short of a lynching was equally unthinkable. This is not to minimize the way in which race was indelibly inscribed on black bodies through legal as well as extralegal practices that upheld the system of white supremacy in all public domains. It is to underscore that whiteness was not monolithic and that the system of white supremacy could exist in robust form *even without lynchings*.

In Rwanda, the line that genocide leaders were inscribing was political, not ethnic, in nature, even if the official aim of the genocide was to exterminate an entire *ethnic* group. In targeting Hutu moderates first and foremost, the genocidal regime was, as in Bosnia, trying to create political homogeneity where it had never existed. Hutu as such had never been a unified group politically, either during the colonial period or during the period of multiparty politics. It is no wonder, then, that so many Hutu (and Tutsi) farmers misunderstood at first what the violence was about, who exactly was the target, and how they were supposed to respond. Ambiguity continued to operate in unforeseen ways, allowing Tutsi to take prominent positions in the genocidal regime and other leaders to protect certain Tutsi.

Violent display, as this book has argued, rewrites what it means to belong to a given social category and in doing so, recategorizes people—victims as well as perpetrators and participants. But even during the most widespread violence and terror, as this chapter shows, violence and violent displays are incapable of keeping everyone on "their" side of the line at all times. Even amidst violence, the line remains porous and permeable. Social engineering through violence can never succeed because personal impulses can still trump political ideologies and mandates.

Epilogue

Elisabeth Jean Wood

In this profound book, Lee Ann Fujii asks why neighbors sometimes engage in gratuitous, collective, "extralethal" violence against their neighbors, including public lynching, public rape, torture, and humiliation of victims before killing; the public mutilation of corpses; and the later display of body parts. Given its risks and costs, why engage in such violence—violence that may be counterproductive to overarching goals?

To address this puzzle, Fujii explores a category of violence she terms "violent display," violence that is *performed* for an audience, often in public spaces. She does so through detailed analysis of specific events of ethnic cleansing in Bosnia, lynching of African Americans in the United States, and genocide in Rwanda.

Fujii shows how violent display is an assertion of a preferred social order through the redrawing (or reconfirming) of social categories in order to resolve ambiguous boundaries of ethnic and racial difference or to respond to transgressions of those boundaries. It reaffirms the salience of the social order's categories by "inscribing" racial/ethnic hierarchies not just on the body of the immediate victim, but on others from the victim's social group, for whom that body also stands.

Moreover, violent display asserts those ideas about a new social order, power, and belonging, for perpetrators and onlookers, Fujii argues. It transforms the meaning and sometimes the boundaries of those categories, as when those who fail to participate with their coethnic perpetrators thereby no longer count as *real* members of their ethnic group. In short, participation in violence becomes "the basis of belonging," supplanting hitherto accepted bases of belonging such as birth into a family recognized as having a particular ethnicity. Violent display may continue after death in the treatment of bodies in ways that perpetuate the preferred narrative of violence, asserting new meanings of racial or ethnic categories.

Throughout the book, Fujii draws on field research in Rwanda, Bosnia, and Maryland's Eastern Shore (birthplace of abolitionists Harriet Tubman and Frederick Douglass), as well as various archives, to illustrate how participants *staged* an episode of violent display as a performance toward a new social order (the "main attraction.") The inclusion of lynching in the United States is both compelling and important as it deflects any possible presumption on the part of readers from the global North that violent display occurs "over there." She draws on this core concept—violent display as a performance—to analyze the history and earlier events leading up to each episode (the "rehearsal"), as well as other episodes of violent display in less public settings ("sideshows"), and the subsequent deployment of bodies toward a dominant narrative ("aftermath"). And in the "intermission," she describes the challenges of carrying out field research in the aftermath of violence. It includes an exemplary analysis of her own positionality, a demonstration that obstacles encountered during field research are themselves a form of data, and a discussion of the importance of narrative silences and revisions. The writing is powerful —it is a rare social science book that compels the reader to turn the pages.

In this epilogue, I briefly lay out what I see as the book's main contributions to our understanding of political violence and the research agenda it suggests before describing the conversation I wish I could have had with Fujii about the book's argument, method, evidence, and relevance for violence beyond violent display.

But before doing so, I would like to reflect briefly on what I learned from Lee Ann over the years. I met her more than a decade and a half ago when she introduced herself at a conference as a doctoral student interested in studying political violence. She asked some penetrating questions about the methodological and ethical challenges of ethnography in such settings. I answered as best I could, impressed by her insight. She left me reflecting on the advantages of entering graduate school after years of work in other occupations—in her case, in theater. I had no inkling that those years would provide the theoretical grounding of her second book.

Since then I have learned much more from Lee Ann than she ever learned from me about political violence and ethnographic method. She asked the most difficult of questions. She was relentless in pursuing the answers, always probing for a deeper meaning beyond some superficial explanation. To explore why neighbors kill, sometimes with violent display, Lee Ann became a remarkably skilled ethnographer. She understood much more clearly than most social scientists—particularly most political scientists, for whom ethnography all too often means only semistructured interviews and often only with elites—that ethnographic data arises from the working relationship forged between researcher and her interlocutors. I learned a lot about ethnography from her several articles and important—and very wise—book on interpretive method, *Relational Interviewing* (2017). The book is very relevant for all scholarly approaches to ethnography, whether interpretivist or not, as well as for other types of field research, including semistructured interviews. In my experience teaching field research, doctoral students—and the few particularly motivated undergraduates who take the course—find it among the most engaging and effective texts.

Like many scholars who work on political violence, particularly those engaged in intensive field research on political violence who were part of Lee Ann's social network, I continue grieving Lee Ann's tragically early death in 2018. I was very moved when Roger Haydon and Martha Finnemore asked me to write this epilogue. I hope it does Lee Ann's work justice in its assessment of its contributions, and in the questions that I so wish I could ask Lee Ann herself—the kind of serious engagement with her work in which she would have reveled.

Contributions of *Show Time* toward Scholarly Understanding of Political Violence

Fujii's most important insight was that political violence is very often a *social process*, indeed a *performative* one, not some rote following of orders. Other scholars of political violence, particularly those who document and analyze lynching, gang rape, and violence that is unordered and unauthorized, have noted this aspect of violence in some settings. But few have focused on the theoretical and empirical implications of approaching violence as a performance—that is, a social process for an audience—and none with Fujii's depth of insight.

On Violence as a Social Process that Transforms Participants

Violent display, Fujii argues, is a *collective* effort to *stage* violence: participants make and implement decisions about lighting, positioning, editing, and costumes. In short, an aesthetic "logic" informs the performance. Fujii focuses on the interactions among participants, namely, how they set the stage for violence, assume various roles, and construct an escalating trajectory—always projecting the performance to those watching.

In focusing on the *enactment* of the new political order through public violence, she shows how participants—often ordinary people—in their performing of identities and narrative central to the asserted political order (e.g., what it means to be a "real" Serb) produce the sequence of actions that comprise the atrocious event.

Moreover, this enactment of the new order *transforms* participants, both the cast who directly participate and also onlookers, she argues. Those in star roles achieve new social status and power (nobodies become somebodies). All participants—even those merely watching—experience the renewal of their dominance over the victim's social category through the ritualized subordination of the victim. In short, violent display *brings alive* a new political order for participants and their audience, not just for the targeted community.

Fujii insists that central to the transformative power of violent display is that it is *embodied*: it is the experience of hearing, smelling, as well as seeing violence that transforms those attending. Further, it transforms those unwillingly or unwittingly drawn into the event as well as those intentionally participating. And the expressive participation of those watching—their laughing, cheering, and encouraging the cast—also socializes the audience to the new political order. (I was initially skeptical of this embodied line of argument—isn't any act necessarily embodied?—but was eventually persuaded in part by reflecting on the power of watching violent events in person over seeing audiovisual images or reading textual description.)

Show Time thus makes another major contribution to the recent literature on socialization and political violence. Violent display *socializes* through participation: violence is an extreme learning-through-doing activity. Fujii also shows that this enactment of a new political order, and socialization into that order and its new norms, may begin well before the violent display, as when neighbors at newly erected barricades check the papers of neighbors very well known to them, when neighbors press others to participate in local patrols, and when those other neighbors acquiesce because it is important to be seen doing so. In Selo, she argues, a teacher became a hero and neighbors became nationalists over the course of a parade that lasted less than twenty minutes.

Fujii develops her theory of violent display as a social and transformative process in the case of violence carried out by neighbors against neighbors. The key insights from approaching violence as a performance constructed by participants—namely, their assumption of roles, their building of the arc of the event, their care to project to an audience (either onlookers or other participants), and the transformative effects of the experience—would also contribute to analysis of violence in other settings.

On Violence as a Dynamic Process

In its emphasis on violent display as a performance, particularly the transformative effects of participation on ordinary people, *Show Time* adds to literature that opens up the "black box" of organizations that engage in violence, including state militaries, rebel organizations, local militias, gangs, and vigilante groups. Recent literature increasingly suggests that patterns of violence by such organizations cannot be adequately understood if they are analyzed as unitary actors in which local agents seamlessly carry out orders from commanders.

Most scholars working in this vein approach the internal dynamics of such organizations though principal agent models that emphasize the differences in preferences and information between commanders and combatants (or leaders and members of militias, gangs, vigilante groups), and the institutions that (to varying degree) mitigate those differences. The approach opens up the "black box," but focuses only on vertical relationships.

In contrast, *Show Time* adds to the more recent body of literature that goes beyond such models in emphasizing horizontal as well as vertical relationships and dynamics. More specifically, she focuses on social dynamics among ordinary people—some of whom take up a commanding role during the episode. This theme is already present in work on gang rape, hazing, and the horizontal socialization of combatants into violence, particularly violence that is neither authorized nor ordered by leaders, but driven by peer dynamics among participants. Scholars working in these other settings might gain traction on those dynamics by considering the extent to which they are captured by Fujii's emphasis on violence as a performance.

In its close focus on the dynamics of violent display, *Show Time* builds powerfully on Fujii's earlier work on political violence. In her first book, *Killing Neighbors: Webs of Violence in Rwanda* (2009), Fujii advanced two important arguments. First, she identified several roles that local people occupy during genocidal violence, from hiding victims, to onlookers, to active participation, and argued that the same person may play distinct roles depending on the context. Drawing on ethnographic research in two case-study areas of Rwanda, including interviews with those imprisoned for their participation in the genocide, she showed that some Rwandans participated in violence against some of their Tutsi neighbors, yet protected others—and sometimes suffered the consequences. In short, the usual dichotomy between victims and perpetrators does not capture that some were both. Second, those who participate in local violence against their neighbors were largely drawn into the killing because they were part of extended family networks with those local officials and militia leaders driving the genocide.

In contrast, *Show Time* focuses on the dynamics of violent display in which "roles" take on a more theatrical meaning. In *Show Time*, the performance of violence is more spontaneous and fluid. Roles emerge from the social interaction of participants and are transformed as the script emerges and evolves. Moreover, whereas the earlier book had an almost structural approach to social networks, in *Show Time* participants and onlookers may be drawn into an episode of violent display for contingent, indeed contagious, reasons as well as by their position in a social network.

The extent to which violence draws on emergent and contingent roles and improvisation merits exploration in other settings. Indeed, the torture of prisoners by US servicemen at Abu Ghraib comes to mind as a case ripe for performative analysis. Fujii's analysis of the torture of prisoners at the Omarska prison camp as a violent display "sideshow" suggests the richness of doing so. She documents the intimacy of the violence carried out there, the performative, ritual nature of interrogation, and how participation affirmed a particular collective identity—real Serbs participated and became new men and women in their status and authority, and even onlookers experienced the power of communal transgression.

On Violence that Transforms the Meaning and Boundaries of Ethnic and Racial Categories

Show Time makes another major contribution to our understanding of violence in its analysis of how violent display transforms ethnic and racial categories. Scholarly work on violence in many disciplines emphasizes that the purpose of much violence is to enforce social boundaries, particularly to punish their transgression. Fujii makes a more subtle argument: violent display does not just communicate the dangers of boundary transgression, but is also *constitutive* of those boundaries and their meaning. Violent display may change the meaning of ethnic and racial categories, as well as sharpen and even shift their boundaries.

In analyzing ethnic and racial difference, Fujii emphasizes the variability in meaning of categories and boundaries over time and across space. Despite state (and, in some settings, elite) efforts to define racial and ethnic categories with clear boundaries, such fixity is a fiction, Fujii argues. Rather, local meanings and practices are varied, malleable, and ambiguous. Families may be mixed, friendships may cross boundaries, and kids often play together without having yet learnt the rules of who gets to inflict and who has to endure subordination.

Moreover, it is from that very ambiguity that violent display draws its power. Because identities are malleable and flexible, she argues, they can be "harnessed" to a political project (elite or not). Or they can be recast for contingent political reasons. For example, before the armed conflict in Bosnia, Muslims were claimed as "lapsed" Serbs by Serbs, and as "really" Croats by Croats. More fundamentally, precisely because who is who is not always obvious, and because some people break the rules, violent display resolves ambiguity by sharpening the salience of boundaries for participant and victimized communities alike. And in the new political order, those boundaries are not just boundaries of difference, but boundaries of racial and ethnic *hierarchy*, one that may invert that of the old order, or introduce a ranking where one was not present before. So violent display, she argues, transforms the *meaning* of ethnic and racial difference. Sometimes it does so by redrawing the boundaries: those who refuse to participate are no longer seen as "real" members of the ethnic group, but as outsiders—beyond the ethnic boundary. (She notes in a later chapter that political actors who overthrow a social order in which they had been subordinate can play on ethnic and racial ambiguity for their own purposes. After defeating the Rwandan regime, for example, the Rwandan Patriotic Front reclassified Hutus who were killed as Tutsi.)

In the final chapter, Fujii returns to the themes of local variation, malleability, and ambiguity and finds some solace there. Violent display despite its power is uneven in its imposition of the meaning of ethnic and racial difference and of the categories and boundaries of the new political order. Moreover, even where those meanings and differentiations are successfully imposed, they do not necessarily endure. Even white supremacy in the US South was asserted through "confounding" patterns across the Eastern Shore: transgressions in Maryland were met with lynching; in Virginia, state authorities, even small-town sheriffs, rejected lynching by the early twentieth century. Even violence cannot prevent some members of the newly dominant group from crossing boundaries and breaking norms, thereby violating the new political order by helping those enduring violence and subordination.

Social engineering through violence can therefore never succeed because it cannot keep everyone on the "right" side of the line for long, Fujii insists.

Questions for a Dialogue about *Show Time* with Lee Ann Fujii

Despite sharp differences in the three settings of ethnic cleaning, genocide, and a highly racialized "peace," and in the degree of stagecraft across the three episodes, Fujii shows how violent display should be understood as a performance that works to inscribe and redraw social categories and boundaries. Here are the questions that I wish I could have raised with Fujii to deepen my understanding of her theory, her method, her empirical analysis of episodes of violent display, and its potential extension to other settings.

On the Theory

While I am deeply persuaded by Fujii's theory of violent display as a performance, I am less persuaded by her theory of "casting." The idea seems to be that *casting* transforms a murder into a lynching, detention into pornographic spectacle, etc. (see the opening paragraphs of chapter 3). But her theory of violent display as a performance intended as a spectacle for an audience seems to me to already imply such transformation. What precisely does the theory of casting add?

Fujii returns to the theme of the ambiguity and malleability of ethnic and racial difference in the final chapter, as mentioned above. Violent display may assert a new political order, but that order and its associated meanings and identities may be fleeting. So I would ask her under what conditions do episodes of violent display contribute to a new political order that endures? What other factors are necessary?

Does the theory of violent display include episodes in which only the *meaning* of categories was changed, but the boundaries of the categories and the membership of each were not? I believe the answer should be yes, but the text is ambivalent on this point, at times insisting that violent display necessarily transforms boundaries.

On Method

To approach violence as a social process entails documenting and analyzing the emergent social meaning of acts of violence and the evolving understanding on the part of participants of the social implications of their participating in violence—and of their *not* participating. I would like to ask Fujii to say more about how she addressed the challenges of inferring the motivations of social actors. Participant violence may have the *effect* of reasserting categories, their meanings and their ordering, but some of *Show Time*'s empirical material offers more direct evidence of these outcomes as also *intended* than other episodes.

Fujii motivates her focus on violent display in part by noting its risks and costs and that it may be counterproductive. Do participants themselves see violent display as counterproductive? Or are they necessarily swept up in the dynamics she emphasizes?

Finally, I would like to ask Fujii to say more about how as social science scholars we can know whether participants and onlookers were "transformed" by violent display in some more-than-passing way.

On the Episodes of Violent Display Analyzed in *Show Time*

Fujii argues that lynching on the Eastern Shore of Maryland was the assertion of a new order through its usurpation of the role of the state as adjudicator and punisher of transgressions. That is true in the immediate setting—lynching is after all, a form of mob violence—but its *enduring* effect was to reassert a long-standing racial order in the US South (since the seventeenth century, although of course it varied in form over time). What would be lost by widening the concept of violent display to include the reassertion of an older order, rather than insisting on its role in a new one?

I would also like to ask Fujii why of the many episodes of violent display in Bosnia she chose to analyze the parade in Selo. I found her analysis of this event less compelling than that of the events in Rwanda and the Eastern Shore, in large part because the violence itself was carried out by actors other than those who orchestrated the parade, and in private. What advantage did the Selo parade offer over other choices that arguably would be more natural pairings with the Armwood lynching and the Ngali violence?

On Possible Extensions of her Theory

Fujii analyzed episodes of violent display in three settings; all were cases of ethnic conflict. Yet the theory should clearly hold in conflicts that do not take place along ethnic and racial lines but on class or ideological lines. For example, some of the public violence against landlords in the course of some social revolutions would seem to be violent display as Fujii defines its. Under what conditions should we expect violent display to occur in various types of conflicts, from ongoing social domination along various lines (ethnic, racial, class, ideological) to open warfare?

There is of course a long history of violent display by the state, for example, public executions. Under what conditions does state violence follow the logic of violent display? Should we expect less improvisation and more adherence to an existing pattern when carried out by the state?

Given its usefulness in consolidating a new political order, what explains variation in the extent of violent display on the part of armed organizations? Some like ISIS carry out elaborately scripted violent displays (e.g., beheadings) that appear to be ordered or at least authorized by commanders. The literature on terrorism has largely analyzed these and other events as intended to communicate messages to an audience of onlookers and national and international officials. How much variation, perhaps through improvisation, occurs in staging, the script, and other aspects of performance across such violent displays by those organizations that engage in them as a matter of organizational policy? Do events of violent display in such contexts have constitutive as well as communicative effects? Do they have similarly transformative effects on participants?

Relatedly, how do the effects on observers of violent display disseminated via social and other media differ from those who experience in person as embodied participation? In contrast, some violent displays may occur as a "practice," that is, without orders or authorization yet are tolerated by commanders. In still greater contrast, some armed organizations would appear to engage in restraint, engaging in very little violent display.

What accounts for these contrasts? Do we need Fujii's theory of violent display, or do other theories adequately account for this variation? I so wish I could brainstorm with Fujii about this.

Should we understand some types of domestic violence as violent display, in which the perpetrator performs violence on the targeted spouse or child for an audience of other family members (or perhaps just those targeted)?

Finally, to what extent does Fujii consider the puzzle of extralethal violence resolved by her theory of violent display? That is, does violent display sometimes occur for other reasons, driven by other logics? Relatedly, in an earlier publication (*Perspectives on Politics*, 2013), Fujii distinguished three types of extralethal violence: *spectacle* (an earlier term for *violent display*), *carnival*, and the *one-man show*. As the latter two are also public performances, which insights from the theory of violent display are relevant for understanding these other types?

Lee Ann Fujii's *Show Time* makes an original, profound, and formative contribution to our understanding of political violence, particularly the lived experience of participants, through its approach to violence as a social process, and more specifically, through its theory of violent display as a performance. I think differently about episodes of political violence after reading this remarkable book, asking new questions and seeking out new types of evidence. I look forward to discussing it with my undergraduate and graduate students.

In Memoriam

McNulty, Stephanie, Erin Tolley, and Robin Turner. 2018. "Lee Ann Fujii." *PS: Political Science and Politics* 51 (3): 678–80.

Selected Works by Lee Ann Fujii

2018. "Show Time: The Logic and Power of Violent Display with Lee Ann Fujii." Seminar at School of Advanced International Studies, Johns Hopkins University. February 21. https://www.youtube.com/watch?v=m3mgt2WSzXI.

2018. *Interviewing in Social Science Research: A Relational Approach*. Edited by Dvora Yanow and Peregrine Schwartz-Shea. New York: Routledge.

2017. "'Talk of the Town': Pathways to Participation in Violent Display." *Journal of Peace Research* 54 (5): 661–73.

2015. "Five Stories of Accidental Ethnography: Turning Unplanned Moments in the Field into Data." *Qualitative Research* 15 (4): 525–39.

2013. "The Puzzle of Extra-Lethal Violence." *Perspectives on Politics* 11 (2): 410–26.

2012. "Research Ethics 101: Dilemmas and Responsibilities." *PS: Political Science and Politics* 45 (4): 717–23.

2010. "Shades of Truth and Lies: Interpreting Testimonies of War and Violence." *Journal of Peace Research* 47 (2): 231–41.

2009. *Killing Neighbors: Webs of Violence in Rwanda.* Ithaca: Cornell University Press.

Notes

INTRODUCTION

1. The RUF stands for the Revolutionary United Front, led by Foday Sankoh and backed by Liberian rebel leader-turned-president, Charles Taylor. The RUF engaged in its signature atrocity of cutting off villagers' hands and arms during two years of the war (personal communication, Paul Richards, September 2013).

2. In Rwanda, my interpreter translated to and from Kinyarwanda and French; in Bosnia, between Bosnian-Croatian-Serbian (hereinafter BCS) and English. Before the wars of dissolution, the language common to all the Yugoslav republics was called Serbo-Croatian. After the wars, each republic renamed the language. In Bosnia, it became "Bosnian," in Croatia, "Croatian," and in Serbia, "Serbian." The International Criminal Tribunal for the former Yugoslavia used the acronym BCS to capture all three variants of the name. The language, however it is called, remains the same linguistically (Bugarski 2004, 2013).

3. The Dayton Accords (so named because the negotiations took place at an Air Force Base near Dayton, Ohio) brought the war to an end and gave every Bosnian the right to return to his or her prewar home. The extent to which people have claimed that right has varied considerably over time and place (Toal and Dahlman 2011).

4. This partisanship is not part of some bygone era. In 1955, two whites from the local Citizens' Council shot Reverend George Lee at point blank range with a shotgun just as he was returning home in Midnight, Mississippi. The next day, the headline in the *Jackson Clarions-Ledger* read, "Negro Leader Dies in Odd Accident" (Tyson, chap. 11).

1. FIXATIONS

1. To be sure, NDH officials did not allow all groups to become "Croats" by converting to Catholicism. They denied this option to Jews and Gypsies (Bergholz 2016, 83).

2. "Ethnicity" is a crude translation for terms used in Bosnia and Rwanda, such as *narod*, which is commonly translated "nation" or "ethnic group," and *nacionalnost* often translated as "ethnicity." As Bringa (1995, 25) explains: "None of these translations conveys the accurate meaning in the original usage of the term." The same problem applies to the Kinyarwanda word *ubwoko*, which outsiders translate as "ethnicity." Its actual meaning is "the type of" some person or thing (e.g., a tree or car). See also Burnet 2012, 232n2.

3. During the precolonial period, the schooling system was established and run mainly by Catholic missionaries, who eventually allied with the colonial state in favoring Tutsi over Hutu catechists (Linden 1977).

4. Beth Roy found similar practices in her rural village in South Asia. As Roy (1994, 155) notes: "Stories abounded of wild times had by Muslims during the Hindu festival of Holi, or Hindus bearing gifts to well-liked Muslim neighbors at the time of Eid."

2. REHEARSAL

1. The fact that in my three sites, those who assumed new roles were all men is mere coincidence, for women, too, can become new "men" as well, as the case of Pauline

Nyiramasuhuko shows. Nyiramasuhuko was minister of sports, gender, and women in the Habyarimana regime and a hardliner. She was tried and found guilty of genocide and crimes against humanity by the International Criminal Tribunal for Rwanda (Guichaoua 2010; Landesman 2002).

2. Silber and Little (1997, 177) tell the story of one soldier who could not decide whether to flee the front or maintain his position so instead, he shot himself dead. For a picture of a JNA unit deserting the front in Slavonia (Croatia), see photo no. 36 in Judah (2009).

3. See also Brdjanin indictment at https://www.icty.org/en/case/brdanin.

4. For a UN report describing the situation in Prijedor, see Greve 1994.

5. I am using the nomenclature "Brdj" in brackets to denote ICTY transcripts from the trial of Radoslav Brdjanin and Momir Talic (*The Prosecutor versus Radoslav Brdjanin and Momir Talic*, IT-99-36-T). All page numbers refer to the English-language transcripts available online at www.icty.org.

6. Other references in brackets refer to interviews I conducted in and around the town of Ključ and the nearby village of "Selo."

7. Journalist Tom Gjelten (1995, 143) notes the same pattern occurred in Sarajevo: "When Nazif Merzić went to his company to collect his paycheck, he was told Muslims and Croats would no longer be paid. Serb neighbors who before the war had been 'perfectly normal' toward Nazif and his wife suddenly began avoiding them, *even looking the other way when they met on the streets and stairways*" (my emphasis).

8. The denial of space to non-Serbs was not unique to Ključ. Journalist Peter Maass witnessed a similar scene outside Biljeljina in northeast Bosnia, when he and some colleagues were trying to locate a Serb-run prison camp in the area. When their escort stopped at a café to make a call, he began yelling at a middle-aged Muslim man drinking coffee at one of the outdoor tables: "I told you never to come here! Get out of here, you filth!" He then proceeded to beat the man senseless, stopping only when the man's wife came and intervened (Maass 1996, 20). Gjelten (1995, 143) remarked on the same phenomena in Serb-controlled sections of Sarajevo: "Signs saying, 'No entrance to Muslims and Croats,' were posted on the front doors of the city hall, the police station, the post office, and all other public buildings."

9. The name is a pseudonym for my research site which encompassed neighboring villages and *mahale* (sections of a village). Selo (pronounced "SAY-low") means "village" in the local language.

10. Selo was comprised mainly of Serbs and Muslims but there were also a few Croats and a few people from outside the Balkans who had married local women and settled there long before the 1990s war.

11. Both Rwanda and Burundi have similar demographic makeups; and both were part of the single territory of Ruanda-Urundi administered by Belgium. Their social and political histories are quite different, however (Lemarchand 1970; 2009).

12. There were many stereotypes of Tutsi physiology, such as being tall or having thin noses; most people I interviewed in 2004 were familiar with them but also knew that in many cases, they did not hold. This did not prevent people from deploying these stereotypes during the genocide with deadly consequences (Fujii 2009).

13. Like the name "Selo" for my research site in Bosnia, "Ngali" is also a pseudonym. I am using the same name for this community that I used in *Killing Neighbors*.

14. In the Rwandan context, nephews are the sons of Jude's sisters. The sons of his brothers would be considered "sons."

15. Not all of Jude's family members were MDR members, however. One family member claimed Jude never joined any political party [Has, 16 Aug 2011]. It is likely that support of Jude was ultimately more important than party affiliation.

16. According to two interviewees, Rwandan government soldiers may have also been involved in organizing these patrols [Je, 16 June 2009; Em, 10 June 2009, #5/6].

17. Exceptions were made in some instances. One man was "excused" because his wife was gravely ill at the time [Sa #2/2]. Another man was able to refuse because he had a brother in the army; this connection constituted him as someone "important" [Eli, 22 Dec 2011]. Another was able to avoid amarondo duty by not having a fixed residence [C #2/2].

18. The MDR was the biggest opposition party and hence the biggest threat to the President's own MRND party. The MDR was rooted in Gitarama, which is why it was dominant in Ngali and most likely, across the entire préfecture. For an excellent overview of party formation in the 1990s, see Bertrand 2000. For an historical overview, see Newbury 1988, Lemarchand 1970, and Reyntjens 1985.

19. Ethnicity in Rwanda is patrilineal, meaning a child "inherits" her ethnicity from her father, regardless of the ethnicity of the mother. And because notions of ethnicity are gendered, a Hutu woman married to a Tutsi man would not offer her spouse similar protections to that of a Hutu man married to a Tutsi spouse. A Tutsi husband with a Hutu wife will not spared; neither will his children because they would be Tutsi, too, given their father's ethnicity.

20. The route to Baltimore from the Lower Eastern Shore in 1931 would have gone north through Delaware up old Route 13 to Newark (the site where locals recall police beating up Euel Lee, according to Moore [2006, 209]) and down Hwy 40 to Baltimore. Using an estimated cruising speed of 35–40 mph, this trip would have taken about five hours. The *Baltimore Sun* ("Eastern Shore Family" 1931) also reported that State Police left Snow Hill with Jones in custody at 4:30 and arrived in Baltimore "shortly after 9 o'clock."

3. MAIN ATTRACTION

1. This section draws from Fujii 2017.

2. The characterization of the tortures that American soldiers committed at Abu Ghraib as "pornography" comes from Norton 2011.

3. I cite the version from the *Afro-American* (Jolley 1933b). The local Princess Anne newspaper, the *Marylander and Herald* also covered this story. Their account is quite different. The *Marylander and Herald* depicts the woman as driving into the ditch to avoid hitting the girl and does not mention that she was driving on the wrong side of the road. This version also ends with reference to the Coroner awaiting "the pleasure of State's Attorney John B. Robins, who will investigate the case" as if a formal inquiry were imminent, whereas the *Afro* notes that "officials of Princess Anne refused to conduct a hearing in the matter." In both versions, the woman is neither held nor (yet) charged with any crime.

4. For Richardson, the arrangement may have been more about obtaining cheap labor than taking care of a young black boy from a poor family. During Richardson's trial on charges of being an accessory to a crime (by helping Armwood elude law enforcement), Richardson repeatedly referred to Armwood as "that n—r" ("Epithets" 1933).

5. I refer to the page numbers on the original transcript, which start with Sheet 1 and end with Sheet 20. The transcripts came from the private papers of John B. Robins IV, https://hdl.handle.net/1813/102784.

6. State Police accounts come from sworn affidavits officers gave after the lynching. Hereinafter I refer to the source as "Police Statements" in brackets. Page numbers refer to those in the original source.

7. According to the *Baltimore Sun*, Duer was accompanied by Dr. George W. Jarman, a "prominent physician of Princess Anne." Jarman, too, tried to speak to the crowd but like Duer, the response was "jeers mingled with friendly jibes" (Player 1933b).

8. Euel Lee was a black man tried and convicted for the murder of a white family of four in a neighboring county two years before the Armwood lynching. The reason Lee was not lynched is that State Police kept him in Baltimore and never returned him to Worcester County, where the crime had occurred (Ifill 2007; Moore 2006). At the time of Armwood's lynching, Lee was awaiting his execution by hanging, scheduled for ten days hence.

9. These may have been rounds loaded with gas shells that police fired from their guns (Serman Statement, 425).

10. Page numbers refer to those in the original. Hereinafter, I refer to this document as "Inquest."

11. Frank Spencer (1933) recalls that the boy who threw the rope over the tree branch was the same young man who jumped on Armwood's back and cut off his ear just outside the jail.

12. In his official statement, Officer Schlueter says he recognized three of the men holding the rope.

13. The Scottsboro trial was also taking place in Alabama at the same time but there is no indication that Eastern Shore whites were following this case or linked it to Armwood. Grace Elizabeth Hale (1999, 222) argues that the Scottsboro case did resonate for those involved in the lynching of Claude Neal in Marianna, Florida, in 1934.

14. Testimony was in Serbo-Croatian. I obtained audio files from the State Court of Bosnia and Herzegovina, some of which I had transcribed. The translations are my own with the help of Ajla Omerspahić, a native speaker of the local language who is also fluent in English. I use brackets to mark off the name of the witness whom I am citing.

15. In the trial transcripts, attorneys use the word *vod* to refer to Samardžija's unit, which can be translated as "squad," "platoon," or "company." In an English language version of the proceedings from September 28, 2006, official translators refer to Samardžija as a "company" commander (2006), but the size his "company" seems to have been closer to a platoon in the American military lexicon.

16. If available, I use the page numbers from the written transcript obtained from the State Court of Bosnia-Herzegovina.

17. In an interview with Birte Weiss (2000), a Danish investigator who interviewed Samardžija in 1999, he would claim he had sixty-two soldiers under him. It is quite possible he did have that many in his unit, but that not all were taking part in the mission on July 10, 1992.

18. In the defendant's opening statement, Samardžija stated that a man with diabetes asked if he could go home to get his medication and Samardžija told him yes and told him to stay home.

19. Bihać was an exception; it was under the leadership of Fikret Abdić, a Muslim, who was not a member of the main Muslim party, the SDA, which was headed by Izetbegović. Abdić positioned himself as a rival to the SDA and struck a deal with Bosnian Serb forces, thereby maintaining his own brand of "home rule" over Bihać. Abdić's presence meant that local Muslims who backed him had better access to food and security, but it also meant that more Muslims in this area died at the hands of other Muslims than of Bosnian Serbs. For a superb analysis of the situation, see Christia 2008.

4. INTERMISSION

1. I am using Linda's real name with her permission.

2. Among the evidence Linda cited was a secondhand account written by Rev. Asbury Smith, a copy of which Linda left on the man's doorstep. She never heard back from him after that (personal communication, May 11, 2017).

3. For another take on this exchange that emphasizes the implications for interview-based research more generally, see Fujii 2018.

4. The list is quite long. See, for example, Pottier 2002; Reyntjens 2010, 2015; Thomson 2013; Sundaram 2016; and Straus and Waldorf 2011.

5. SIDESHOW

1. For a view from the perspective of humanitarian medical personnel, see Bradol and Le Pape 2017, who enumerate the many field hospitals, city hospitals, and medical facilities where militia killed local staff and patients they deemed to be Tutsi or Tutsi supporters.

2. A commune is made up of subunits called *secteurs*. Ngali is one such secteur in the commune headed by Joseph. I do not name the commune to maintain anonymity.

3. I use the nomenclature "Tad" to refer to the trial of Duško Tadić (The Prosecutor v. Dusko Tadic, Case No. IT-94-1-T) and "Kv" to refer the trial of Miroslav Kvočka et al. (*The Prosecutor v. Miroslav Kvocka, Milojica Kos, Mladjo Radic, and Zoran Zigic*, Case No. IT-98-30-T). The numbers in the brackets refer to the page numbers in the English language transcripts, which are available at icty.org. When quoting directly from the English-language transcripts, I follow the spellings as they appear in the transcripts. They sometimes follow British conventions (e.g., "tyre" instead of "tire") and do not include diacritics (e.g., "Kvocka" instead of "Kvočka").

4. Hukanović (1996, 68) also mentions this incident in his memoir.

5. The English translations were done by native speakers of Serbo-Croatian, which explains certain word choices that might sound odd to a native (American) English speaker. In this case, "spraying" or "hosing down" is probably a more accurate translation than "sprinkling."

6. For a similar story of a young boy's idealization of his karate coach and his shock at his coach's change in behavior, see Trebinčević and Shapiro 2014. This story takes place in the town of Brčko in northeastern Bosnia, which also fell under Bosnian Serb control from the spring of 1992.

7. *Canals* is the word used in the English version of the ICTY transcripts. I use the same word to keep the vocabulary consistent.

6. ENCORE

1. I thank my former student, Jenna Mohammed, for this title.

2. The practice of using latrines was not unique to Rwanda. Both sides in the American Civil War also used "natural trenches and existing declivities" to bury the dead quickly and easily (Faust 2008).

3. Ruzibiza fled Rwanda to Norway in 2001. In addition to writing and publishing his book on the RPF, he testified at the ICTR, as part of the Bruguière inquiry in Paris, and before a Spanish judge in Madrid. He died in 2010 (Reyntjens 2015, 240).

4. In addition, Ruzibiza (2005, 348, 352–64) lists countless instances where the RPF knew about Tutsi who were in danger of being killed, but did nothing to save them.

5. According to an informal conversation Linda Duyer had with the granddaughter of William James, he initially refused the town's request to remove the body, but when the Armwood family asked him to do so, he agreed (Linda Duyer, personal communication, January 28, 2018).

6. In one version of the "crime," Richardson put Armwood up to the assault, instructing Armwood how to lie in wait and rob Denston as she walked home. Richardson rehearsed the instructions several times with Armwood so the latter would know what

to do (Wennersten nd, 352–53). This version came from black informants with whom Wennersten talked. I myself never came across any corroborating evidence of this version.

7. Copies of these oral histories can be found at the Nabb Center, in the papers of Polly Stewart. The folder number for these is FK69.099.

7. FICTIONS

1. Estimates vary as do the time periods that scholars use. Brundage (1993, 8) counts 723 whites and 3,220 blacks lynched in the South between 1880–1930. Yohuru Williams (2001, 3) estimates that 3,405 lynchings occurred between 1882 and 1921.

2. Unless otherwise noted, all citations in the Lee case refer to Barnes 2006.

3. According to Maass (1996, 159), "the literary elite" of Sarajevo looked down on Karadžić's writing (poetry) and that contributed to Karadžić's desire to "punish the city that turned its back on him." Being a true Sarajevan, or *Sarajlija*, meant "being 'cultured,' well educated, open-minded, witty, and superior in ways of dressing, acting, and speaking" (Toal and Dahlman 2011, 73). Until the late 1980s, Karadžić seemed to be trying his best to be a true Sarajevan (Donia and Fine 1994, 6–7).

4. Founded by Adil Zulfikarpašić, an émigré who returned to Bosnia and broke from Izetbegović's SDA (the Muslim nationalist party), the MBO was a party with a "non-religious programme" (Malcolm 1996, 219).

5. The term comes from John Austin's (1962) discussion of speech acts as performatives.

6. The news of Omer's death also reached the US State Department, which wrote in its March 1993 report submitted to the United Nations: "On July 29, a high-ranking member of the Bosnian Muslim party was also beaten to death by guards" (US State Department 1993). This incident most likely refers to the killing of Omer Filipović.

7. Pauline's background was not at all unusual. In my research site in Gitarama, I encountered several interviewees with a similar family history. The family had been Tutsi at one time but then became Hutu. The recategorization tended to occur as people's fortunes rose or fell. A Hutu man who married into a Tutsi family, for example, might become known as Tutsi; or a Tutsi family might become known as Hutu on losing its wealth. The other method of "conversion" was to obtain new identity cards (Fujii 2009; de Lame 1996; Newbury 1988).

References

Alexander, Jeffrey C. 2011. *Performance and Power*. Cambridge: Polity Press.

Apel, Dora, and Shawn Michelle Smith. 2008. *Lynching Photographs: Defining Moments in American Photography*. Berkeley: University of California Press.

Appadurai, Arjun. 1998. "Dead Certainty: Ethnic Violence in the Era of Globalization." *Development and Change* 29: 905–25.

Austin, John L. 1962. *How to Do Things with Words*. Cambridge: Harvard University Press.

Banks, Jerome W. 1993. Letters to the Editor. *Daily Times*, December 21.

Barnes, Brooks Miles. 2006. *Gallows on the Marsh: Crime and Punishment on the Chesapeake, 1906*. Eastville, VA: Hickory House.

Bayart, Jean-François. 2006. *L'état en Afrique: La politique du ventre*. 1989; reprint Paris: Fayard.

Beik, William. 2007. "The Violence of the French Crowd from Charivari to Revolution." *Past & Present* 59: 51–91.

Berezin, Mabel. 1997. *Making the Fascist Self: The Political Culture of Interwar Italy*. Ithaca: Cornell University Press.

Bergholz, Max. 2010. "The Strange Silence: Explaining the Absence of Monuments for Muslim Civilians Killed in Bosnia During the Second World War." *East European Politics and Societies* 24 (3): 408–34.

Bergholz, Max. 2016. *Violence as a Generative Force: Identity, Nationalism, and Memory in a Balkan Community*. Ithaca: Cornell University Press.

Bertrand, Jordane. 2000. *Rwanda: Le piège de l'histoire*. Paris: Karthala.

"Blonde Youth Tells How Mob Acted in Princess Anne Jail." 1933. *Afro-American*, October 28, 4.

Bougarel, Xavier. 1996. *Anatomie d'un conflit*. Paris: La Découverte.

Bourke, Joanna. 1999. *An Intimate History of Killing*. New York: Basic Books.

Bowman, Glenn. 2001. "The Violence in Identity." In *Anthropology of Violence and Conflict*, edited by Bettina E. Schmidt and Ingo W. Schröder, 25–46. New York: Routledge.

Bradol, Jean-Hervé, and Marc Le Pape. 2017. *Humanitarian Aid, Genocide, and Mass Killings: Médecins Sans Frontières, the Rwandan Experience, 1982–97*. Manchester: Manchester University Press.

Brandstetter, Anna-Maria. 2010. "Contested Pasts: The Politics of Remembrance in Post-Genocide Rwanda." The Sixth Ortelius Lecture, Netherlands Institute for Advanced Study in the Humanities and Social Sciences, April 1.

Bringa, Tone. 1993. "Nationality Categories, National Identification and Identity Formation in 'Multinational' Bosnia." *Anthropology of East Europe Review* 11 (1–2): 80–89.

Bringa, Tone. 1995. *Being Muslim the Bosnian Way: Identity and Community in a Central Bosnian Village*. Princeton: Princeton University Press.

Bringa, Tone. 2002. "Averted Gaze: Genocide in Bosnia-Herzegovina, 1992–1995." In *Annihilating Difference*, edited by Alexander Laban Hinton, 194–227. Berkeley: University of California Press.

Brubaker, Rogers. 2004a. "Ethnicity without Groups." In *Facing Ethnic Conflicts: Toward a New Realism*, edited by Andreas Wimmer, Richard J. Goldstone, Donald L. Horowitz, Ulrike Joras, and Conrad Schetter, 34–52. Lanham, MD: Rowman & Littlefield.

Brubaker, Rogers. 2004b. *Ethnicity without Groups.* Cambridge: Harvard University Press.

Brugger, Robert J. 1988. *Maryland: A Middle Temperament.* Baltimore: Johns Hopkins University Press.

Brundage, W. Fitzhugh. 1993. *Lynching in the New South: Georgia and Virginia, 1880–1930.* Urbana: University of Illinois Press.

Buckley-Zistel, Susanne. 2006. "Remembering to Forget: Chosen Amnesia as a Strategy for Local Coexsitence in Post-Genocide Rwanda." *Africa* 76 (2): 131–50.

Bugarski, Ranko. 2004. "Language and Boundaries in the Yugoslav Context." In *Language, Discourse, and Borders in the Yugoslav Successor States*, edited by Brigitta Busch and Kelly Kelly-Holmes, 21–37. Buffalo: Multilingual Matters.

Bugarski, Ranko. 2013. "What Happened to Serbo-Croatian?" In *After Yugoslavia: The Cultural Spaces of a Vanished Land*, edited by Radmila Gorup, 160–68. Stanford: Stanford University Press.

Burg, Steven L., and Paul S. Shoup. 2000. *Ethnic Conflict and International Intervention: The War in Bosnia-Herzegovina.* London: Routledge.

Burke, Peter. 2005. "Performing History: The Importance of Occasions." *Rethinking History* 9 (1): 35–52.

Burnet, Jennie E. 2012. *Genocide Lives in Us: Women, Memory and Silence in Rwanda.* Madison: University of Wisconsin Press.

Butler, Judith. 1999. *Gender Trouble: Feminism and the Subversion of Identity.* New York: Routledge.

Byrd, James E. 1933. "Who Took Armwood to Baltimore?" *Marylander and Herald*, October 28, 2.

Callimachi, Rukmini. 2014. "Obama Calls Islamic State's Killing of Peter Kassig 'Pure Evil.'" *New York Times*, November 16. http://nyti.ms/1q8GVw3.

Caputo, Philip. 1977. *A Rumor of War.* New York: Ballantine Books.

Carr, Cynthia. 2006. *Our Town: A Heartland Lynching, a Haunted Town, and the Hidden History of White America.* New York: Crown Publishers.

Cell, John W. 1982. *The Highest Stage of White Supremacy: The Origins of Segregation in South Africa and the American South.* Cambridge: Cambridge University Press.

Chafe, William H., Raymond Gavins, and Robert Korstad, eds. 2001. *Remembering Jim Crow: African Americans Tell About Life in the Segregated South.* New York: The New Press.

Checkel, Jeffrey T. 2017. "Socialization and Violence—Introduction and Framework." *Journal of Peace Research* 54 (5): 592–605.

Chretien, J.P. 1995. *Rwanda: Les medias du genocide.* Paris: Karthala.

Christia, Fotini. 2008. "Following the Money: Muslim Versus Muslim in Bosnia's Civil War." *Comparative Politics* 40 (4): 461–80.

Clark, John Louis. 1933. "Desk Man Tells How Afro Staff Covered Princess Anne Lynching." *Afro-American*, October 28, 4.

CNN Library. 2016. "Iraq Prison Abuse Scandal Fast Facts." *CNN.com*. March 12. Accessed February 18, 2017. http://www.cnn.com/2013/10/30/world/meast/iraq-prison-abuse-scandal-fast-facts/.

Cohen, Dara Kay. 2016. *Rape during Civil War.* Ithaca: Cornell University Press.

Cole, Catherine M. 2010. *Performing South Africa's Truth Commission: Stages of Transition.* Bloomington: Indiana University Press.

Coll, Steve. 2000. "The Other War." *Washington Post*, January 9, W08. Accessed February 2, 2017. http://www.washingtonpost.com/wp-srv/WPcap/2000–01/09/097r-010900-idx.html.

Collins, Randall. 2006. "Micro-Interactional Dynamics of Violent Atrocities." *Irish Journal of Sociology* 15.1: 40–52.

Collins, Randall. 2008. *Violence: A Micro-Sociological Theory*. Princeton: Princeton University Press.

Cook, Susan E. 2006. "The Politics of Preservation in Rwanda." In *Genocide in Cambodia and Rwanda: A New Perspective*, edited by Susan E. Cook, 281–99. New Brunswick, NJ: Transaction.

Cooper, Brittney C. 2017. *Beyond Respectability: The Intellectual Thought of Race Women*. Urbana: University of Illinois Press.

Corddry, George H. 1981. *Wicomico County History*. Salisbury, MD: Peninsula Press.

"Coroner Probed Only 7 Minutes, No Decision." 1933. *Afro-American*, October 28, 3.

Danner, Mark. 2004. "Torture and Truth." *New York Review of Books*, June 10.

Davis, F. James. 2001. *Who is Black?* Tenth anniversary ed. University Park: Pennsylvania State University Press.

Davis, Julie Hirschfeld. 2014. "After Beheading of Steven Sotloff, Obama Pledges to Punish ISIS." *New York Times*, September 3. http://nyti.ms/1pHxWAD.

de Lame, Danielle. 1996. *Une colline entre mille ou le calme avant la tempête: Transformations et blocages du Rwanda rural*. Tervuren: Musée royal de l'Afrique centrale.

de Lame, Danielle. 2003. "Deuil, commémoration, justice dans les contextes rwandais et Belge." *Poliique africaine* 92 (décembre): 39–55.

Des Forges, Alison. 1999. *Leave None to Tell the Story: Genocide in Rwanda*. New York: Human Rights Watch and Fédération internationale des ligues des droits de l'homme.

Des Forges, Alison Liebhafsky. 2011. *Defeat Is the Only Bad News: Rwanda under Musinga, 1896–1931*. Madison: University of Wisconsin Press.

Donia, Robert J., and John V. A. Fine Jr. 1994. *Bosnia and Hercegovina: A Tradition Betrayed*. New York: Columbia University Press.

Dorsey, Jennifer Hull. 2011. *Hirelings: African American Workers and Free Labor in Early Maryland*. Ithaca: Cornell University Press.

Douglas, Mary. 1966. *Purity and Danger: An Analysis of Concepts of Pollution and Taboo*. London: Routledge.

Douglas, Mary. 1996. *Natural Symbols: Explorations in Cosmology*. 2d ed. New York: Routledge.

Douglas, Mary. 2003. *Purity and Danger: An Analysis of Concepts of Pollution and Taboo*. e-Library ed. London: Routledge.

Downey, Dennis, and Raymond Hyser. 1991. *No Crooked Death: Coatesville, Pennsylvania, and the Lynching of Zachariah Walker*. Urbana: University of Illinois Press.

Drakulić, Slavenka. 2004. *They Would Never Hurt a Fly*. New York: Penguin Books.

Dray, Philip. 2003. *At the Hands of Persons Unknown*. New York: Modern Library.

Duyer, Linda. 2007. '*Round the Pond: Georgetown of Salisbury, Maryland*. Salisbury: Self-published.

"Eastern Shore Family of Four Killed in Beds." 1931. *Baltimore Sun*, October 13, 1.

"Epithets Fly at the Trial of Armwood Boss." 1933. *Afro-American*, December 2, 3.

"Euel Lee Hangs for Murder of Two Years Ago." 1933. *Baltimore Sun*, October 27, 24.

"Eye Witness to Lynching Tells How Mob Acted." 1931. *Afro-American*, December 12, 1.

Fair, Eric. 2016. *Consequence: A Memoir*. Kindle ed. New York: Henry Holt.

"Family Murder Suspect Sped to Baltimore." 1931. *Baltimore Sun*, October 14, 24.

Faust, Drew Gilpin. 2008. *The Republic of Suffering: Death and the American Civil War.* Kindle ed. New York: Alfred A. Knopf.

Ferme, Mariane C. 2001. *The Underneath of Things: Violence, History, and the Everyday in Sierra Leone.* Berkeley: University of California Press.

Fisher, Ian. 2004. "Iraqi Recounts Hours of Abuse by US Troops." *New York Times,* May 5.

Foucault, Michel. 1995. *Discipline and Punish: The Birth of the Prison.* Translated by Alan Sheridan. New York: Vintage Books.

Fujii, Lee Ann. 2009. *Killing Neighbors: Webs of Violence in Rwanda.* Ithaca: Cornell University Press.

Fujii, Lee Ann. 2010. "Shades of Truth and Lies: Interpreting Testimonies of War and Violence." *Journal of Peace Research* 47 (2): 231–41.

Fujii, Lee Ann. 2013. "The Puzzle of Extra-Lethal Violence." *Perspectives on Politics* 11 (2): 410–26.

Fujii, Lee Ann. 2014. "Five Stories of Accidental Ethnography: Turning Unplanned Moments in the Field into Data." *Qualitative Research* 15 (4): 525–39.

Fujii, Lee Ann. 2017. "'Talk of the Town': Pathways to Participation in Violent Display." *Journal of Peace Research* 54 (5): 661–73.

Fujii, Lee Ann. 2018. *Interviewing in Social Science Research: A Relational Approach.* New York: Routledge.

Fuoss, Kirk W. 1999. "Lynching Performances, Theatres of Violence." *Text and Performance Quarterly* 19: 1–37.

Gagnon, V. P., Jr. 2004. *The Myth of Ethnic War: Serbia and Croatia in the 1990s.* Ithaca: Cornell University Press.

Garot, Robert. 2007. "'Where You From!' Gang Identity as Performance." *Journal of Contemporary Ethnography* 36 (1): 50–84.

Garot, Robert. 2010. *Who You Claim: Performing Gang Identity in School and on the Streets.* New York: New York University Press.

Gasana, James K. 2002. *Rwanda: Du parti-état à l'état-garnison.* Paris: L'Harmattan.

Gjelten, Tom. 1995. *Sarajevo Daily: A City and Its Newspaper under Siege.* New York: HarperCollins.

Glenny, Misha. 1996. *The Fall of Yugoslavia: The Third Balkan War.* 3d rev. ed. New York: Penguin Books.

Goldstein, Daniel M. 2004. *The Spectacular City: Violence and Performance in Urban Bolivia.* Durham, NC: Duke University Press.

Gourevitch, Peter. 1986. *Politics in Hard Times: Comparative Responses to International Economic Crises.* Ithaca: Cornell University Press.

"Governor Puts Responsibility on Duer and State's Attorney." 1933. *Baltimore Sun,* October 19, 1.

Gravel, Pierre Bettez. 1968. *Remera: A Community in Eastern Ruanda.* The Hague: Mouton.

Greene, Sandra E. 2003. "Whispers and Silences: Explorations in African Oral History." *Africa Today* 50 (2): 41–53.

Greiner, Bernd. 2009. *War without Fronts: The USA in Vietnam.* Translated by Anne Wyburd and Victoria Fern. New Haven: Yale University Press.

Greve, Hannae Sophie. 1994. "Annex V: The Prijedor Report: Final Report of the United Nations Commission of Experts Established Pursuant to Security Council Resolution 780 (1992)." United Nations.

Griffin, Larry J., Paula Clark, and Joanne C. Sandberg. 1997. "Narrative and Event: Lynching and Historical Sociology." In *Under Sentence of Death: Lynching in the South,* edited by W. Fitzhugh Brundage, 24–47. Chapel Hill: University of North Carolina Press.

Grmek, Mirko, Marc Gjidara, and Neven Simac, eds. 1993. *Le nettoyage ethnique: Documents historiques sur une idéologie serbe*. Paris: Fayard.

Grossman, Dave. 1995. *On Killing: The Psychological Cost of Learning to Kill in War and Society*. Boston: Little, Brown.

Guichaoua, André. 2005. *Rwanda 1994: Les politiques du génocide à Butare*. Paris: Karthala.

Guichaoua, André. 2010. *Rwanda de la guerre au génocide: Les politiques criminelles au Rwanda (1990–1994)*. Paris: La Découverte.

Guss, David M. 2000. *The Festive State: Race, Ethnicity, and Nationalism as Cultural Performance*. Berkeley: University of California Press.

Gutman, Roy. 1993. *A Witness to Genocide*. New York: Macmillan.

Guyer, Sara. 2009. "Rwanda's Bones." *boundary 2* 36 (2): 155–75.

Hagen, Ryan, Kinga Makovi, and Peter Bearman. 2013. "The Influence of Political Dynamics on Southern Lynch Mob Formation and Lethality." *Social Forces* 92 (2): 757–87.

Hale, Grace Elizabeth. 1999. *Making Whiteness: The Culture of Segregation in the South, 1890–1940*. New York: Vintage Books.

Hammer, Richard. 1970. *One Morning in the War: The Tragedy at Son My*. New York: Coward-McCann.

Handelman, Don. 1997. "Rituals/Spectacles." *International Social Science Journal* 49 (153): 387–99.

Hanson, Dorothea. 2009. "Bosnian Serb Crisis Staffs, War Presidencies and War Commissions, 1991–1995." Prepared for the case of RADOVAN KARADŽIĆ (IT-95-5/18).

Harris, J. William. 1995. "Etiquette, Lynching, and Racial Boundaries in Southern History: A Mississippi Example." *American Historical Review* 100 (2): 387–410.

Hawkesworth, Mary. 2016. *Embodied Power: Demystifying Disembodied Politics*. New York: Routledge.

Hayden, Robert M. 2000. "Muslims as 'Others' in Serbian and Croatian Politics." In *Neighbors at War: Anthropological Perspectives on Yugoslav Ethnicity, Culture and History*, edited by Joel Halpern and David Kideckel, 116–24. University Park: Pennsylvania State University Press.

Hayman, Juanita. 1980. "That Awful Day." Unpublished memoir.

Hayman, Sidney. 1992. Interview for TV program "The Great Depression." Episode 6, "To Be Somebody" at about 3:40. https://www.youtube.com/watch?v=MI6Y5vN xCag&list=PLNKKKWWQywFNZh4xL9Okf3xkZc0g0spND&index=7&t=235s The uncut interview is at https://www.youtube.com/watch?v=zvsFO6zeZsw.

Helsinki Watch. 1992. *War Crimes in Bosnia-Hercegovina*. New York: Human Rights Watch.

Helsinki Watch. 1993. *War Crimes in Bosnia-Herzegovina*. Vol. 2. New York: Human Rights Watch.

Hersh, Seymour M. 1970. *My Lai 4: A Report on the Massacre and Its Aftermath*. New York: Random House.

Hersh, Seymour M. 2004. "Torture at Abu Ghraib." *The New Yorker*, May 10.

Hinton, Alexander Laban, ed. 2002. *Annihilating Difference*. Berkeley: University of California Press.

Hinton, Alexander Laban. 2005. *Why Did They Kill?* Berkeley: University of California Press.

Hoare, Marko Attila. 2013. *The Bosnian Muslims in the Second World War: A History*. New York: Oxford University Press.

Hoffman, Danny. 2011. *The War Machines: Young Men and Violence in Sierra Leone and Liberia*. Durham, NC: Duke University Press.

Horowitz, Donald L. 2001. *The Deadly Ethnic Riot.* Berkeley: University of California Press.

Hukanović, Rezak. 1996. *The Tenth Circle of Hell: A Memoir of Life in the Death Camps of Bosnia.* Translated by Colleen London and Midhat Ridjanović. New York: Basic Books.

Ifill, Sherrilyn A. 2007. *On the Courthouse Lawn: Confronting the Legacy of Lynching in the Twenty-First Century.* Boston: Beacon Press.

Inquest. 1933. Coroner's Inquest on the lynching of George Armstrong.

Jackman, Mary R. 2002. "Violence in Social Life." *Annual Review of Sociology* 28: 387–415.

Jarman, Neil. 1997. *Material Conflicts: Parades and Visual Displays in Northern Ireland.* Oxford: Berg.

Jolley, Levi. 1933a. "Armwood Quit School in 5th Grade, Says Pal." *Afro-American,* October 28, 2.

Jolley, Levi. 1933b. "Child Is Killed as Mob Seeks Prey to Lynch." *Afro-American,* October 28, 3.

Jones, Bruce. 2001. *Peacemaking in Rwanda: The Dynamics of Failure.* Boulder: Lynne Rienner.

Jones, Jacqueline. 2013. *A Dreadful Deceit: The Myth of Race from the Colonial Era to Obama's America.* New York: Basic Books.

Judah, Tim. 2009. *The Serbs: History, Myth, and the Destruction of Yugoslavia.* 3rd ed. New Haven: Yale University Press.

Kabagema, Édouard. 2001. *Carnage d'une Nation.* Paris: L'Harmattan.

Kagabo, José. 1994. "Après le génocide. Notes de voyage: Août 1994." *Les Temps Modernes* 583 (Juillet–Août): 102–25.

Kalyvas, Stathis N. 1999. "Wanton and Senseless? The Logic of Massacres in Algeria." *Rationality and Society* 11 (3): 243–85.

Kalyvas, Stathis N. 2003. "The Ontology of 'Political Violence': Action and Identity in Civil Wars." *Perspectives on Politics* 1 (3): 475–94.

Kalyvas, Stathis N. 2006. *The Logic of Violence in Civil War.* Cambridge: Cambridge University Press.

Karemano, Charles. 2003. *Au-delà des barrières: Dans les méandres du drame rwandais.* Paris: L'Harmattan.

Kimonyo, Jean-Paul. 2008. *Rwanda: Un génocide populaire.* Paris: Karthala.

Klusemann, Stefan. 2010. "Micro-Situational Antecedents of Violent Atrocity." *Sociological Forum* 25 (2): 272–95.

Koff, Clea. 2005. *The Bone Woman: A Forensic Anthropologist's Search for Truth in Rwanda, Bosnia, and Kosovo.* Toronto: Vintage Canada.

Krech, Shepard, III. 1981. *Praise the Bridge That Carries You Over: The Life of Joseph Sutton.* Cambridge: Schenkman Books.

Krupa, Christopher. 2009. "Histories in Red: Ways of Seeing Lynching in Ecuador." *American Ethnologist* 36 (1): 20–39.

Landesman, Peter. 2002. "A Woman's Work." *New York Times Magazine,* September 15, 82–134.

Lemarchand, René. 1970. *Rwanda and Burundi.* New York: Praeger.

Lemarchand, René. 2009. *The Dynamics of Violence in Central Africa.* Philadelphia: University of Pennsylvania Press.

Linden, Ian. 1977. *Church and Revolution in Rwanda.* Manchester: Manchester University Press.

Lockwood, William G. 1975. *European Moslems: Economy and Ethnicity in Western Bosnia.* New York: Academic Press.

Longinović, Tomislav Z. 2013. "Post-Yugoslav Emergence and the Creation of Difference." In *After Yugoslavia: The Cultural Spaces of a Vanished Land*, edited by Radmila Gorup, 149–59. Stanford: Stanford University Press.

Longman, Timothy. 2011a. *Christianity and Genocide in Rwanda*. Cambridge: Cambridge University Press.

Longman, Timothy. 2011b. "Limitations to Political Reform." In *Remaking Rwanda: State Building and Human Rights*, Kindle ed., edited by Scott Straus and Lars Waldorf, 25–47. Madison: University of Wisconsin Press.

"Lynchers in Salisbury Had Right-of-Way." 1931. *Afro-American*, December 12, 1.

Maass, Peter. 1996. *Love Thy Neighbor: A Story of War*. New York: Vintage Books.

"Mad Mobsters Pick out Victim's Gold Teeth." 1933. *Afro-American*, October 28, 1.

Malcolm, Noel. 1996. *Bosnia: A Short History*. Updated ed. New York: New York University Press.

Malkki, Liisa. 1995. *Purity and Exile: Violence, Memory, and National Cosmology among Hutu Refugees in Tanzania*. Chicago: University of Chicago Press.

Marx, Anthony W. 1998. *Making Race and Nation: A Comparison of South Africa, the United States, and Brazil*. Cambridge: Cambridge University Press.

"Maryland Prisoner Snatched from Ready Eastern Shore Mob." 1933. *Afro-American*, October 21, 1.

Matthews, Ralph. 1933. "Potter's Field Gets Last Remains of Mob Victim." *Afro-American*, October 28.

McAdam, Doug, Sidney Tarrow, and Charles Tilly. 2001. *Dynamics of Contention*. Cambridge: Cambridge University Press.

McCall, Nathan. 1995. *Makes Me Wanna Holler: A Young Black Man in America*. New York: Vintage Press.

McCord, Edward A. 2001. "Burn, Kill, Rape, and Rob: Military Atrocities, Warlordism, and Anti-Warlordism in Republican China." In *Scars of War: The Impact of Warfare on Modern China*, edited by Diana Lary and Stephen MacKinnon, 18–47. Vancouver: University of British Columbia Press.

Meierhenrich, Jens. 2011. "Topographies of Remembering and Forgetting: The Transformation of *Lieux de Mémoire* in Rwanda." In *Remaking Rwanda: State Building and Human Rights after Mass Violence*, edited by Scott Straus and Lars Waldorf, 283–96. Madison: University of Wisconsin Press.

Melson, Robert. 1996. *Revolution and Genocide*. Chicago: University of Chicago Press.

Milicevic, Aleksandra. 2004. "Joining Serbia's Wars: Volunteers and Draft-Dodgers, 1991–1995." PhD, diss., University of California at Los Angeles.

Mironko, Charles. 2004. "*Igitero*: Means and Motive in the Rwandan Genocide." *Journal of Genocide Research* 6 (1): 47–60.

Mitchell, Clarence. 1933a. "Crowd Outside Makes Merry as Lee Dies." *Afro-American*, November 4, 11.

Mitchell, Clarence. 1933b. "Mob Members Knew Prey Was Feeble-Minded." *Afro-American*, 1.

Mitchell, Clarence. 1986. "Reminiscences of Clarence Mitchell." Edited by Ed Edwin. Oral History Research Office, Columbia University.

"Mob Described by Brockman." 1931. *The Baltimore News*, December 5.

"Mob Storms County Jail Wednesday Night; Lynches Negro Accused of Attacking White Woman Monday." 1933. *Crisfield Times*, October 20, 1.

Moody, Anne. 2011. *Coming of Age in Mississippi*. New York: Bantam Dell.

Moore, Joseph E. 2006. *Murder on Maryland's Eastern Shore: Race, Politics and the Case of Orphan Jones*. Charleston: The History Press.

Mueller, John. 2000. "The Banality of "Ethnic War." *International Security* 25 (1): 42–70.

"Negro Admits Shore Attack, Police Claim." 1933. *Baltimore Sun*, October 17, 24.

Newbury, Catharine. 1988. *The Cohesion of Oppression: Clientship and Ethnicity in Rwanda, 1860–1960*. New York: Columbia University Press.

Newbury, Catharine, and David Newbury. 1999. "A Catholic Mass in Kigali: Contested Views of the Genocide and Ethnicity in Rwanda." *Canadian Journal of African Studies* 33 (2/3): 292–328.

Newbury, David. 1980. "The Clans of Rwanda: An Historical Hypothesis." *Africa* 50 (4): 389–403.

Newbury, David. 1995. "The Invention of Rwanda: The Alchemy of Ethnicity." 38th Annual Meeting of the African Studies Association, Orlando, FL, November 3–6.

"No Fear of Lynching on 'Shore Says Princess Anne Head." 1933. *Afro-American*, October 21, 2.

Norton, Anne. 2011. "On the Uses of Dogs: Abu Ghraib and the American Soul." In *Performances of Violence*, edited by Austin Sarat, Carleen R. Basler, and Thomas L. Dumm, 98–117. Amherst: University of Massachusetts Press.

"Officers and Posses Hunt Somerset Woods for Negro Assailant of Aged Woman." 1933. *Salisbury Times*, October 16, 1.

Papenfuse, Eric Robert. 1997. *The Evils of Necessity: Robert Goodloe Harper and the Moral Dilemma of Slavery*. Philadelphia: American Philosophical Society.

Perloff, Richard M. 2000. "The Press and Lynchings of African Americans." *Journal of Black Studies* 30 (3): 315–30.

Pervanić, Kemal. 1999. *The Killing Days: My Journey through the Bosnian War*. London: Blake Publishing.

Pfeifer, Michael J. 2004. *Rough Justice: Lynching and American Society 1874–1947*. Urbana: University of Illinois Press.

Phillips, Branche H. 1950. "Somerset—Our Nook in the Nation." In *The Eastern Shore of Maryland and Virginia*, edited by Charles B. Clark, 991–1011. New York: Lewis Historical Publishing.

Phillips, Patrick. 2016. *Blood at the Root: A Racial Cleansing in America*. New York: W. W. Norton.

Player, William O. 1933a. "Capt. Johnson, of State Police, and Eight Others Hurt Defending Prisoner." *Baltimore Sun*, October 19.

Player, William O. 1933b. "Shore Mob Lynches Negro." *Baltimore Sun*, October 19, 1.

Player, William O., Jr. 1933c. "Shore Judges Hold Conference over Probe of Lynching." *Baltimore Sun*, October 20, 1.

"Police Squads Escort Negro Back to Shore." 1933. *Baltimore Sun*, October 18, 22.

Portelli, Alessandro. 1991. *The Death of Luigi Trastulli and Other Stories: Form and Meaning in Oral History*. Albany: State University of New York Press.

Pottier, Johan. 2002. *Re-Imagining Rwanda: Conflict, Survival and Disinformation in the Late 20th Century*. Cambridge: Cambridge University Press.

Prunier, Gérard. 1995. *The Rwanda Crisis: History of a Genocide*. New York: Columbia University Press.

"Punishment for the Crime of Lynching: Hearings before a Subcommittee of the Committee on the Judiciary, United States Senate, Seventy-Third Congress, Second Session on S. 1978." 1934. Washington, DC: Government Printing Office.

Pusey, David. 1961. "Princess Anne Ties a Noose." Princess Anne Home Prize essay, Somerset County.

Ramet, Sabrina P. 2006. *The Three Yugoslavias: State-Building and Legitimation 1918–2005*. Bloomington: Indiana University Press.

Raper, Arthur. 1933. *The Tragedy of Lynching*. Chapel Hill: University of North Carolina Press.

Redzic, Enver. 2005. *Bosnia and Herzegovina in the Second World War*. London: Frank Cass.

Reyntjens, Filip. 1985. *Pouvoir et Droit au Rwanda*. Tervuren: Musée Royale de l'Afrique Centrale.

Reyntjens, Filip. 2010. *The Great African War: Congo and Regional Geopolitics, 1996–2006*. Cambridge: Cambridge University Press.

Reyntjens, Filip. 2015. *Political Governance in Post-Genocide Rwanda*. Cambridge: Cambridge University Press.

Richards, Paul. 1996. *Fighting for the Rain Forest: War, Youth, and Resources in Sierra Leone*. Oxford: James Currey.

"Ritchie Sets Date of Euel Lee Execution." 1933. *Salisbury Times*, October 20, 1.

Ritterhouse, Jennifer. 2006. *Growing Up Jim Crow: How Black and White Southern Children Learned Race*. Chapel Hill: University of North Carolina Press.

Roache, George W., Jr. 1993a. "Crowd Watches as Lynch Mob Hangs Victim." *Daily Times*, December 19, A9, Local.

Roache, George W., Jr. 1993b. "Vigilantes Took the Law in Their Own Hands." *Daily Times*, December 12, A11, Local/State.

Robins, John B. 1933. "Typewritten First Person Account."

Rodgers, Dennis. 2017. "*Bróderes* in Arms: Gangs and the Socialization of Violence in Nicaragua." *Journal of Peace Research* 54 (5): 648–60.

Roediger, David R. 2007. *The Wages of Whiteness: Race and the Making of the American Working Class*. London: Verso.

Roy, Beth. 1994. *Some Trouble with Cows: Making Sense of Social Conflict*. Berkeley: University of California Press.

"Rush Suspect to City for Safe Keeping." 1933. *Afro-American*, 1.

Ruzibiza, Abdul Joshua. 2005. *Rwanda: L'histoire Secrète*. Paris: Éditions du Panama.

Sanders, Edith R. 1969. "The Hamitic Hypothesis: Its Origin and Functions in Time Perspective." *Journal of African History* 10 (4): 521–32.

Schiff, Stacy. 2015. *The Witches: Suspicion, Betrayal, and Hysteria in 1692 Salem*. New York: Little, Brown.

Schwartz-Shea, Peregrine. 2014. "Judging Quality: Evaluative Criteria and Epistemic Communities." In *Interpretation and Method: Empirical Research Methods and the Interpretive Turn*, 2nd ed., edited by Dvora Yanow and Peregrine Schwartz-Shea, 120–46. Armonk, NY: M. E. Sharpe.

Scott, James C. 1998. *Seeing Like a State: How Certain Schemes to Improve the Human Condition Have Failed*. New Haven: Yale University Press.

Seligman, C. G. 1930. *Races of Africa*. London: Thornton Butterworth.

"Sho' Mob Waits for Accused Orphan Jones." 1931. *Afro-American*, October 31.

"Shore Mob Hangs, Burns Negro." 1931. *Baltimore Post*, December 5, 1.

"Shore Mob Lynches Negro: Salisbury Killer is Hanged from Tree at Courthouse." 1931. *Baltimore Sun*, December 5, 1.

Sikavica, Stipe. 1997. "The Army's Collapse." In *Burn This House: The Making and Unmaking of Yugoslavia*, edited by Jasminka Udovički and James Ridgeway, 130–52. Durham, NC: Duke University Press.

Silber, Laura, and Allan Little. 1997. *Yugoslavia: Death of a Nation*. Revised ed. New York: Penguin Books.

Sim, Kevin. 1989. *Four Hours in My Lai*. United Kingdom.

Sivac-Bryant, Sebina. 2016. *Re-Making Kozarac: Agency, Reconciliation, and Contested Return in Post-War Bosnia*. London: Palgrave Macmillan.

Sledge, E. B. 1981. *With the Old Breed: At Peleliu and Okinawa.* Oxford: Oxford University Press.

Smead, Howard. 1986. *Blood Justice: The Lynching of Mack Charles Parker.* New York: Oxford University Press.

Smith, Fraser. 2008. *Here Lies Jim Crow: Civil Rights in Maryland.* Baltimore: Johns Hopkins University Press.

"Snow Hill Mob Beats Lawyer Aiding Negro." 1931. *Baltimore Sun,* November 5.

Snyder, Timothy. 2010. *Bloodlands: Europe between Hitler and Stalin.* New York: Basic Books.

SoRelle, James M. 1983. "The "Waco Horror": The Lynching of Jesse Washington." *Southwestern Historical Quarterly* 86 (4): 517–36.

Spencer, Frank. 1933. "Robins and Daugherty Told Armwood Would Be Lynched." *Afro-American,* October 28, 1.

Spijker, Gerard van 't. 1990. *Les usages funéraires et la mission de l'église: Une étude anthropologique et théologique des rites funéraires au Rwanda.* Kampen: Uitgeversmaatschappij J.H. Kok.

"A Statement." 1931. *Salisbury Times,* December 5.

Steflja, Izabela. 2017. "The Production of the War Criminal Cult: Radovan Karadžić and Vojislav Šešelj at the Hague." *Nationalities Papers:* 1–17. doi: http://dx.doi.org/10.1080/00905992.2017.1354365.

Stewart, Polly. 1990. "Regional Consciousness as a Shaper of Local History: Examples from the Eastern Shore." In *Sense of Place: American Regional Cultures,* edited by Barbara Allen and Thomas J. Schlereth, 74–87. Lexington: University Press of Kentucky.

Stone, Dan. 2004. "Genocide as Transgression." *European Journal of Social Theory* 7 (1): 45–65.

Stovel, Katherine. 2001. "Local Sequential Patterns: The Structure of Lynching in the Deep South, 1882–1930." *Social Forces* 79 (3): 843–80.

Straus, Scott. 2006. *The Order of Genocide: Race, Power, and War in Rwanda.* Ithaca: Cornell University Press.

Straus, Scott, and Lars Waldorf, eds. 2011. *Remaking Rwanda: State Building and Human Rights after Mass Violence.* Madison: University of Wisconsin Press.

Stump, Brice. N.d. "Somerset Joe." *Daily Times,* F1–F2.

Su, Yang. 2011. *Collective Killings in Rural China During the Cultural Revolution.* Cambridge: Cambridge University Press.

Sud Bosne i Hercegovine. 2006. "Trial of Marko Samardžija, Case No. X-Kr-05/07." Sarajevo.

Sundaram, Anjan. 2016. *Bad News: Last Journalists in a Dictatorship.* Toronto: Random House Canada.

Swain, Robert L., Jr.,. 1950. "Origin of the County Names." In *The Eastern Shore of Maryland and Virginia,* edited by Charles B. Clark, 909–15. New York: Lewis Historical.

Taylor, Diana. 1997. *Disappearing Acts: Spectacles of Gender and Nationalism in Argentina's "Dirty War."* Durham, NC: Duke University Press.

Taylor, Diana. 2016. *Performance.* Translated by Abigail Levine. Kindle ed. Durham, NC: Duke University Press.

Tertsakian, Carina. 2008. *Le Château: The Lives of Prisoners in Rwanda.* London: Arves Books.

Tesser, Lynn M. 2013. *Ethnic Cleansing and the European Union: An Interdisciplinary Approach to Security, Memory and Ethnography.* New York: Palgrave Macmillan.

Testimony Given before Coroner Edgar A. Jones, at the Inquest of George Armwood on October 24, 1933. Johnny Robins IV private papers. https://hdl.handle. net/1813/102784.

Theidon, Kimberly. 2007. "Gender in Transition: Common Sense, Women, and War." *Journal of Human Rights* 6 (4): 453–78.

Thomson, Susan. 2013. *Whispering Truth to Power: Everyday Resistance to Reconciliation in Postgenocide Rwanda.* Madison: University of Wisconsin Press.

Tilly, Charles. 1985. "War Making and State Making as Organized Crime." In *Bringing the State Back In*, edited by Peter B. Evans, Dietrich Rueschemeyer and Theda Skocpol, 169–91. Cambridge: Cambridge University Press.

Tilly, Charles. 2008. *Contentious Performances.* Cambridge: Cambridge University Press.

Toal, Gerard, and Carl T. Dahlman. 2011. *Bosnia Remade: Ethnic Cleansing and Its Reversal.* Oxford: Oxford University Press.

Tolnay, Stewart E., and E. M. Beck. 1995. *A Festival of Violence: An Analysis of Southern Lynchings, 1882–1930.* Champaign: University of Illinois Press.

"Town Flooded with Curiosity Seekers." 1933. *Afro-American*, October 28, 3.

Trebinčević, Kenan, and Susan Shapiro. 2014. *The Bosnia List: A Memoir of War, Exile, and Return.* New York: Penguin Books.

"Trial of Marko Samardžija, Case No. X-Kr-05/07. 2006. Testimony of Nikola Kuridža."

Turse, Nick. 2013. *Kill Anything That Moves: The Real American War in Vietnam.* New York: Metropolitan Books.

Tyson, Timothy B. 2017. *The Blood of Emmett Till.* New York: Simon & Schuster.

Umutesi, Marie Béatrice. 2000. *Fuir ou mourir au Zaïre: Le vécu d'une réfugiée rwandaise.* Paris: L'Harmattan.

US State Department. 1992. "Second Report on War Crimes in the Former Yugoslavia." Supplemental United States Submission of Information to the United Nations Security Council in Accordance with Paragraph 5 of Resolution 771 (1992).

US State Department. 1993. "Eighth Report on War Crimes in the Former Yugoslavia." Supplemental United States Submission of Information to the United Nations Security Council in Accordance with Paragraph 5 of Resolution 771 (1992) and Paragraph 1 of Resolution 780 (1992).

Verdery, Katherine. 1999. *The Political Lives of Dead Bodies: Reburial and Postsocialist Change.* New York: Columbia University Press.

Vidal, Claudine. 1995. "Le génocide des rwandais Tutsi: Trois questions d'histoire." *Afrique Contemporaine* 174: 8–20.

Vidal, Claudine. 2004. "La commémoration du génocide au Rwanda: Violence symbolique, mémorisation forcée et histoire officielle." *Cahiers d'Études africaines* 175: 575–92.

Vidal, Claudine. 2005. "Preface." In *Rwanda: L'histoire Secrète.* Paris: Éditions du Panama.

Vietnam Veterans against the War. 1972. *The Winter Soldier Investigation: An Inquiry into American War Crimes.* Boston: Beacon Press.

Vinikas, Vincent. 1999. "Specters in the Past: The Saint Charles, Arkansas, Lynching of 1904 and the Limits of Historical Inquiry." *Journal of Southern History* 65 (3): 535–64.

Vulliamy, Ed. 2012. *The War Is Dead, Long Live the War: Bosnia, The Reckoning.* London: Bodley Head.

Wagner, Michelle D. 1998. "All the Bourgmestre's Men." *Africa Today* 45: 25–36.

Waldorf, Lars. 2011. "Instrumentalizing Genocide." In *Remaking Rwanda: State Building and Human Rights*, edited by Scott Straus and Lars Waldorf, 48–66. Madison: University of Wisconsin Press.

Walker, Barrington. 1997. "'This Is the White Man's Day': The Irish, White Racial Identity, and the 1866 Memphis Riots." *Left History* 5 (2): 31–55.

Weiss, Birte. 2000. "Witness to Madness." Unpublished ms.

Wennersten, John R. 1992. *Maryland's Eastern Shore: A Journey in Time and Place.* Centreville, MD: Tidewater.

Wennersten, John R. nd. "Tidewater Somerset, 1850–1970."

Wesselingh, Isabelle, and Arnaud Vaulerin. 2005. *Raw Memory: Prijedor, Laboratory of Ethnic Cleansing.* London: Saqi Books in association with The Bosnian Institute.

Wilkinson, Steven I. 2004. *Votes and Violence.* Cambridge: Cambridge University Press.

Williams, Yohuru R. 2001. "Permission to Hate: Delaware, Lynching, and the Culture of Violence in America." *Journal of Black Studies* 32 (1): 3–29.

Winslow, Donna. 1999. "Rites of Passage and Group Bonding in the Canadian Airborne." *Armed Forces and Society: An Interdisciplinary Journal* 25 (3): 429–57.

"Witness Stand Proves Hot Seat for Shore Sheriff." 1933. *Afro-American*, December 2, 3.

"Woman's Assailant Confesses Crime; Accused Man Now in Baltimore Jail." 1933. *Salisbury Times*, October 17.

Wood, Amy Louise. 2009. *Lynching and Spectacle: Witnessing Racial Violence in America, 1890–1940.* Chapel Hill: University of North Carolina Press.

Wood, Elisabeth Jean. 2000. *Forging Democracy from Below: Insurgent Transitions in South Africa and El Salvador.* Cambridge: Cambridge University Press.

Wood, Elisabeth Jean. 2003. *Insurgent Collective Action and Civil War in El Salvador.* Cambridge: Cambridge University Press.

Woodward, C. Vann. 1955. *The Strange Career of Jim Crow.* New York: Oxford University Press.

Yankovitch, Paul. 1971. "Yugoslavia: In Belgrade, There Are Serbs, Croats but Not a Yugoslav to Be Found." *The Globe and Mail*, March 6, 9.

Index

Abdić, Fikret, 198n19
Abu Ghraib
  active engagement in, 9
  fate of perpetrators at, 5
  impact of, 4
  possible performative analysis of, 189
  purpose of violent displays at, 7
  and staging of violent displays, 3
accidental ethnography, 17, 96
Ades, Bernard, 65–66, 163
Adkins, Irving, 77
Afro-American, 15, 42, 64, 74, 75, 81, 82,
  152–53, 154, 157–59, 197n3
Akayesu, Jean-Paul, 57
Alić, Eno, 130, 131, 133–34
Alić, Meho, 130
amarondo duty, 60–61, 197n17
ambiguity
  ethnic, 181–82, 197n19, 200n7
  in racial classification, 41–43
  in Rwandan genocide, 177–82, 183
  in social categories, 19–21
  violent display draws power from, 189–90
Armwood, George, 72–85
  assumed guilt of, 160–62
  commemoration of lynching of, 162–63
  as instructed to carry out assault,
    199–200n6
  and policing of past, 104–5
  sources on lynching of, 15, 16, 100
  staging of lynching of, 11
  surnames at site of lynching of, 102
  treatment of body of, 151–63
Arusha Accords, 55
assassinations, and Rwandan genocide,
  178–80
Austin, John, 7

Babić, Milan, 48
Baltimore Sun, 159–60
Banks, Jerome W., 105–6
Barnes, Miles, 102, 168, 169
Basomingera, Alberto, 150
Bayart, Jean-François, 96–97
beatings, in Omarska prison camp, 124–26, 128

Beck, E. M., 167
Beik, William, 13
"belly, politics of the," 96–97
belonging
  in Eastern Shore, 103–5
  and extralethal violence in Krajina, 127–28
  and groupness, 9
  participation in violence as basis of,
    184–85
  See also social categories
Bender, Esad, 174–75
Bergholz, Max, 26, 28
Bihać, 53, 198n19
birthright, and determination of Eastern
  Shoreman, 103–4
body
  communicative power of, 8–9, 165
  as potent signifier, 163–64
  See also dead, treatment of; embody/
  embodied action
bones, display of genocide victims', 149–51,
  163
Bosnia
  author's research in, 96–99
  comparison of extralethal violence in, and
    other settings, 134–38
  context of, 12
  enactment of new political order in, 47–54,
    196nn7–8
  extralethal violence in, 116–17, 119–34
  friendship across ethnic divide in, 39–40,
    182–83
  history of group making in, 24–28
  languages spoken in, 97, 195n2
  local deviations from official social
    categories in, 31–34
  microviolations of nationalist line in,
    169–77, 182–83
  parade and murder of Muslims as violent
    display in, 85–91, 192
  religious borrowing in, 25–26
  sources in, 14–15
  staging in, 11
Bosnian Muslim Organization (MBO),
  200n4